COUNSELING STRATEGIES THAT WORK!

Evidence-Based Interventions for School Counselors

RICHARD D. PARSONS

West Chester University of Pennsylvania

Boston ■ New York ■ San Francisco
Mexico City ■ Montreal ■ London ■ Madrid ■ Munich ■ Paris
Hong Kong ■ Singapore ■ Tokyo ■ Cape Town ■ Sydney

For Dr. William Morton . . .
A man who blended head, heart, and hands
in service to others. A true healer.
RP
2006

Executive Editor: *Virginia Lanigan*
Series Editorial Assistant: *Matthew Buchholz*
Marketing Manager: *Kris Ellis-Levy*
Composition and Prepress Buyer: *Linda Cox*
Manufacturing Buyer: *Linda Morris*
Manufacturing Manager: *Megan Cochran*
Cover Coordinator: *Joel Gendron*
Editorial-Production Coordinator: *Mary Beth Finch*
Editorial-Production Service: *Modern Graphics, Inc.*
Electronic Composition: *Modern Graphics, Inc.*

For related titles and support materials, visit our online catalog at www.ablongman.com

Copyright © 2007 Pearson Education, Inc.

All rights reserved. No part of the material protected by this copyright notice may be reproduced or utilized in any form or by any means, electronic or mechanical, including photocopying, recording, or by any information storage and retrieval system, without written permission from the copyright owner.

To obtain permission(s) to use material from this work, please submit a written request to Allyn and Bacon, Permissions Department, 75 Arlington Street, Boston, MA 02116 or fax your request to 617-848-7320.

Between the time Web site information is gathered and then published, it is not unusual for some sites to have closed. Also, the transcription of URLs can result in unintended typographical errors. The publisher would appreciate notification where these errors occur so that they may be corrected in subsequent editions.

Library of Congress Cataloging-in-Publication Data

Parsons, Richard D.
Counseling strategies that work! : evidence-based interventions for school counselors / Richard D. Parsons.
p. cm.
Includes bibliographical references and index.
ISBN 0-205-44558-6
1. Educational counseling—United States. 2. Student Counselors—United States. I. Title.
LB1027.5.P3177 2006
371.4—dc22

2006040143

Printed in the United States of America.
10 9 8 7 6 5 12

CONTENTS

PREFACE

Some have suggested that our society is in crisis (e.g., Lockhart & Keys, 1998). Statistics on divorce, poverty, sexism, racism, violence within and outside of our families and institutions, drug and alcohol abuse, sexual abuse, joblessness, and homelessness appear to support this notion and suggest that by almost any demographic yardstick mental and emotional distress are taking an alarming toll on our students. Statistics from the Substance Abuse and Mental Health Services Administration (SAMHSA, 1998) and the National Institute of Mental Health (2005) (see Table 1) point to the fact that our students are in need of psycho-emotional support. These statistics suggest that over 20 percent of our children and adolescents have significant emotional impairment requiring treatment, and yet given noted shortages in community-based services (Luongo, 200), many in need fail to get the services they require.

COUNSELING IS MORE THAN AN ANCILLARY SERVICE

Although some may feel that school counseling programs are ancillary to the real business of educating our youth, data on the changing psycho-emotional needs of students make it clear that school counseling programs and services are a *must* if we truly are to leave "no student behind."

Today's school counselors deal routinely with complicated situations in which students have acute counseling needs, including cases of severe depression and suicide ideation, pregnancy, substance abuse, school violence, and child abuse (Page, Pietrzak, & Sutton, 2001). The importance of the school counselor's role in the removal of social and emotional barriers to learning has prompted some to call for a redefinition of the role and function of school counselors to that of "school mental health counselors" (e.g., Frye, 2005; Lockhart & Keys, 1998).

School counselors face many hurdles in their attempts to meet the social and emotional needs of the students within their charge. Caseloads in excess of 500 students for each counselor (U.S. Department of Education, 1998), along with the assignment of extensive quasi-administrative and non-counseling-related tasks, make it difficult for counselors to work with all of the students in need. In addition to workload issues, the ability of school counselors to respond to this ever-growing crisis may be impeded by their limited awareness and training in the utilization of brief, effective intervention strategies.

TABLE 1 Children's Mental Health Statistics

GENERAL

- Mental health problems affect one in every five young people at any given time. (Department of Health & Human Services)
- An estimated two-thirds of all young people with mental health problems are not getting the help they need. (Department of Health & Human Services)
- Studies indicate that 1 in 5 children and adolescents (20 percent) may have a diagnosable disorder. Estimates of the number of children who have mental disorders range from 7.7 million to 12.8 million. (Department of Health & Human Services)

ANOREXIA NERVOSA

- Anorexia affects one in every 100 to 200 adolescent girls and a much smaller number of boys. (Department of Health & Human Services)
- Approximately 1 percent of adolescent girls develop anorexia nervosa. One in 10 cases lead to death from starvation, cardiac arrest, or suicide. (National Institute of Mental Health)

ANXIETY DISORDERS

- As many as 1 in 10 young people may have an anxiety disorder. (U.S. Department of Health & Human Services).
- Studies suggest that children or adolescents are more likely to have an anxiety disorder if their parents have anxiety disorders. (U.S. Department of Health & Human Services)

ATTENTION DEFICIT/HYPERACTIVITY DISORDER (AD/HD)

- Thirty to 40 percent of children diagnosed with AD/HD have relatives with the same type of problem. (*Clinical Pediatrics*)
- AD/HD is the most common psychiatric condition affecting children; estimates of prevalence in childhood range from 5 to 10 percent. (*Clinical Pediatrics*)
- As many as 50 percent of children with AD/HD are never diagnosed. (*Harvard Mental Health Letter*)

BIPOLAR DISORDER (MANIC-DEPRESSION)

- Almost one-third of 6- to 12-year-old children diagnosed with major depression will develop bipolar disorders within a few years. (*Journal of the American Academy of Child and Adolescent Psychiatry*)

BULIMIA NERVOSA

- Reported rates of bulimia nervosa vary from 1 to 3 out of 100 young people. (Department of Health and Human Services)

CONDUCT DISORDER

- As many as 1 in 10 children and adolescents may have conduct disorder. (Department of Health and Human Services)

(continued)

TABLE 1 Continued

DEPRESSION

- Recent studies show that, at any given time, as many as one in every 33 children may have clinical depression. The rate of depression among adolescents may be as high as one in eight. (Department of Health and Human Services)
- Recent studies have shown that greater than 20 percent of adolescents in the general population have emotional problems and one-third of adolescents attending psychiatry clinics suffer from depression. (*The Canadian Journal of CME*)

JUVENILE JUSTICE

- It is estimated that between 118,700 and 186,600 of youths who are involved in the juvenile justice system have at least one mental disorder. (The National Coalition for the Mentally Ill in the Criminal Justice System)
- According to a 1994 OJJDP study of juveniles' response to health screenings conducted at the admission of juvenile facilities, 73 percent of juveniles reported having mental health problems and 57 percent reported having prior mental health treatment or hospitalization.
- Of the 100,000 teenagers in juvenile detention, estimates indicate that 60 percent have behavioral, mental, or emotional problems. (Department of Justice)

LEARNING DISORDERS

- It is thought that anywhere from 15 to 20 percent of children with AD/HD have a condition known as a "Specific Learning Disability"—and perhaps 50 percent of children with learning disability have AD/HD. (*Hyperactivity and Attention Deficit Disorder in Children*)

SCHIZOPHRENIA

- Schizophrenia is rare in children under 12, but occurs in about 3 out of every 1,000 adolescents. (Department of Health & Human Services)

SERIOUS EMOTIONAL DISTURBANCES

- Serious emotional disturbances affect 1 in every 10 young people at any given time. (Department of Health & Human Services)

SUICIDE

- Suicide is the third leading cause of death for 15- to 24-year-olds (approx 5,000 young people) and the sixth leading cause of death for 5- to 15-year-olds. (American Academy of Child and Adolescent Psychiatry)
- The rate of suicide for this age group has nearly tripled since 1960, making it the third leading cause of death in adolescents and the second leading cause of death among college age youth. (American Academy of Child and Adolescent Psychiatry)
- More teenagers and young adults died as a result of suicide in 1999 than of cancer, heart disease, HIV/AIDS, birth defects, stroke, and chronic lung disease combined. (U.S. Centers for Disease Control & Prevention)
- For every older teen and young adult who takes his or her own life, 100 to 200 of their peers attempt suicide. Between 500,000 and 1 million young people attempt suicide each year. (American Association of Suicidology)

Source: National Institute of Mental Health (2005). Retrieved from www.nmha.org/children/prevent/stats.cfm.

INTERVENTIONS OF CHOICE

When presented with a child in need of counseling services, how should the counselor respond? What intervention method should be utilized? Often, and perhaps most typically, the intervention choice is made on the basis of the counselor's chosen theory or system of counseling, This method of treatment selection appears to be changing.

In recent years, a shift has occurred toward the promotion of specific approaches for specific problems or diagnoses based on empirically supported treatments (Deegear and Lawson, 2003). For example, the Surgeon General has called for increased development and proliferation of evidence-based intervention (U.S. Public Health Service, 2000).

The use of research evidence as the base from which to select and employ counseling interventions reflects the simple belief that treatments with good outcomes revealed by a substantial number of sound studies are more likely to prove efficacious than those without such support (Nathan & Gorman, 2002; Massey, Armstrong, Boroughs, Henson, & McCash, 2005). This approach to treatment selection is not only intuitively appealing but reflects the Ethical Standards of the American Counseling Association, which states that counselors have the ethical responsibility to use "individual counseling plans that offer reasonable promise of success" (American Counseling Association, 1995, Section A.1.c). Certainly, counselors searching for intervention plans that offer "reasonable promise of success" need to consult current research on empirically supported techniques.

The goal of *Counseling Strategies That Work! Evidence-Based Interventions for School Counselors* is to help school counselors select and employ efficacious interventions. *Counseling Strategies That Work! Evidence-Based Interventions for School Counselors* will assist school counselors in their understanding and valuing of the need to be critical consumers of the research. Further, this book challenges school counselors to test more rigorously the adequacy of their own techniques as a means of ensuring current accountability and future success.

It is this author's belief, as well as that of others (e.g., Brown & Trusty, 2005), that the use of well thought out and carefully designed and implemented interventions will increase the likelihood that counselors' efforts will prove effective in increasing the academic performance of those children under their charge. The studies included in the following chapters provide a good basis for just such well thought out, carefully designed interventions.

FOCUS OF TEXT

Counseling Strategies That Work! offers interventions that have been applied to those problems most often encountered by the school counselor and for which empirical support is available. In selecting interventions for inclusion, the author attempted to follow the criteria outlined by Lonigan, Elbert, and Johnson (1998) in *identifying established and probably effective interventions for children.* Although interventions that were supported by methodologically and statistically sound research were those first sought, the limitations to current research methodology in the area of mental health intervention necessitated the inclusion of strategies for which abundant, convergent literature supported their effectiveness, even in the absence of scientific rigor. Although seeking to present interventions for which randomized, control group studies have demonstrated effectiveness, often the interventions employed and embraced within the professional community are those supported by single-case or small-sample studies. As such, each technique described within this text is identified as being supported by research that may range from pure experiments with requisite design and control to those with less rigor and those that represent more-clinical case studies. The nature of the research supporting the strategy, along with its limitations, is noted, and suggestions for monitoring the effectiveness of the technique when employed within the reader's own setting and practice are provided.

In addition to providing research-supported interventions, each chapter offers a look at strategies being employed in the workplace. In the section entitled "From the Field," the reader will find suggestions and recommendations from counselors who have "successfully" intervened with the type of student and student difficulty discussed in the chapter. Because these suggestions reflect just that—suggestions from colleagues—they should be employed with due caution, and when they are employed, their effectiveness should be evaluated. Finally, because counselors often act as consultants as well as direct service providers, strategies that have been successfully employed by counselors in collaborative consultation with teachers and parents are also provided.

TEXT FORMAT AND CHAPTER STRUCTURE

Each chapter provides a blending of theory, practice, and guided personalized application. Each chapter includes:

- A brief introduction to the nature of the problems that serve as the focus of the chapter
- Sample research supporting specific intervention techniques
- Detailed presentation of the application of an intervention strategy, including this author's reflections on the intervention
- A list of field-tested recommendations for use by the school counselor
- A list of Web- and literature-based resources and additional material

The text is broken down into three major sections. In the first section, "Assisting Students Navigate Academic Demands," the reader is provided specific intervention strategies targeted to the following issues: student distractibility, disruptive and attention-seeking behaviors, off-task behavior, dishonesty, low motivation, and task-completion difficulties. The second section of the text, "Assisting Students with Interpersonal Relationships," identifies interventions that have been shown to be effective when working with issues of shyness, aggression, defiance, antisocial behavior, sexual inappropriateness, and prejudice. The final section, "Helping Students with Emotional Difficulties," includes strategies for working with children experiencing anxiety, stress, obsessive-compulsive tendencies, low self-esteem, cutting, depression, suicide ideation, grief responses, eating disorders, and substance abuse.

REFERENCES

American Counseling Association. (1995). *Code of ethics and standards of practice*. Alexandria, VA: Author.

Brown, D., & Trusty, J. (2005). School counselors, comprehensive school counseling progams, and academic achievement: Are school counselors promising more than they can deliver? *American School Counselor Association, 9*(10), 1–8.

Deegear, J., & Lawson, D. M. (2003). The utility of empirically supported treatments. *Professional Psychology: Research and Practice, 34*(3), 271–277.

Frye, H. N. (2005). How elementary school counselors can meet the needs of students with disabilities. *Professional School Counseling, 8*(5), 442–450.

Lockhart, E. J., & Keys, S. G. (1998). The mental health counseling role of school counselors. *Professional School Counseling, 1*, 3–6.

Lonigan, C. J., Elbert, J. C., & Johnson, S. B. (1998). Empirically supported psychosocial interventions for children. An overview. *Journal of Clinical Child Psychology, 27*, 138–145.

Luongo, P. F. (2000). Partnering child welfare, juvenile justice and behavioral health with schools. *Professional School Counseling, 3*, 308–314.

Massey, O. T., Armstrong, K., Boroughs, M., Henson, K., & McCash, L. (2005). Mental health services in schools: A qualitative analysis of challenges to implementation, operation, and sustainability. *Psychology in the Schools, 42*(4), 361–372.

Nathan, P. E., & Gorman, J. M. (Eds.). (2002). *A guide to treatments that work* (2d ed.). New York: Oxford University Press.

National Institute of Mental Health. (2005). Children's mental health statistics. Retrieved from www.nmha.org/children/prevent/stats.cfm.

Page, B. J., Pietrzak, D. R., & Sutton, J. M. (2001). National survey of school counselor supervision. *Counselor Education and Supervision, 41*, 142–150.

Substance Abuse and Mental Health Services Administration. (1998). *National expenditures for mental health, alcohol and other drug abuse treatment*. Washington, DC: SAMHSA, Department of Health and Human Services.

U.S. Department of Education. (1998). *Digest of educational statistics*. Washington, DC: Author.

U.S. Public Health Service. (2000). *Report on the Surgeon General's conference on children's mental health: A national action agenda*. Washington, DC: U.S. Government Printing Office.

ACKNOWLEDGMENTS

I am grateful to all of my graduate students, my colleagues, and most importantly those clients who gave me the gift of their trust for pushing me to reflect on the degree of professionalism, efficacy, and accountability that I bring to all I do. You have made me not just a better counselor . . . but a better person.

I appreciate the comments by the following reviewers of the manuscript: Charles Barke, Missouri State University; Patricia Goodspeed, State University of New York at Brockport; Brenda Hall, North Carolina A&T State University; Martha Hall, Hampton University; Carol Hoheisel, North Dakota State University; Beverly Klecker, Morehead State University; Dennis Pelsma, Emporia State University; Jan Stalling, Stephen F. Austin State University; Carolyn Suppa, Marshall University; and Linda Wilson, Northeastern University.

A special "thank you" goes to Virginia Lanigan and Scott Blaszak at Pearson Education and Marty Tenney and the people at Modern Graphics for their support, expertise, and valuable input. I would also like to thank my colleagues, especially Dr. Trish Broderick, for the ongoing engagement in discussion and reflection on empirically supported techniques—the potential and the limitations. And, finally a very special thank you to my graduate assistant, Tammi Schulman. Without her assistance, this project would still be "in progress."

SECTION 1

ASSISTING STUDENTS NAVIGATE ACADEMIC DEMANDS

For some students, the academic and "schooling" demands found within the classroom are simply too difficult, too challenging to navigate. For these students, issues of distractibility, the need for attention, low motivation and self-efficacy, and difficulty with task completion may impede their ability to achieve. The interventions presented within Section I have been demonstrated to be effective in assisting students with such difficulties.

CHAPTER 1

ATTENTION-DEFICIT/ HYPERACTIVITY DISORDER: INTERVENTIONS FOR STUDENT DISTRACTIBILITY, INATTENTIVENESS, AND TIME ON TASK

Attention to task is essential to academic achievement. Historically, research (e.g., Berliner, 1988; Rosenshine, 1979) has shown that time on task is an important correlate of classroom performance and academic achievement. Although many students may experience transient flights of attention, for those students identified as having Attention-Deficit/Hyperactivity Disorder, these flights of inattentiveness are neither transient nor benign and can result in academic and social difficulties.

Attention-Deficit/Hyperactivity Disorder (AD/HD) is a relatively recent addition to the *Diagnostic and Statistical Manual of Mental Disorders,* Fourth Edition, Text Revision (DSM-IV-TR: American Psychiatric Association, 2000). The DSM-IV-TR (2000) defines AD/HD as persistent, developmentally inappropriate problems with attention, impulsivity, and hyperactivity. Historically AD/HD has been included under the category of behavior disorders, along with Oppositional Defiant Disorder and Conduct Disorder. DSM-IV-TR differentiates AD/HD from these other conditions based on the presence of the prominent symptoms of difficulty with attention and overactivity.

AD/HD is an impairing, persistent condition that can significantly affect a student's academic and social development. Children with AD/HD are prone to serious accidents and injuries, are likely to be academic underachievers, are often rejected by peers, and typically present with lowered self-esteem (Hinshaw & Melnick, 1995; Slomokoski, Klein, & Mannuzza, 1995). Further, longitudinal research studies have found that those with AD/HD, when compared to those without the disorder, are at higher risk for academic, behavioral, and social problems across their lifespan (Barkley, 1997a; Goldstein, 1999; Weyandt, 2001).

Although the specific etiology of AD/HD remains an area of debate, most researchers generally believe it involves some type of brain dysfunction. Barkley (1997a) suggested that individuals with AD/HD have impairment to key neurobiological areas of the brain that are responsible for directing "executive control." Although such neurobiological models predominate, most agree that interaction patterns at home and at school are relevant to the exacerbation of symptoms and functional impairment (Tannock, 1998). This broader view of possible etiology and contributing factors has given shape to the development and implementation of a multimodal, multidisciplinary form of intervention.

Widespread support exists for the multimodal, multidisciplinary form of intervention (Barkley, 1998; DuPaul & Stoner, 1994; Goldstein, 1996). The intervention model includes four major areas: (1) educational accommodations, (2) promotion of appropriate behavior, (3) medical management, and (4) ancillary support services for children and parents (e.g., counseling, parental support groups).

This intervention model has found support through what has been called the largest and most comprehensive clinical research study ever undertaken in the United States (Barkley, 2000a)—the Collaborative Multimodal Treatment Study of Children with Attention-Deficit/Hyperactivity Disorder, sponsored by the National Institute of Mental Health (MTA Cooperative Group, 1999). The MTA study found that the use of intensive multifaceted behavioral interventions along with well-developed pharmacological agents renders better treatment outcomes than either intervention by itself (Erk, 2000; Goldstein, 1996; Richters et al., 1995; Wells et al., 2000). Further, it was reported that although combined treatment (i.e., medicine and behavioral interventions) may not always prove superior to medication alone, it was the only treatment that normalized behavior patterns among children with AD/HD (Hinshaw, Klein, & Abikoff, 2002). With the inclusion of these behavioral and psycho-educational components in the treatment of AD/HD, the school counselor becomes much more pivotal in the overall treatment schema.

School counselors, as behavioral and relationship specialists, can provide support for AD/HD students and their teachers. The American School Counselor Association (ASCA) published a position statement that strongly encourages the involvement of school counselors in the multidimensional treatment of students with AD/HD (ASCA, 1994). Others in the field (Erk, 1995; Lavin, 1997; Schwiebert, Sealander, & Tollerud, 1995) also have addressed the important role of school counselors in the treatment of AD/HD. The school counselor is able to work not only with the student, but also with the student's parents, teachers, and other school-support personnel. Therefore, it is very important that the counselor identify the treatment that brings about changes in the child's most problematic areas of functioning (Hoza & Pelham, 1993).

Treatment strategies that have been employed and that fall within the training and job definition of a school counselor include parent counseling and training (Barkley, 1997b, 2000b), client education (Levine, 1993a, 1993b), individual and group counseling (Robin, 1990), social-skills training (Sheridan, Dee, Morgan, McCormick, & Walker, 1996), and specific interventions targeted to academic and school difficulties (DuPaul & Ekert, 1997; DuPaul & Stoner, 1994; Goldstein, 1999; Pfiffner, 1996). In addition to assisting the child with the most problematic areas of functioning, it is also important for counselors to emphasize the positive qualities exhibited by a child or adolescent with AD/HD. Explicating these qualities can help ease the negative messages often received from peers, teachers, and parents (Murphy, 1998).

Counselors who would like more information on specific interventions and strategies should refer to the works of Barkley (1998), Erk (2000), and Teeter (1998).

The following are but a few examples of effective interventions for students who manifest attention difficulties. The interventions to be discussed employ contextual, behavioral, and cognitive strategies for increasing focused attention and on-task behavior (see Table 1.1). Further, the nature of the problems addressed range from simple distraction, which appears to be the result of boredom, to the more serious and persistent AD/HD.

TABLE 1.1 Overview of Studies Presented

TARGET PROBLEM	REFERENCE	K–6	6–9	9–12	OTHER SPECIFICATIONS
Improving social skills	Sheridan, Dee, Morgan, McCormick, & Walker (1996)	Yes	No	No	Multiple baseline design (n = 5)
The effects of self-monitoring of academic productivity and accuracy on academic performance and on-task behavior	Shimabukuro, Prater, Jenkins, & Edelen-Smith (1999)	No	Yes	No	Multiple baseline design across three academic areas
Increasing academic achievement scores and enhanced classroom behavior of students with AD/HD	Miranda, Presentacion, & Soriano (2002)	No	Yes	No	Large study employing 52 teachers and the counselor as teacher trainer
Providing a cognitive-behavioral approach for self-management	Webb & Myrick (2003)	No	Yes	No	Employed control group pre- and post-test design

SAMPLE INTERVENTIONS

A Multimethod Intervention for Social-Skills Deficits in Children with AD/HD and Their Parents

Authors: Susan M. Sheridan and Candace C. Dee

Précis: The implementation of a social-skills intervention program for five boys with AD/HD and their parents.

Introduction

Students with AD/HD are sometimes described as being socially disruptive and may become the target of peer social harassment (Erk, 2000). It is often in this arena of peer-group entry and social interaction that students with AD/HD encounter great difficulty (Barkley, 1998). Certainly, the development of a more successful repertoire of social skills seems to be essential for children and adolescents with AD/HD. The current study provides an illustration of an effective social-skills program.

Intervention

The authors employed a 10-week intervention focusing on skills involved with social entry, maintaining interactions, and social problem solving. The study was implemented with five boys who had been diagnosed with AD/HD and their parents. The boys ranged in age from 8 to 10 years (M = 9.0) and were enrolled in grades 2 through 5 (M = 4).

Two 10-week training groups served as the independent variables in this study. One group was a social-skills training group for children; the other was a skills-based group for parents. Each group session was 75 minutes, with a booster session conducted 6 weeks following the last group meeting. Sessions were held over 10 consecutive weeks.

Each of the student group sessions followed a similar pattern: a review of homework and home programs with parents, identification of personal goals, introduction and discussion of a new skill, modeling, behavioral rehearsal, performance feedback by leaders and peers, reinforcement for appropriate within-group behavior and for returning homework, and establishment of a weekly home contract. Topics covered in the student sessions included body basics and starting conversations, joining in, maintaining interactions, playing cooperatively, solving problems/arguments, dealing with teasing, using self-control, and accepting "no."

The parents group met at the same time as the children's group. Parents were taught the skills of debriefing, problem solving, and goal setting.

The study employed a multiple baseline across behaviors design. The authors reported positive changes in the students' behavior as well as improved parent skills in debriefing, problem solving, and goal setting. All of the students reported improvements of at least one standard deviation on self-report social-skills rating scales, and parent and teacher reports also suggested general improvement for most subjects.

Reflection

Interventions designed to improve social skills and social competency have been shown to reduce peer-interaction difficulties for those with AD/HD (Barkley, 1998; Teeter, 1998). This study certainly supports the value and need for such social-skills training of those students diagnosed with AD/HD.

Social-skills training should be considered an important element of any multidimensional AD/HD treatment plan. Because the school serves as the primary arena for peer interaction, it would appear to be the logical setting for such social-skills training, and the group modality described here would make such training appropriate to the counselor role and function.

To increase potential effectiveness, a counselor may wish to consider the inclusion of peers not diagnosed with AD/HD in the social groups. Inclusion of nondiagnosed peers has been found not only to provide additional appropriate social models, but has resulted in the improvement of social status for those with AD/HD (Teeter, 1998). Further, it may prove helpful for the counselor to assess the students' functional skills, prior to intervention, as a base for targeting intervention strategies. Such an assessment would help the counselor place emphasis on the training in those skill areas where deficits were identified.

Finally, a caveat regarding the application of these findings needs to be stated. As with all studies with small sample sizes (in this case five students), the ability to generalize findings to other students and other settings is limited. Therefore, counselors employing this method need to consider this limitation and closely monitor the impact on the specific group targeted.

Source: Sheridan, S. M., & Dee, C. C. (1996). A multimethod intervention for social skills deficits in children with ADHD and their parents. *School Psychology Review, 25*(1), 57–76.

SAMPLE INTERVENTIONS

The Effects of Self-Monitoring of Academic Performance

Authors: Serena M. Shimabukuro, Mary Anne Prater, Amelia Jenkins, and Patricia Edelen-Smith

Précis: The effects of self-monitoring of academic productivity and accuracy on academic performance and on-task behavior.

Introduction

The authors cite research that indicates that self-management procedures, such as self-monitoring of attention, are effective not only for increasing time on task, but also for improving academic productivity. Although behavioral interventions have been reported to have decreased disruptive and off-task behaviors in children with AD/HD, the authors of the current study noted that reduction of such behaviors is not sufficient. They proposed that interventions should focus on improving academic behaviors rather than inattentiveness, disruptiveness, and excessive motor activities.

The current study investigated the effects of self-monitoring of academic productivity and accuracy on the academic performance of students with learning disabilities and ADD/ADHD during independent class assignments using curricular materials already in place and to determine the effects of academic self-monitoring on attentional behaviors. The self-monitoring intervention was implemented for three students using a single group, multiple baseline design across three academic areas. The authors reported gains in on-task behavior, academic productivity, and accuracy for all three students.

Intervention

Participants included three male students, one sixth grader and two seventh graders diagnosed with AD/HD. The three students were members of a self-contained, mixed-grade class in a private school for students with learning disabilities. The classroom teacher taught the self-monitoring strategies. The teacher helped students learn to manage their independent work through progress graphs and other self-monitoring procedures. Students were taught to compute completion scores as a percentage and to graph the completion scores to establish trends. A similar process was used to teach students to self-monitor and track the accuracy of their scores.

Reflection

The current study was included within this text even though the intervention was applied by a classroom teacher in a classroom setting because it provides a simple, clear illustration of a strategy that could be used by teachers with the consultative support of the school counselor. Moving from direct service models to consultative ones can increase counselors' potential for working with a larger number of students in a more preventive framework. In reviewing the specifics of this study, it is clear that a major limitation is the fact that not only was the sample small ($n = 3$), but that the research was conducted in a unique educational setting.

Source: Shimabukuro, S. M., Prater, M. A., Jenkins, A., & Edelen-Smith, P. (1999). The effects of self-monitoring of academic performance on students with learning disabilities and ADD/ADHD. *Education and Treatment of Children, 22*(4), 397–414.

SAMPLE INTERVENTIONS

School-based Multicomponent Program for Treating AD/HD

Authors: Ana Miranda, Maria Jesus Presentacion, and Manuel Soriano

Précis: Evaluation of the efficacy of a multicomponent program for treating attention deficit/hyperactivity disorder carried out by teachers in a classroom context.

Introduction

With the increasing movement toward full inclusion within our schools, teachers are finding that they are called upon to teach and manage children who present with exceptional needs and for whom the teacher is ill prepared. The lack of training is the barrier most often cited by teachers as the reasons for their limited effectiveness when working with AD/HD students. As such, the current study tested the effectiveness of training teachers in the use of behavior modification techniques, cognitive behavior strategies, and instructional management strategies as a means of increasing academic achievement scores and enhanced classroom behavior of students with AD/HD.

Intervention

The study employed a non-randomly assigned pre-test, post-test, control group design. Initially 52 children meeting the criteria for AD/HD were selected for the study. However, only 29 children were employed in the experimental group (one was not completely assessed and thus dropped from the analysis), with the remaining 22 children assigned to a control group. The teachers of these 29 students were trained using small groups of 10 teachers. The first session included information on the nature, effect, and basic features of AD/HD. The second training session focused on procedures directed toward increasing desirable behavior (e.g., positive reinforcement, token economy, Premack, etc.). The third session focused on methods to decrease inadequate behavior (e.g., extinction, response cost, time out). In the fourth session, specific guidelines concerning instructional management procedures for students with AD/HD were presented. Sessions 5 and 6 focused on cognitive behavioral strategies to stimulate self control (such as Think Aloud). Teachers also were assisted in setting classroom rules, training students in the classroom to evaluate levels of behavioral and academic performance, and developing and employing a token economy system.

Parents' and teachers' observational ratings indicated increased academic scores; enhanced classroom behavior; and reduced inattentiveness, hyperactivity, and impulsivity for the experimental group when compared to both their own pre-test scores and with the control group.

Reflection

The study provides an effective and efficient approach to increasing school performance of children with AD/HD. Of special note for school counselors is that the approach—that is, training teachers—allows the school counselor to maximize their impact by sharing their knowledge and expertise with those in the trenches. Hopefully, the increased competency of the teacher to manage and teach the child with AD/HD will reduce the need for one-on-one counseling by the school counselor.

Source: Miranda, A., Presentacion, M. J., & Soriano, M. (2002). Effectiveness of a school-based multicomponent program for the treatment of children with ADHD. *Journal of Learning Disabilities, 35*(6), 546–562.

DETAILED INTERVENTIONS

Group Counseling Intervention for Children with AD/HD

Introduction

In addressing the counseling needs of students with AD/HD, Resnick (2005) suggested that it is important to help students with AD/HD understand the diagnosis and how it can positively affect their lives. The current study employs a group counseling intervention model that focuses on helping students understand AD/HD and how it impacts school performance. Further, the intervention highlights that the disorder by itself will not keep students from their personal, academic, or career goals. The authors emphasize that the secret to success is being able to manage one's thoughts, feelings, and behaviors; thus, they provide a cognitive-behavioral approach for self-management.

Method

The intervention involved 14 elementary school counselors from one school district. The intervention consisted of six small-group sessions with about six students in each group.

Each session had a specific objective related to thoughts, behaviors, and skills that focused on school and personal achievement. Each session began with a review of the previous session and a check on the application of skills learned in that session. Sessions ended with tasks for practice and an encouraging summary statement. The unit culminated with snacks, juice, and talk about the group experience as well as a review of plans for utilizing strategies.

The sessions were based on the theme of a journey. The metaphor of a journey provided opportunities to construct group activities that were fun and that enabled participants to reflect on goals and goal setting, the influence of personal characteristics on achieving goals, and personal management skills.

Students were helped to see that the journey required preparation and the ability to recognize certain road signs and to manage the vehicle in such a way that they would arrive safely at the final destination. Further, it was highlighted that given their AD/HD, they would, at times, take a different route than others, although they would eventually arrive at the same destination. As the students considered the skills needed to move along on their imaginary journey, they also thought about how the skills were related to the academic, personal, social, and career goals shared by all students their age.

The study employed a control group, pretest, posttest design. Teachers completed a pre- and post-intervention Likert-type scale. Teachers rated students based on exhibited behaviors. Teacher ratings improved by an average of 13.55 points. Dependent t tests found both improvements to be significant ($\alpha = .05$).

Interventions

As noted, a psycho-education model emphasizing the development of behaviors and cognitions to facilitate academic achievement were imparted in six small-group sessions. A brief description of the focus of each session follows.

Preparing for the Journey

The counselor begins the unit by telling students that they have been selected for the group because they have been identified as being a different kind of learner: They have AD/HD. Students are asked, "What do you know about AD/HD?"

Discussion and clarification help the students identify AD/HD symptoms and how the symptoms are manifested in school, which often makes them learn in different ways than others. They are, in one sense, a different traveler in the education world.

Session 1: Beginning the Journey

Counselors open the discussion of "journey" by having the students explore a variety of paths to reach a single destination in MapQuest; they talk about goals and places to go. Counselors then help the students realize that everyone does not have to follow the same road to reach the same final destination. Summary statements include: "Having AD/HD doesn't mean you can't be successful as a student; however, it does mean that you might have to find some ways to get there (success) that will be a little different than the routes others take. You will need to learn to be a different kind of traveler and do some things to help yourself become successful. If you do, you will have more control over where you are going and how you will get there."

Session 2: Pack It Up

The counselor begins the session by rummaging through a bag or backpack, throwing things left and right and creating havoc. It is a demonstration of the chaos that comes from being cluttered and disorganized. Students explore their own bags and the need for organization. Organizational skills are introduced, demonstrated, and practiced. The session closes with a brief summary statement: "Keeping things organized is important. It is one way for you to help yourself on your journey to school success."

Session 3: Stop Lights and Traffic Cops

Students embark on an imaginary "car ride" to heighten their awareness of the need to pay attention to the signs around them. As they pretend to drive a car, signs are flashed in front of them, and they have to navigate obstacles in the room. They then play the "paying attention" game. A participant wins the game by keeping his or her eyes focused on a moving object, book, or perhaps person, such as the teacher, for various time intervals. Time intervals are increased from a few seconds until a 1-minute interval is reached. The counselor summarizes by saying, "Having AD/HD makes paying attention and listening more difficult, but it can be done. Learning and remembering strategies like we practiced today help us notice important things along the way and let us take control during our journey."

Session 4: Using Road Signs as a Guide

Students identify familiar road signs (cards) that cue behavior on the road. They then develop their own cues to help them to be more successful in the classroom. Summarizing remarks include, "Students with AD/HD can be successful in school and get things done—using cues and reminders in your classroom and making up your own are ways to do it."

Session 5: Road Holes and Detours

Students brainstorm ideas about what could go wrong on a road trip, obstacles that could make it difficult for them to get to their destination. Students then generate school situations that may be obstacles to their success. The counselor teaches and demonstrates selected cognitive-behavioral strategies for handling these obstacles. The counselor closes with, "We know there will be holes in the road for AD/HD students. There are holes in the road for all students, but your map is marked and you can expect them. You are learning ways to get around obstacles and difficult situations at school and go on with your journey."

Session 6: Roadside Help and Being Your Own Mechanic

Using the metaphor of breaking down on the road, students consider the skills they have learned that they can use on their journey but also recognize that sometimes help is needed. The session emphasizes that students oftentimes can fix things on their own, thus making them more responsible and empowered. This session also discusses medication and helps those taking medication to recognize that it is a needed tool in their toolbox.

Summary Session

This session highlights that students have the right to take different routes, but that they need to be organized and use cues and strategies to help them remember to pay attention and think before acting. The session focuses on being positive and hopeful about reaching one's goal.

Reflection

The cognitive reframing and behavioral strategies developed in the short, six-week program appeared to empower the students. Because students are in the best position to recognize indications that problems may be occurring, they are also in a position to respond in ways that are immediately helpful. This, of course, assumes that they possess the attitude, knowledge, and skills to get back on track.

The current intervention appeared to be effective in helping students develop the needed tools to deal with AD/HD. The program provided students a language of self-help that enabled them to be more responsible for their actions and to manage themselves in the school environment.

The six-week group model should appeal to counselors who operate under time and task constraints, especially if it is part of a multidimensional treatment approach. Of special note is the authors' reference to the fact that a longer, 12-week intervention that included teachers' reinforcement of success skills in the classroom yielded significant improvement in student and teacher ratings of school-success behaviors. Perhaps, counselors should consider and evaluate the effectiveness of expanding this program into classroom guidance units and/or in conjunction with teacher training to assist in the reinforcement of the new attitudes and skills exhibited by the students.

Source: Webb, L. D., & Myrick, R. D. (2003). A group counseling intervention for children with attention deficit hyperactivity disorder. *Professional School Counseling,* 7(2), 108–115.

FROM THE FIELD

As with each of the chapters to follow, the recommendations provided in this section, "From the Field," reflect methods and practices currently employed within our schools. The recommendations are suggestions based on the experience and anecdotal reporting of counselors working within our schools. They have not been tested for internal validity or generalizability. Thus, implementation of any of the following should be done with caution and their impact monitored closely.

Working with the Student

- Engage the student in study skills groups, including those focused on note taking, test taking, organization, and time management.
- Work with the student to develop a system for organizing and planning, with a focus on recording assignments, breaking long-term assignments into smaller units, and keeping a calendar of due dates.
- Require the student to check with a teacher or counselor before leaving school to check that all materials needed for that evening's work are in the student's book bag and that all assignments are listed.
- Look for positives and provide reinforcement each time the desired behavior and/or task is achieved—no matter how small the accomplishment.
- Communicate with parents on the plan, intervention strategies, and noted successes using a weekly note or information sheet.
- Reinforce teachers for support provided.
- Help the AD/HD student to understand and accept the realities of the condition and the value of the various intervention strategies (including medication).
- Teach the student techniques for maintaining attention in class.
- Create psycho-educational/counseling groups in which issues such as social skills, problem-solving techniques, anger management, and peer relationships can be discussed.
- Teach anger-control strategies such as positive self-talk, time outs, relaxation breathing, and stress-reduction techniques.
- Teach students self-management skills such as self-monitoring, taking breaks, active listening and learning, and self-reinforcement.

Working with Teachers: Reducing Distraction

- Provide the student with a quiet, distraction-free area for quiet study time, seat work, and test taking.
- Keep the student in close proximity to the teacher and instructional materials in order to reduce interference from other stimuli.
- Place the student near positive role models—those not only modeling attention to task, but also those who can resist invitation to distraction.
- Arrange the classroom so that desks face away from distractions (e.g., exterior windows, hallways).

- Place high-interest equipment (e.g., computers, lab materials, animal cages) in designated areas away from the student's immediate proximity.
- In their research of on-task behavior in second- and third-grade classrooms, Bonus and Riordan (1998) found that students remained engaged in learning longer when desks were arranged appropriately for the task at hand: U-shaped arrangements for class discussions, rows for test taking, etc.

Working with Teachers: Supporting the Student

- Provide soft reprimands when the student is off task. For example, walk near the student's desk and point to the text or worksheet or softly remind the student to continue the task.
- Provide the student with forewarning of transitions. For example, announcing "when we finish this, we will begin that" is a helpful way to focus the student on the next task rather than merely completing one task and assuming that the transition to another is downtime or play time.
- During highly active, physical class activities, the student should remain close so that verbal and nonverbal prompts can be provided.
- Develop a routine when ending the day. Prompt all students to review the homework they have been assigned and to check that they have all needed materials. During this time, walk around the class checking that students, especially those who have difficulty focusing on instructions, have the materials they will need.
- Provide AD/HD students with short tasks and allow them to run errands. Some form of physical exercise may prove helpful. If you have a co-teacher, you can send the student to ask that person a question or give them a note.
- For students with AD/HD, it sometimes helps to provide a "reward" upon completion of a task, such as allowing them to play with something small and nondistracting (e.g., a push puzzle, an etch-a-sketch), while waiting for the next task to begin.
- Use little signals, or private cues, to remind the student not to call out.
- Praise in public, reprimand in private.
- Provide a highly structured environment with clearly defined routines, rules, procedures, and consequences. Use immediate consequences for students' behavior. Enforce preestablished consequences consistently with these students. However, make sure the consequence fits the offense and avoid public ridicule or criticism.

Working with Teachers: Tasks and Task Assignment

- Most people attend to things that are emphatically oriented (i.e., that have been emphasized via changes in voice or via cues or reminders). When providing direction or instruction, be clear and use voice inflection to draw attention to important points.
- When giving assignments, present the information both orally and in written form and request that the students repeat back what has been requested.

- Use the board for highlighting important notes, concepts, and directives.
- Move about the class, remaining in close proximity to the student(s).
- Provide students with severe AD/HD with outlines, syllabi, or assignment listings in advance of instruction.
- Deliver instruction in short, sequential steps using mini-assignments and tasks rather than one long-term project or presentation.
- With long-term projects, help students set schedule and task deadlines. Check to see that students remain on schedule.
- Given the elements that foster attention, employ creative visuals and lively presentations to maintain high interest and novelty.
- Develop materials that relate to students' lives.
- Employ teaching strategies that highlight ways learning can be applied in real-life situations.
- Assign challenging but achievable tasks for all students; assignments that seem impossible discourage learners, as do those that are rote and repetitive.
- Arouse curiosity. Use a detective or mystery approach; give students hints as to where the lesson is leading, but allow them to hypothesize as to where it will go. People attend to things that are provocative (i.e., that engage our cognitive disequilibrium), such as "mystery of life questions" or "why are driveways places where we park and parkways places where we drive?"

REFERENCES

American Psychiatric Association. (2000). *Diagnostic and statistical manual of mental disorders* (4th ed.). Washington, DC: Author.

American School Counselor Association. (1994). *Position statement: Attention deficit hyperactivity disorder*. Alexandria, VA: Author.

Barkley, R. A. (1997a). *AD/HD and the nature of self-control.* New York: Guilford Press.

Barkley, R. A. (1997b). *Defiant children: A clinician's manual for assessment and parent training.* New York: Guilford Press.

Barkley, R. A. (1998). *Attention-Deficit Hyperactivity Disorder: A handbook for diagnosis and treatment* (2nd ed.). New York: Guilford Press.

Barkley, R. A. (2000a). Commentary on the multimodal treatment study of children with AD/HD. *Journal of Abnormal Psychology, 28,* 595–599.

Barkley, R. A. (2000b). Commentary: Issues in training parents to manage children with behavior problems. *Journal of the American Academy of Child and Adolescent Psychiatry, 39,* 1004–1007.

Berliner, D. (1988). Simple views of effective teaching and a simple theory of classroom instruction. In D. Berliner & B. Rosenshine (Eds.), *Talks to teachers* (pp. 93–110). New York: Random House.

Bonus, M., & Riordan, L. (1998). Increasing student on-task behavior through the use of specific seating arrangements. Non Masters Action Research Project, Saint Xavier University and URI/Skylight Field-Based Masters Program. (Eric Document Reproduction Service No. 422129).

DuPaul, G. J., & Ekert, T. (1997). School-based interventions for students with attention-deficit hyperactivity disorder. A meta-analysis. *School Psychology Review, 26,* 5–27.

DuPaul, G. J., & Stoner, G. (1994). *ADHD in the school.* New York: Guilford Press.

Erk, R. R. (2000). Five frameworks for increasing understanding and effective treatment of Attention-Deficit/Hyperactivity Disorder: Predominately inattentive type. *Journal of Counseling and Development, 78*(4), 389–400.

Erk, R. R. (1995). *Elementary School Guidance & Counseling, 29*(4), 243–248.

Goldstein, S. (1996). *Managing attention and learning disorders in children: A guide for practitioners.* New York: John Wiley & Sons.

Goldstein, S. (1999). Attention-Deficit/Hyperactivity Disorder. In S. Goldstein & C. R. Reynolds (Eds.), *Handbook of neurodevelopmental and genetic disorders in children* (pp. 154–188). New York: Guilford Press.

Henderson, H. S., Jensen, W. R., Erken, N. E., Davidsmeyer, P. L. (1986). Variable interval reinforcement as a practical means of increasing and maintaining on-task behavior in classrooms. *Techniques, 2*(3), 217–229.

Hinshaw, S. P, Klein, R. G., & Abikoff, H. B. (2002). Childhood attention-deficit hyperactivity disorder. In P. E. Nathan & J. M. Gorman (Eds.), *A guide to treatments that work* (2nd ed.) (pp. 3–23). London: Oxford University Press.

Hinshaw, S. P., & Melnick, S. M. (1995). Peer relationships in boys with attention-deficit hyperactivity disorder with and without comorbid aggression. *Development and Psychopathology, 7,* 627–647.

Hoza, B., & Pelham, W. E. (1993). Attention-deficit hyperactivity disorder. In T. Ammerman, C. G. Last, & M. Hersen (Eds.), *Handbook of prescriptive treatments for children and adolescents* (pp. 64–84). Boston: Allyn and Bacon.

Lavin, P. (1997). A daily classroom checklist for communicating with parents of children with attention deficit. *School Counselor, 44*(4), 315–318.

Levine, M. D. (1993a). *All kinds of minds.* Cambridge, MA: Educators Publishing Service.

Levine, M. D. (1993b). *Guidelines for all kinds of minds.* Cambridge, MA: Educators Publishing Service.

MTA Cooperative Group. (1999). A 14-month randomized clinical trial of treatment strategies for attention deficit hyperactivity disorder. *Archives of General Psychiatry, 56*(12), 1073–1086.

Murphy, K. R. (1998). Psychological counseling of adults with AD/HD. In R. A. Barkley (Ed.), *Attention Deficit Disorder: A handbook for diagnosis and treatment* (pp. 582–591). New York: Guilford Press.

Pfiffner, L. (1996). *All about ADHD: The complete practical guide for classroom teachers.* New York: Scholastic.

Resnick, R. J. (2005). Attention deficit hyperactivity disorder in teens and adults: They don't all outgrow it. *Journal of Clinical Psychology, 61*(5), 529–533.

Richters, J. E., Arnold, L. E., Jensen, P. S., Abikoff, H., Conners, C. K., Greenhill, L. L., Hechtman, L. T., Hinshaw, S. P., Pelham, W. E., & Swanson, J. M. (1995). The National Institute of Mental Health Collaborative Multisite Mutimodal Treatment Study of Children with Attention-Deficit Hyperactivity Disorder (MTA): 1. Background and rational. *Journal of the American Academy of Child and Adolescent Psychiatry, 34,* 987–1000.

Robin, A. L. (1990). Training families with ADHD adolescents. In R. A. Barkley (Ed.), *Attention-deficit hyperactivity disorder: A handbook for diagnosis and treatment* (pp. 462–497). New York: Guilford Press.

Schwiebert, V. L., Sealander, K. A. & Tollerud, R. R. (1995). Attention-deficit hyperactivity disorder: an overview for school counselors. *Elementary School Guidance & Counseling, 29,* 249–259.

Sheridan, S. M., Dee, C. C., Morgan, J. C., McCormick, M. E., & Walker, D. (1996). A multimethod intervention for social skills deficits in children with ADHD and their parents. *School Psychology Review, 25,* 57–76.

Shimabukuro, S. M., Prater, M. A., Jenkins, A., Edelen-Smith, P. (1999). The effects of self-monitoring of academic performance on students with learning disabilities and ADD/ADHD. *Education and Treatment of Children, 22*(4), 397–414.

Slomokoski, C., Klein, R. G., & Mannuzza, S. (1995). Is self-esteem an important outcome in hyperactive children? *Journal of Abnormal Child Psychology, 23,* 303–315.

Tannock, R. (1998). Attention deficit hyperactivity disorder: Advances in cognitive, neurobiological and genetic research. *Journal of Child Psychology and Psychiatry, 39*, 65–99.

Teeter, P. A. (1998). *Interventions for AD/HD: Treatment in developmental context.* New York: Guilford Press.

Webb, L. D., & Myrick, R. D. (2003). A group counseling intervention for children with attention deficit hyperactivity disorder. *Professional School Counseling, 7*(2), 108–115.

Wells, K. C., Pelham, W. E., Kotkin, R. A., Hoza, B., Abidoff, H. B., Abramowitz, A., et al. (2000). Psychosocial treatment strategies in the MTA study: Rationale, methods, and critical issues in design and implementation. *Journal of Abnormal Child Psychology, 28*, 483–505.

Weyandt, L. L. (2001). *Attention Deficit/Hyperactivity Disorders: An AD/HD primer*. Boston: Allyn and Bacon.

ADDITIONAL RESOURCES

INTERNET

www.chadd.org. Web site for Children and Adults with Attention-Deficit/Hyperactivity Disorder (CHADD). CHADD is a national organization providing education, advocacy, and support for individuals with AD/HD. The Web site provides excellent resources for professional, educational, and family communities.

www.wings.buffalo.edu/adhd/. Established by SUNY Buffalo, the Center for Children and Families is an interdisciplinary center that disseminates new information to the professional, educational, and family communities and provides state-of-the-art treatments for families whose children have mental health and learning problems.

www.4teachers.org/4teachers/profd/motivtrack.shtml. Classroom management tracks are resource sites developed by educators. The information provided is practical and comes from the experience of those within the classroom.

PRINTED MATERIALS

Dendy, C. (2000). *Teaching teens with ADD and ADHD: A quick reference guide for teachers and parents*. Bethesda, MD: Woodbine House.

DuPaul, G. J., & Stoner, G. (2003). *AD/HD in the schools: Assessment and intervention strategies* (2nd ed.). New York: Guilford Press.

Power, T. J., Karustis, J. L., Habboushe, D. F. (2001). *Homework success for children with ADHD: A family–school intervention program*. New York: Guilford Press.

Rief, S. F., & Heimburge, J. A. (2002). *How to reach and teach ADD/AD/HD children: Practical techniques, strategies and interventions for helping children with attention problems and hyperactivity.* San Francisco: Jossey-Bass.

Weyandt, L. L. (2001). *Attention Deficit/Hyperactivity Disorders: An AD/HD primer*. Boston: Allyn and Bacon.

CHAPTER 2

DISRUPTIVE BEHAVIOR: TANTRUMS, OUT-OF-SEAT, AND CLOWNING

Disruptive behavior can appear in many forms and serve many functions. Disruption can take the form of behavior that is not only off task, but that also interferes with the ability of the student and others within the classroom to attend to the lesson at hand. Common examples of disruptive behavior include tantrums, getting out of one's seat without permission, talking with others, clowning, or simply pestering and annoying others within the class. Such behaviors result in the loss of lesson time for both the disruptive student and the others within the classroom. The disruptive behavior of a single student can consume a disproportionate amount of teacher time and attention, thus interfering with the normal flow of the curriculum.

Regardless of the nature of the disruptive behavior, it can be assumed that it is serving a purpose for the student who is being disruptive, one that is counterproductive to the goals of the lesson and the class. O'Neill, Horner, Albin, Storey, and Sprague (1990) suggested that disruptive behavior is a means to either (1) obtain something desirable or (2) escape or avoid something undesirable. It is not unusual, for example, for a student to engage in disruptive behavior to gain the attention of teacher and/or peers. In this situation, the teacher's attention (even when it appears to be negative attention, such as a reprimand) may serve as the reinforcement to maintain the undesirable behavior. Under these conditions, contingent withdrawal of that form of attention is the treatment strategy of choice, along with the differential reinforcement of appropriate on-task behavior (Hovert & Zeiler, 1995). However, as demonstrated in the article by Umbriet, Lane, and Dejud (2004), which is summarized later in the chapter, off-task behavior can also serve the purpose of helping the student escape or avoid something undesirable, in which case an alternative form of intervention (rather than extinction and differential reinforcement) would be needed. Because the purpose or reason for the disruptive behavior is so pivotal to the creation of an efficient intervention, the first step in intervening may be the performance of a functional behavioral assessment.

A functional behavior analysis is an assessment method of identifying the relationship between behaviors and the setting, antecedent, and consequent events that maintain those behaviors (see Kahn, 1999). The goals of the functional analysis are to understand the functions served by a particular behavior and to plan interventions based on those functions (Derby et al., 1992; Dunlap, Kern-Dunlap, Clarke, & Robbins, 1991).

OVERVIEW

The interventions presented in this chapter (Table 2.1), although targeting varying forms of disruptive classroom behaviors (i.e., tantrums, out-of-seat behavior), demonstrate the value of a functional behavioral analysis as the first step in intervention planning.

As with much of the research in the area of counseling, single cases or studies with small samples are most often employed. Although such designs can offer adequate control for threats to internal validity, their findings often cannot be generalized. Thus, when employing these strategies counselors need to carefully monitor the impact of an intervention in order to ensure its effectiveness.

TABLE 2.1 Overview of Studies Presented

TARGET PROBLEM	REFERENCE	K–6	6–9	9–12	OTHER SPECIFICATIONS
Reducing classroom disruption	Wilkinson (2003)	Y	N	N	Employed a behavioral consultation model to assist teacher in reducing the tantrum behavior of a 7-year-old, first-grade student
Reducing off-task, attention-seeking behavior	Umbriet, Lane, & Dejud (2004)	N	Y	N	Case study, reversal design with 10-year-old student, using modification in task difficulty to reduce off-task behavior
Decreasing occurrence of out-of-seat behavior, incomplete assignments, and talking out (including talking with peers)	Lohrmann & Talerico (2004)	Y	N	N	Classwide intervention/prevention program using peers as reinforcing agents
Single-case intervention with two students using short-term counseling model	Yarbrough & Thompson (2002)	N	Y	N	Employed a time-series design with a statistical procedure for assessing significance of behavioral change

SAMPLE INTERVENTIONS

Contingency Contracting: Reducing Classroom Tantrums

Author: Lee A. Wilkinson

Précis: This article demonstrates the effectiveness of a teacher-implemented behavioral intervention (contingency contracting) for reducing "challenging" behavior in the classroom.

Introduction

The study offers an example of a behavioral consultation with a teacher in order to develop, implement, maintain, and assess the effectiveness of a contingency management program targeted at reducing the tantrums and off-task behaviors of a 7-year-old, first-grade student. Intervention effectiveness was assessed using an A-B design with direct observation and the use of a behavior checklist to measure changes in disruptive behavior from baseline to treatment. Positive treatment effects were maintained at a four-week follow-up.

Intervention

The counselor, using a behavioral consultation model outlined by Kratochwill & Bergan (1990), assisted the teacher in gathering and analyzing baseline data and implementing a behavioral contract with the student. Because the goal of the student's disruptive behavior appeared to be attention seeking and social control, adult attention was employed as one of the reinforcements for appropriate behavior. The contract was presented as a game in which the student had the opportunity to earn rewards such as stickers, home–school notes, teacher attention, and freedom to engage in preferred classroom activities. The student could earn these rewards by (1) completing assignments, (2) interacting appropriately with other students, and (3) complying with teacher requests and classroom rules.

Reflection

Contingency management procedures targeting the reduction of inappropriate behavior by reinforcing more appropriate, yet equally functional, responses has been well documented in the literature (e.g., Scott, DeSimone, Fowler, & Webb, 2000). The added value of this study was the outlining of the steps employed in the consultation, including the problem-identification interview, the problem-analysis interview, and the treatment-implementation phase. The value of good consultation processes, along with research-based behavioral interventions, is clearly demonstrated.

Source: Wilkinson, L. A. (2003). Using behavioral consultation to reduce challenging behavior in the classroom. *Preventing School Failure, 47*(3), 100–105.

SAMPLE INTERVENTIONS

Modifying Task Difficulty

Authors: John Umbreit, Kathleen L. Lane, and Carlos Dejud

Précis: Modification of a student's off-task, attention-seeking behavior by adjusting task difficulty.

Introduction

This case study of a 10-year-old, fourth-grade male student demonstrated the effective use of increasing task difficulty as an intervention for reducing disruptive behaviors such as wandering around the classroom and talking with other students. Previous use of negative consequences failed to modify the student's behavior. As a result, the authors employed a functional behavioral assessment, collecting data on the antecedents and consequences that affected the student's off-task behavior. Results from the functional behavior assessment revealed that the student's off-task behaviors increased when the task at hand was, according to the student, "almost too easy." This observation led to the creation and implementation of the task adjustment as intervention.

Intervention

Using an A-B-A-B (reversal) design, the author identified the conditions under which the disruptive attention-seeking behavior was exhibited. The data revealed that each of the observed off-task behaviors occurred after the student had completed his assignments. During the baseline phase, the task assigned was the same as that given to the entire class. The treatment phase involved assignments of greater difficulty. The results indicated that during each baseline phase, the student was on task an average of 50 percent of the time, whereas during intervention phases time on task increased to an average of 77 percent.

Reflection

Research has pointed to the influence of curricular variables on the occurrence of in-class behavioral problems (e.g., Kern, Delaney, Clarke, Dunlap, & Childs, 2001). Task difficulty has been identified as one of the primary curricular variables associated with problem behaviors in the classroom (Gunter, Denny, Jack, Shores, & Nelson, 1993). The current study extended this research to demonstrate the effectiveness of modifying task difficulty as a means of increasing on-task behavior and thus reducing off-task, attention-seeking, and self-stimulating behaviors. As suggested by the authors, if the tasks assigned were stimulating, then alternatives would most likely not be sought.

In addition to the presentation of an interesting intervention, the study is useful in that it provides a clear, cogent example of the effective use of functional behavioral assessment as a tool for identifying the conditions that result in undesirable behaviors. The assessment was effective in targeting the specific conditions under which the identified behaviors were likely to occur and provided a direct link to the development of a function-based intervention.

Although the single-subject design employed lends to the validity of the conclusions drawn regarding the treatment effect, generalization of these findings to other students or other settings should be done with caution. As with all research, application to other settings needs to be done with caution, and the effectiveness of the intervention should be monitored closely.

Source: Umbriet, J., Lane, K. L., & Dejud, C. (2004). Improving classroom behavior by modifying task difficulty. *Journal of Positive Behavior Interventions, 6*(1), 13–20.

SAMPLE INTERVENTIONS

Group Contingency to Manage Disruptive Behavior

Authors: Sharon Lohrmann and Janet Talerico

Précis: An example of the use of group contingency on a classwide basis.

Introduction

This study employed an intervention that was designed to systematically teach and reinforce consistent behavior expectations. The intervention program, "Anchor the Boat," employs positively stated behavioral expectations, teacher-directed instruction, and group-based contingencies. Group-based contingency relies on peers functioning as change agents, influencing each other's behaviors by providing reminders, prompts, and encouragement (Gable, Arllen, & Hendrickson, 1994).

Intervention

Baseline data were collected on the aggregate occurrence of out-of-seat behavior, incomplete assignments, and talking out (including talking with peers). The "Anchor Your Boat" program was explained to the students. They were told that they could earn points by staying in their seats, completing assignments, and talking when it was their turn. The teacher hung a picture of a boat and anchor that were separated by approximately 20 inches. She informed the class that they would earn rewards if they could anchor the boat. The anchoring would be accomplished by attaching 10 paper clips from the anchor to the boat. A paper clip could be earned by having 50 or fewer aggregate incidents of disruption per class period. The use of 50 incidents was determined because of the high rate of disruption recorded during baseline.

The use of variable interval reinforcement appeared to result in an increase in on-task behavior and academic achievement. Once the class had "anchored the boat," each student was able to select one reward (e.g., toys, bookmarks, games) from a reward box. The chain was then removed, and the process began again.

The classwide intervention resulted in a substantial and steady decrease in level and rate of talk-out behaviors yet was somewhat less effective for reducing incomplete assignments and out-of-seat behavior.

Reflection

The small sample and absence of a randomized control group design requires caution when interpreting the apparent success of this program. Even with its limitations, the current study provides a look at a simple and positive intervention strategy that appears suitable for implementation by a classroom teacher. A counselor suggesting such an approach may experience less resistance from the classroom teachers because the group-contingency process is considered to be more acceptable than individualized interventions, which are often viewed as "special treatment" (Turco & Elliot, 1990). Further, the focus on earning points for positive behaviors enables the teachers to avoid coercive interaction cycles that often lead to the creation of a negative and combative classroom environment.

Source: Lohrmann, S., & Talerico, T. (2004). Anchor the Boat: A classwide intervention to reduce problem behavior. *Journal of Positive Behavior Interventions, 6*(2), 113–120.

DETAILED INTERVENTION

Reality Therapy and Solution-Focused Counseling for Student Off-Task Behavior

Introduction

Teachers report that failure to complete schoolwork or homework assignments, along with behavior that disrupts the class, are some of their primary concerns (Langdon, 1997). Off-task behaviors that restrict student's completion of academic assignments and that disrupt others within the class often demand the counselor's attention.

The current study investigated the efficacy of two short-term counseling approaches (i.e., Reality Therapy and Solution-Focused Brief Counseling) for elementary school students engaged in excessive off-task behaviors. The time-series design employed enabled the researchers to demonstrate significant positive changes in students' on-task behaviors when treated with either approach.

Method

The study took place in a suburban elementary school that mainly serves families of middle socioeconomic status. Participants included two children recruited from a suburban elementary school. The participants were selected based on the school counselor's recommendation, teacher reports, and willingness to participate. The first student was an 8-year-old African American male who was in the third grade at the time of the study. The second student was a 9-year-old Caucasian female enrolled in the fourth grade.

The first student's teacher reported that the student exhibited a variety of off-task behaviors, such as daydreaming and doodling, a lack of interaction with the classroom teacher, and a failure to complete and turn in schoolwork. The teacher of the second student reported similar behaviors of daydreaming, talking to friends in class, and failing to complete assignments.

Individual counseling sessions employing either a Reality Therapy or Solution-Focused Brief Counseling took place once a week over a two-month period. Each session lasted between 20 and 40 minutes.

An A-B design was used with goal-attainment scaling as the dependent measure. Data were collected in a time-series format over eight weeks. Baseline data were gathered during the first three weeks of the study followed by five weeks of the treatment phase.

Interventions

During the three-week baseline period, the counselor met with the students once a week to construct goal-attainment scales, build rapport, and collect data on the students' current level of performance on each of their goals. The baseline period was followed by the five-week counseling phase.

The first student received Solution-Focused Brief Counseli scribed by Sklare (1997). The following steps were used by the SFBC approach with the student:

1. Focused on solutions rather than problems.
2. Used scaling to determine how much of the problem had been solved.
3. Used the miracle question to identify what the student would be doing if the problem were magically solved.
4. Reviewed the miracle and identified what the student would be doing differently when the miracle happened, focusing on exceptions.
5. Used positive blame to assist student in identifying what would go into making this exception.
6. Aimed for a 10-percent improvement each week. Engaged the student to identify what he would have to do to move up the scale (e.g., from a 5 to a 6 on a 10-point scale).
7. Reviewed with the student things that could interfere with moving from a 5 to 6 in a particular week—flagged the minefield.
8. Reinforced the things the student was already doing to make the miracle happen.
9. Had the student identify his level of motivation to work on solving the problem.
10. Each session ended with a written reminder highlighting the connection between the student's abilities and talents and the demands of the assigned task.

The second student received counseling from a Reality Therapy orientation, as described by Glasser (2000). The following Reality Therapy steps were used by the counselor in her counseling approach with the second student:

1. Focused on what the student was doing rather than on why she was doing it.
2. Helped student evaluate whether her choices and behavior helped or hindered her getting what she wanted.
3. Asked the student if she would be willing to stop doing things that were not helping her get what she wanted.
4. Brainstormed alternatives to try to solve the problem or get what she wanted.
5. Had the student commit to trying some of the new behaviors for one week and report on how well they worked.
6. Focused on logical consequences rather than punishment when the student did not meet her commitments.
7. Focused on the student's responsibility for meeting her own needs.
8. Focused on the fact that only the student could control her own behavior and that she had a choice in what behaviors she choose.

The authors reported that both students showed statistically significant improvement in on-task behavior when compared to baseline. Using a T score analysis method, the authors reported that the first student improved to 65.96 (1.6 SD above the mean) following treatment, having had a baseline initial T score of 26.95. Behaviorally, the student was submitting all weekly assignments in three of his four school subjects. Similar improvements were found for the second student, whose T scores went from 23.25 at intake to a high of 75.15 following treatment. Similarly, her behavior was reported to have progressed from completing no homework to completing all assignments in three of her four subjects. Of special note was that during the follow-up interview during the fall semester of the following year, the students' teachers reported that both students continued to maintain the goals they had attained at the time of the study.

Reflection

The results offer support for the use of individual counseling with either a Reality Therapy or SFBC orientation when working with students struggling with off-task behavior. Each method enabled the children to set specific goals, track their progress, and experience positive changes in behavior and in classroom performance. The fact that both of the interventions employed in this study are designed to be used over relatively short periods of time and appear to demonstrate rapid impact make them attractive to the school counselor, who typically fails to have the luxury of providing long-term interventions.

One particularly interesting facet of this study is the use of a single-participant design. Such a method appears to be a user-friendly approach for school counselors seeking to employ strategies to assess the validity of their interventions. Although such designs provide for control of the threats to internal validity, the ability to generalize these findings to other settings and students is limited. As such, counselors employing these intervention strategies should do so with caution and strictly monitor their impact.

Source: Yarbrough, J. L., & Thompson, C. L. (2002). Using single-participant research to assess counseling approaches on student's off-task behavior—statistical data included. *Professional School Counseling, 5*(5), 308–315.

FROM THE FIELD

The following recommendations and suggestions reflect the experience and anecdotal reporting from counselors working "in the field." They are provided as suggestions to be employed by the school counselor as they interact with the classroom teacher in their role as consultant. Each strategy should be monitored and assessed for effectiveness.

Attention Getting—Boasting

- The boastful student may be seeking to compensate for feelings of inferiority; therefore, providing the student with opportunities for gaining attention with appropriate behaviors may reduce the need for such boastfulness. For example, providing the student with the opportunity to take a classroom leadership role—such as distributing papers, collecting projects, or acting as class monitor—as a reward for reduced boastful attention-seeking behavior may reduce inappropriate acting out.
- Ignore the boastful behavior but provide recognition and social praise when the student acts in ways that are socially acceptable.
- Be sure the tasks assigned are within the student's level of functioning.
- Provide the student with opportunities for attention getting that are appropriate to the classroom. For example, allow the student to read aloud, go to the board, run an errand, take care of plants or animals, and so on.

Attention Getting—Tantrums

- Ask the student to leave the room until he or she can gain control and act appropriately. Tantrum behavior as a means of attention getting requires an audience, removing the audience may help to stop the behavior.
- Do not threaten the student with punishment, simply point out the inappropriateness of the behavior, direct the student to gain control, and verbally praise the student for responding appropriately.
- Provide the student with a quiet, distraction-free area for quiet study time, seat work, and test taking.

Clowning and Annoying Others

- Provide soft reprimands when the student is off task. For example, walk near the student's desk and point to the text or worksheet or softly remind the student to continue the task.
- Use the Premack principle. Allow the student to "perform" at the end of a certain amount of on-task, appropriate behavior.
- When the student acts up, with antics targeted to get classmate response, stand close to the student and point to classwork or gently touch the student's shoulder. Eventually, the student will recognize that when the teacher begins to walk toward him or her, it is a cue to calm down.

- Make time for humor and laughter. If the student is attempting to rile the teacher with humorous statements, note that humor is a good thing when done at the right time. Further, allowing for a few seconds for the student to take center stage once work is complete would disarm the student.
- Bring the student closer to the teacher or place the student next to another student who can resist the student's disruptive behavior and comments and model proper behavior.
- Disruptive behavior such as clowning may increase during quiet, reflective times. The use of hands-on learning may help to reduce the need for alternative forms of stimulation.

REFERENCES

Barlow, D. H., & Hersen, M. (1984). *Single case experimental designs: Strategies for studying behavior change* (2nd ed.). Elmstead, NY: Pergamon Press.

Dunlap, G., Kern-Dunlap, L., Clarke, S., & Robbins, F. R. (1991). Functional assessment, curricular revision and severe behavior problems. *Journal of Applied Behavior Analysis, 24*, 387–397.

Gable, R. A., Arllen, N. L., & Hendrickson, J. M. (1994). Use of students with emotional/behavioral disorders as behavior change agents. *Education & Treatment of Children, 17*(3), 267–276.

Glasser, W. (2000). *Reality therapy in action*. New York: Harper Collins.

Gunter, P., Denny, R. K., Jack, S., Shores, R., & Nelson, C. M. (1993). Aversive stimuli in academic interactions between students with serious emotional disturbances and their teachers. *Behavioral Disorder, 18*, 265–274.

Horner, R. H., Day, H. M., Sprague, J. R., O'Brien, M., & Heathfield, L. T. (1991). Interspersed requests: A nonaversive procedure for reducing aggression and self-injury during instruction. *Journal of Applied Behavior Analysis, 24*, 265–278.

Kahn, W. (1999). *The A-B-C's of Human Experience: An integrative model*. Belmont: CA: Brooks Cole.

Kratochwill, T. R., & Bergan, J. R. (1990). *Behavioral consultation in applied settings: An individual guide*. New York: Plenum.

Kazdin, A. E. (1982). *Single-case research designs*. New York: Oxford University Press.

Langdon, C. A. (1997). The fourth Phi Delta Kappa poll of teachers' attitudes toward the public schools. *Phi Delta Kappan, 79*(3), 212–220.

Lohrmann, S., & Talerico, T. (2004). Anchor the Boat: A classwide intervention to reduce problem behavior. *Journal of Positive Behavior Interventions, 6*(2), 113–120.

O'Neill, R., Horner, R., Albin, R. Storey, K., & Sprague, J. (1990). *Functional analysis of problem behavior: A practical assessment guide*. Sycamore, IL: Sycamore.

Scott, T. M., DeSimone, C., Fowler, W., & Webb, E. (2000). Using functional analysis to develop interventions for challenging behaviors in the classroom: Three case studies. *Preventing School Failure, 44*, 51–56.

Sklare, G. B. (1997). *Brief counseling that works: A solution-focused approach for school counselors. Practical skills for counselors*. Thousand Oaks, CA: Corwin Press.

Turco, T. L., & Elliot, S. N. (1990). Acceptability and effectiveness of group contingencies for improving spelling achievement. *Journal of School Psychology, 28*, 27–37.

Umbriet, J., Lane, K. L., & Dejud, C. (2004). Improving classroom behavior by modifying task difficulty. *Journal of Positive Behavior Interventions, 6*(1), 13–20.

Wilkinson, L. A. (2003). Using behavioral consultation to reduce challenging behavior in the classroom. *Preventing School Failure, 47*(3), 100–105.

Yarbrough, J. L., & Thompson, C. L. (2002). Using single-participant research to assess counseling approaches on student's off-task behavior—statistical data included. *Professional School Counseling, 5*(5), 308–315.

ADDITIONAL RESOURCES

INTERNET

http://pbis.org. The Web site of the National Technical Assistance Center on Positive Behavioral Interventions and Support provides schools with information and assistance for identifying, adapting, and sustaining effective schoolwide discipline practices.

http://cecp.air.org/fba/problembehavior/main.htm. The Web site of the Center for Effective Collaboration and Practice provides an excellent look at functional behavioral assessment and intervention planning.

www.nasponline.org. This Web site provides fact sheets and Web links on positive behavior, zero tolerance, IDEA, and discipline.

PRINTED MATERIALS

Allen, L. D., Gottselig, M., & Boylan, S. (1982). A practical mechanism for using free time as a reinforcer in classrooms. *Education and Treatment of Children, 54*, 347–353.

Liaupsin, C. J., Scott, T. M., & Nelson, C. M. (2000). *Functional behavioral assessment: An interactive training module: User's manual and facilitator's guide* (2nd ed.). Longmont, CO: Sopris West.

Witt, J. C., Daly, E. M., & Noell, G. (2000). *Functional assessments: A step-by-step guide to solving academic and behavioral problems*. Longmont, CO: Sopris West.

CHAPTER 3

DISHONESTY: CHEATING AND STEALING

Dishonesty among school-aged children has been and continues to be on the rise. A survey of 12,000 high-school students by the Josephson Institute of Ethics (2004) found that 74 percent of students had cheated on an exam at least once in 2003. Dishonesty appears to be influenced by several factors, including the potential for gain, the probability of detection, and the degree of sanction if the dishonesty is detected (Covey, Saladin, & Killen, 2001). The current chapter presents interventions targeted to two forms of dishonesty among school-aged children: cheating and stealing.

CHEATING

Academic dishonesty has been a problem for many decades and continues to be of concern in the educational community. Research shows that academic cheating is widespread and becomes increasingly common as students gain more years of schooling (Finn & Frone, 2004).

In-class cheating has gone high tech. Students who cheat have moved beyond reliance on crib sheets. They now use cell phones to instant message questions and answers, and they store notes on their graphing calculators. The Internet is another source of support for cheating. Students can swap projects and homework in online chat rooms and hundreds of sites, such as www.schoolsucks.com and www.evilhouseofcheat.com, provide custom-written term papers.

Cheating is more likely among students who are motivated by a desire to get high grades regardless of learning (Anderman, Griesinger, & Westerfield, 1998; Newstead, Franklyn-Stokes, & Armstead, 1996). Students often employ cheating as a mechanism to avoid failure and appear competent in a particular domain (Calabrese & Cochran, 1990; Michaels & Miethe, 1989; Schab, 1991; Rost & Wild, 1990). This notion finds indirect support in the fact that cheating appears to increase in frequency as students transition from elementary school to middle school and high school, where increased emphasis is placed on grades and academic performance. Anderman, Griesigner, and Westerfield (1998) found that cheating often becomes a mechanism for survival when students are in environments that stress competition and grades. Concerns about performing well may stem from such factors as pressure from parents, heavy school workloads, or inadequate time to study (see Cizek, 1999; Whitley & Keith-Spiegel, 2002). Further, cheating is more likely among students with low academic self-efficacy and performance concerns (Evans & Craig, 1990; Murdock, Hale, & Weber, 2001). However, goal orientation is not the only important situational condition correlated with cheating behavior. Researchers (e.g., Houston, 1977; Corcoran & Rotter, 1987) have found that the probability of detection plays an important role in the presence or absence of cheating behavior.

STEALING

Theft that does not involve confrontation or the use of force with a victim (i.e., nonconfrontational stealing) has been found to be associated with childhood conduct disorders (Miller & Klungness, 1986). Persistent involvement in theft during adolescence may be a precursor to more serious criminality, especially when such behavior is compounded by aggressive tendencies, academic failure, or family maladjustment (Loeber, 1996; Loeber, Tremblay, Gragnon, & Charlebois, 1989; Patterson, 1986). It is essential that intervention and prevention steps be taken before these behaviors become entrenched.

Research suggests that prevention and intervention efforts require a multidimensional approach that attends to peer relationships, attitudes toward school, family relationships, developmental level, and personal history (Moncher & Miller, 1999; Loeber, 1996). Because self-reported stealing correlates with poor school attitudes, one suggested focus for intervention is school performance and achievement (Farrington, 1996; Kagan, 1991). The use of peer models and group interventions that promote healthy socialization and help youths cope with typical developmental stressors and that teach problem-solving skills has also been suggested as an approach to intervention and prevention (Greening, 1997). Finally, it is generally agreed that parents' involvement is necessary because of their potential for influencing the student's attitude toward and participation in school; their role in monitoring activities and providing consequences for misbehavior; and their influence on peer choice (Tremblay & Drabman, 1997; Warr, 1993).

OVERVIEW

Although it is clear that something needs to be done about both cheating and stealing among school-aged children, a review of the current research reveals a real absence of information identifying causes and treatment of such behaviors. The studies found in this chapter, although somewhat dated, remain some of the best of practice that appear in the literature (see Table 3.1). In addition, the studies presented use a single-case-study methodology, typically targeting elementary and middle school children; therefore, attempts to generalize these findings to other students, especially adolescents, must be done with caution. It is clear that more formal research needs to be performed. In the meantime, school counselors need to monitor and assess the impact of their own interventions.

TABLE 3.1 Overview of Studies Presented

TARGET PROBLEM	REFERENCE	K–6	6–9	9–12	OTHER SPECIFICATIONS
Reducing cheating in the classroom	Houser (1982)	Y	Y	N	Employed punishment as means of control
Reducing cheating in the classroom	Murphy (1987)	Y	Y	Y	Preventive programming drawn from correlational research
Stealing	Rosen & Rosen (1983)	Y	N	N	Case study of 7-year-old student using stimulus control and response cost
Stealing	Luisellin & Pine (1999)	N	Y	N	Case study of 10-year-old female; good illustration of the use of a functional behavioral analyses
Stealing	Stumphauzer (1976)	N	Y	Y	Case study of 12-year-old male demonstrating the value of extinction as an intervention when stealing is reinforced by social attention

SAMPLE INTERVENTIONS

Classroom Control as a Means of Reducing Cheating

Author: Betsy Bosak Houser

Précis: The use of coercive power within the classroom was found to produce the least cheating and the most favorable student attitudes when compared to reward and five other power-based strategies.

Introduction

The study tested the differential effect of social power and influence in controlling cheating. French and Raven (1959) identified five types of social power and influence:

1. Coercive power, or the ability to reward and/or punish another
2. Legitimate power, which is power that stems from society's sanctioning of a person's role and authority
3. Informational power, which is power accrued because the information provided by one person is viewed as highly relevant and useful by the second
4. Expert power, or the power given to a person who is perceived as having special knowledge and skill that is valued and necessary by another
5. Referent or identification power, which is the power accrued to a person because he or she is attractive, a person that another wants to be like, in short, a role model

Intervention

The study used French and Raven's conditions of power (except referent) in an attempt to control cheating behavior. Specifically, the conditions of control were:

1. Reward power: For example, allowing those who did not cheat to go to recess early.
2. Coercive power: Sending children who cheat to the office.
3. Referent power: Making reference to others in the classroom who don't cheat (e.g., "your friends who don't cheat").
4. Legitimate power: Relying on the teacher's right to control behavior in the classroom (e.g., "there will be no cheating during the test").
5. Informational power: Suggesting that not-cheating is a way to learn something of value for the future.

The results supported the notion that the teacher's use of coercive power (i.e., the ability to punish the transgressor) not only resulted in the lowest rate of cheating, but also in the most favorable attitudes of the students toward the teacher.

Reflection

It is important to note that although the use of punishment appears to be effective, additional research on punishment (e.g., Kazdin, 1994) suggests that such an approach should be used in moderation. The extensive use of coercive power (i.e., punishment) may lend itself to the creation of a combative classroom environment and disruption of the learning–teaching process.

Source: Houser, B. B. (1982). Student cheating and attitude: A function of classroom control techniques. *Contemporary Educational Psychology, 7,* 113–123.

SAMPLE INTERVENTIONS

Encouraging Schoolwide Honesty

Author: John P. Murphy

Précis: A review of preventive strategies targeted to increasing schoolwide honesty and reducing cheating behaviors.

Introduction

Previous research has shown the existence of a relationship between cheating and variables such as student anxiety about performance, fear of failure, limited experiences of success, school and home pressure, and inappropriate (too easy or too difficult) assignments. The author extrapolates from these findings to provide strategies in the form of primary, secondary, and tertiary preventive measures that are geared toward promoting increased honesty, thus decreasing the occurrence of cheating.

Intervention

The author suggested that each of the following serve as valuable preventive measures:

- Develop policies on cheating that direct staff in their interactions with students in situations conducive to cheating.
- Advocate and model honesty—both informally and within instructional activities.
- Create an environment supportive of honesty.
- Arrange conditions to make cheating risky.
- Reduce chance for cheating by making multiple tasks, varying assignments, or even keeping student papers.
- Organize discussion targeted to fostering moral/value development.
- Employ punishment as a deterrent to cheating.

For students who have already engaged in cheating behavior, the author suggests the following tertiary prevention measures:

- Move beyond punishment to creating strategies that target students' development and employment of honest behavior.
- Connect motivation with intervention. It may be important to alter the effects and/or increase the students' awareness of the effects that cheating has on the perpetrator and others in the classroom.
- Emphasis should be placed on the misbehavior and the emotional/moral implications of this behavior rather than simply focusing on the consequences of the action.

Reflection

The work provides intuitively appealing recommendations for the development of schoolwide strategies targeted at reducing and preventing cheating behaviors. The emphasis is on the need to create an environment within the school that models integrity, honesty, and respect as a means of deterring cheating. This approach appears to be a logical conclusion drawn from the correlational research identifying elements associated with cheating behavior. However, the article provides a clear example of the limitations of research on cheating and interventions.

Numerous correlational studies have identified conditions associated with increased cheating; however, no randomly assigned, control-group studies have been conducted to test the efficacy of a specific intervention strategy. Further research is called for; in the short term, counselors should employ action research strategies (see Parsons & Brown, 2002) that enable them to validate the effectiveness of their own "intuitively appealing" interventions.

Source: Murphy, J. P. (1987). Children and cheating. In A. Thomas & J. Grimes (Eds.), *Children's needs: Psychological perspective* (pp. 83–87). Washington, DC: National Association of School Psychologists.

SAMPLE INTERVENTIONS

Stimulus Control-Reinforcement and Response Cost as a Means of Reducing Stealing

Authors: Howard Rosen and L. Alison Rosen

Précis: Elimination of stealing by a first grader through stimulus-control training.

Introduction

Behavior modification is more difficult when the contingencies are ineffective, inconsistent, or delayed and weak. Too often, stealing results in the acquisition of a desired item and even the attention and support of admiring peers. Negative consequences for stealing and/or positive consequences for restraint and decisions not to steal are not always readily available. The current case study of a 7-year-old first grader demonstrated the importance of both positive and negative consequences in reducing stealing behavior.

Intervention

The authors employed differential reinforcement to reduce stealing by a 7-year-old male in the first grade. Treatment consisted of marking the student's possessions with green circles. Teaching staff would check his person, desk, and supply box every 15 minutes and reinforced him with praise and tokens for having only marked items. However, if items were found that were unmarked, they were considered to be stolen, and a verbal reprimand and a point fine were applied.

An A-B-A-B design was employed in which a baseline of 11 days was followed by the first treatment (points and fines) for 15 days. The points were part of a classroom token-economy system and were exchangeable for items at a classroom store. Stealing behavior decreased from 6.0 to .32 stolen items a day. The authors employed a 12-day fading condition during which time the subject's belongings were checked every 2 hours instead of every 15 minutes. From this point, the token system was systematically eliminated and items were only checked when something was reported as missing. During a 31-day follow-up period, the subject averaged .09 stolen items/day, as contrasted to the initial 6 items per day found during the baseline period.

Reflection

An important element of this intervention is the consistent application of consequences, a process that was made easier by employing the possession of items (marked and unmarked) rather than attempting to catch the behavior in process. What appears to be an obvious limitation to the general utilization of this procedure is that a teacher without the assistance of an aide or aides may find it disruptive and unrealistic to check a student's items every 15 minutes. The other limitation that would need to be addressed is that for this differential reinforcement treatment to work, the reinforcement for the alternative, non-stealing behavior needs to be more desirable (stronger) than that derived from stealing. Thus, although teacher attention and tangibles may work for younger children, the role of peer as reinforcer may need to be considered when working with preadolescent and adolescent clients.

Source: Rosen, H. S., & Rosen, L. A. (1983). Eliminating stealing: Use of stimulus control with an elementary student. *Behavior Modification, 7,* 56–63.

SAMPLE INTERVENTIONS

Extinction as a Means of Controlling Stealing

Authors: James K. Luisellin and Jennifer Pine

Précis: A case study of a 10-year-old female whose stealing behavior was successfully treated using an extinction process.

Introduction

The case study addresses the behavioral treatment of stealing exhibited by a child in a public-school setting. The student was a 10-year-old female diagnosed as having AD/HD and, provisionally, as having an obsessive-compulsive disorder.

Intervention

Data from a functional behavioral assessment suggested that the student's behavior was maintained by the social attention it elicited. Using these data and a hypothesis-driven model of treatment formulation, intervention consisted of eliminating multiple sources of attention (e.g., peers, teacher, parents) in an extinction paradigm. Intervention was associated with a systematic reduction in stealing; results were maintained through a 12-month follow-up.

Reflection

The case provides a good illustration of the diagnostic-intervention link and the value of functional behavioral assessment. This process allows for the matching of intervention to the functional influences that maintain the behavior of concern. The tailoring of treatment to diagnosis, although increasing effectiveness, makes it difficult to generalize the findings of this case study to others, because stealing behavior can be effected by multiple sources of control.

In addition to the limited ability to generalize these findings, it is also important to note that caution needs to be taken when using an extinction process as intervention. When using an extinction paradigm, one must be prepared for an "extinction blip"; that is, the initial increased intensity or frequency of the behavior being extinguished. Because of this, prior to employing such a strategy one must be sure that the escalation in the behavior can be tolerated long enough to allow for extinction to occur. Otherwise, attention may be given to the escalated behavior, thus intermittently reinforcing the behavior of real concern. This results in a situation that increases the difficulty of future extinction.

Source: Luisellin, J. K., & Pine, J. (1999). Social control of childhood stealing in a public school: A case study. *Journal of Behavior Therapy & Experimental Psychiatry, 30*(3), 231–239.

DETAILED INTERVENTION

Family Contracting and Self-Reinforcement of Alternative Behavior

Author: Jerome S. Stumphauzer

Précis: Stealing behavior of 5 years' duration in a 12-year-old girl was overcome by a combination of self-reinforcement of alternative behavior and family contracting.

Introduction

One of the difficulties with attempting to reduce stealing behavior is that the behavior is most often self-reinforcing. The stealing behavior most often results in the acquisition of a desired object, and thus is reinforced. Further, as with other criminal behaviors, aversive controls have proven ineffective. As such, most research on the modification of delinquent behavior has pointed to the use of behavior therapy, contingency management in particular. The current study extends the use of behavioral principles as specifically applied to stealing behavior. The focus of the intervention was on the use of self-reinforcement of an alternative, incompatible response as a means of reducing stealing behavior.

Method

The study focused on the case of a 12-year-old student who exhibited repeated incidences of theft. According to the school and parents, the student exhibited "uncontrollable stealing" almost daily for five years. With the exception of the stealing (mostly of money, which was used for sweets and ice cream), teachers and parents described her as a good student with above average grades. The frequency of stealing during a baseline behavioral analysis was four to five times a week. The behavioral analysis also revealed that in addition to acquiring the desired object, the stealing was also being reinforced by the attention she received from teachers, the principal, and her parents.

Intervention

The intervention developed was a direct result of the behavioral analysis. The intervention involved a combination of self-control techniques (see Meichenbaum & Goodman, 1971) and family contingency contracting (see Stuart, 1971).

Treatment occurred over 15 sessions, initially once a week and later once every 4 weeks for a total of 5 months. Each session included individual and family meetings.

The first three sessions involved the gathering of baseline measures. Frequency of stealing behavior was recorded at home by the client's mother and at school by the client's teacher.

Starting with the fourth session, self-control techniques were introduced. The analysis of the exact circumstances under which the stealing occurred along with identifying what the client said to herself provided the information needed for self-control. Role-play was employed to have the client experience the usual kinds of things that she would steal and then practice shifting her attention to alternative activities. If she engaged in these nonstealing alternatives, she would self-reinforce with comments such as "I'm proud of myself." The technique followed the formula of self-monitoring, self-evaluation, and self-reinforcement. The client was asked to keep a record of her stealing. Initially, data were collected on "the number of times I steal." However, starting with the sixth session, the focus was shifted to more positive behavior, with the client recording the frequency of "I did very well, I did not steal . . . " and then recording the number of times she thought "I have done so well in the past that I did not think to steal."

For the last two months of treatment, the self-evaluation measures were:

- "I'm trustworthy. I keep my hand to myself."
- "At the store I look for what I'm supposed to and not things that will get my interest."

In addition to self-monitoring, a simple family contract was employed in which praise and a 20-cent allowance were given for each day of no stealing. Bonuses for entire weeks of not stealing were used, and these included engaging in special activities or meals on Sunday.

The stealing behavior stopped altogether by the sixth week of treatment and continued at this zero rate through 6-, 12-, and 18-month follow-up periods.

Reflection

Behavioral strategies have successfully been employed to modify a number of delinquent behaviors. Surprisingly, there is a real absence of research on the use of behavioral therapy principles with stealing behavior. The current case study is one of the few that points to the potential value of behavioral intervention with students who steal. The major limitation to this study is its case study format. Although the results are encouraging, generalizability of findings is significantly limited due to the case study methodology employed.

Source: Stumphauzer, J. S. (1976). Elimination of stealing by self-reinforcement of alternative behavior and family contracting. *Journal of Behavior Therapy & Experimental Psychiatry,* 7(3), 265–268.

FROM THE FIELD

As with each of the chapters presented within this text, the recommendations provided in this section—"From the Field"—reflect suggestions based on the experience and anecdotal reporting of counselors working within our schools. Note that the suggestions listed within this chapter emphasize strategies applied within the classroom by the classroom teacher. They are provided as suggestions to be employed by school counselors as they interact with classroom teachers in their role as consultants.

Cheating: General Considerations

- Establish an honor code and develop a climate of honesty within the classroom.
- Consequences for cheating need to be specified. They need to be clear, concrete, and applied consistently.
- Shift focus from emphasis on performance to one of improvement and mastery. Remove the pressure for cheating. Grades, demands for perfection, and parental and/or teacher pressure should be reduced.
- When catching a child cheating, confront the student privately and focus on having the student strategize about how to control him or herself better next time.
- Be sure to reinforce (i.e., publicly display) works that are clearly student productions.
- Make work challenging but within students' reach.
- Discuss academic honesty and integrity. Do not assume students know why cheating is wrong.
- Try to identify the "reason" for the cheating and provide the student an alternative way to achieve this goal. For example, if there is pressure to achieve, provide the student with study skills, extra help, and anxiety-reduction techniques.

Cheating: Tests

- Inform the class that you will monitor behavior during tests by providing alternative forms of the test, moving desks, and moving about the room.
- Use multiple versions of the same test so students don't share the questions and answers with friends in other classes.
- Give verbal warnings before each test.
- Require students to show all work and explain all answers.
- Arrange the room with ample space between seats.
- Circulate around the room.

Cheating: Papers/Projects

- Break work down into smaller steps so that students submit works in progress.
- Inform the students about information and assistance on the Web. Show them you are aware of the resource as a means of deterring its use.
- Tailor assignments to individual course goals.
- Tailor assignments to students' individual goals.
- Have students attach copies of a couple of their resources.

Nonconfrontational Stealing

- Make the student return the items taken or replace them.
- Avoid sermons and moral judgment; calmly and firmly remind the child that the items did not belong to him or her.
- Avoid arguing or forcing confessions. Just direct the student to return the item: "You took it . . . take it back."
- Identify motivation for stealing by talking with the student. Strategize with the student to find more appropriate ways to meet these needs.
- Have the child return the stolen item and provide the "victim" with some form of additional recompense.
- In younger students, taking items from the teacher's desk may be done for attention. Teacher should not overreact but warn the class to safeguard their items and provide the "suspected student" with attention when functioning.
- Reduce the opportunity and "invitation" to stealing by instituting classroom and system-level changes that increase property security, such as the use of locks, warning signs, and even increased monitoring.
- Make the costs of stealing known and undesirable. Defining and publicizing student behavior codes and disciplinary procedures can be effective in reducing nonconfrontative stealing.

REFERENCES

Anderman, E. M., Griesigner, T., & Westerfield, G. (1998). Motivation and cheating during early adolescence. *Journal of Educational Psychology, 90*(1), 84–93.

Calabrese, R. L., & Cochran, J. T. (1990). The relationship of alienation to cheating among a sample of American adolescents. *Journal of Research and Development in Education, 23,* 65–72.

Cizek, G. J. (1999). *Cheating on tests: How to do it, detect it, and prevent it.* Mahwah, NJ: Erlbaum.

Corcoran, K. J., & Rotter, J. B. (1987). Morality-conscience guilt scale as a predictor of ethical behavior in a cheating situation among college females. *Journal of General Psychology, 114,* 117–123.

Covey, M. K., Saladin, S., & Killen, P. J. (2001). Self-monitoring, surveillance, and incentive effects on cheating. *The Journal of Social Psychology, 129*(5), 673–679.

Evans, E. D., & Craig, D. (1990). Teacher and student perceptions of academic cheating in middle and senior high schools. *The Journal of Educational Research, 84,* 44–52.

Farrington, D. P. (1996). The explanation and prevention of youthful offending. In J. D. Hawkins (Ed.), *Delinquency and crime: Current theories*. Cambridge: Cambridge University Press.

Finn, K. V., & Frone, M. R. (2004). Academic performance and cheating: Moderating role of school identification and self-efficacy. *Journal of Educational Research, 97*, 115–123.

French, J. R. P., Jr., & Raven, B. (1959). The bases of social power. In D. Cartwright (Ed.), *Studies in social power*. Ann Arbor, MI: University of Michigan Institute of Social Research.

Greening, L. (1997). Adolescent stealers' and nonstealers' social problem-solving skills. *Adolescence, 32*, 51–55.

Kagan, J. (1991). Etiologies of adolescents at risk. *Journal of Adolescent Health, 12*, 591–596.

Kazdin, A. E. (1994). *Behavior modification in applied settings* (5th ed.). Pacific Grove, CA: Brooks/Cole.

Houser, B. B. (1982). Student cheating and attitude: A function of classroom control techniques. *Contemporary Educational Psychology, 7*, 113–123.

Houston, J. P. (1977). Cheating behavior, anticipated success-failure, confidence, and test importance. *Journal of Educational Psychology, 69*, 55–60.

The Josephson Institute of Ethics. (2004). Eye on cheaters. *Current Events, 103*(15), 1–3.

Loeber, R. (1996). Developmental continuity, change, and pathways in male juvenile problem behaviors and delinquency. In J. D. Hawkins (Ed.), *Delinquency and crime: Current theories*. Cambridge: Cambridge University Press.

Loeber, R., Tremblay, R. E., Gragnon, C., & Charlebois, P. (1989). Continuity and desistance in disruptive boys' early fighting at school. *Development and Psychopathology, 1*, 39–50.

Luisellin, J. K., & Pine, J. (1999). Social control of childhood stealing in a public school: A case study. *Journal of Behavior Therapy & Experimental Psychiatry, 30*(3), 231–239.

Meichenbaum, D., & Goodman, J. (1971). Training impulsive children to talk to themselves: A means of developing self-control. *Journal of Abnormal Psychology, 77*, 115–126.

Michaels, J. W., & Miethe, T. D. (1989). Applying theories of deviance to academic cheating. *Social Science Quarterly, 70*, 870–885.

Miller, G. E., & Klungness, L. (1986). Treatment of nonconfrontative stealing in school-aged children. *School Psychology Review, 15*(1), 24–35.

Moncher, F. J., & Miller, G. E. (1999). Nondelinquent youth's stealing behavior and their perception of parents, school, and peers. *Adolescence, 34*(135), 577–592.

Murdock, T. B., Hale, N. M., & Weber, M. J. (2001). Predictors of cheating among early adolescents: Academic and social motivations. *Contemporary Educational Psychology, 26*, 96–115.

Murphy, J. P. (1987). Children and cheating. In A. Thomas & J. Grimes (Eds.), *Children's needs: Psychological perspective* (pp. 83–87). Washington, DC: National Association of School Psychologists.

Newstead, S. E., Franklyn-Stokes, A., & Armstead, P. (1996). Individual differences in student cheating. *Journal of Educational Psychology, 88*, 229–241.

Parsons, R. D., & Brown, K. A. (2002). *Teacher as reflective practitioner and action researcher*. Belmont, CA: Wadsworth.

Patterson, G. E. (1986). Performance models for antisocial boys. *American Psychologist, 41*, 432–444.

Rosen, H. S., & Rosen, L. A. (1983). Eliminating stealing: Use of stimulus control with an elementary student. *Behavior Modification, 7*, 56–63.

Rost, D. H., & Wild, K. P. (1990). Cheating and achievement-avoidance at school: Components and assessment. *Zeitschrift fur Padagogische Psychologie, 4*, 13–27.

Schab, F. (1991). Schooling without learning: Thirty years of cheating in high school. *Adolescence, 26*, 839–847.

Stuart, R. B. (1971). Behavioral contracting within the families of delinquents. *Journal of Behavior Therapy & Experimental Psychiatry, 2*, 1–11.

Sumphauzer, J. S. (1976). Elimination of stealing by self-reinforcement of alternative behavior and family contracting. *Journal of Behavior Therapy & Experimental Psychiatry, 7*(3), 265–268.

Tremblay, G. C., & Drabman, R. S. (1997). An intervention for childhood stealing. *Child and Family Behavior Therapy, 19*, 33–40.

Warr, M. (1993). Parents, peers, and delinquency. *Social Forces, 72*, 247–264.

Whitley, B. E., Jr., & Keith-Spiegel, P. (2002). *Academic dishonesty: An educator's guide*. Mahwah, NJ: Erlbaum.

ADDITIONAL RESOURCES

INTERNET

www.academicintegrity.org. The Center for Academic Integrity is a consortium of over 200 U.S. colleges and universities through which Donald McCabe, a leading authority on academic dishonesty, has conducted much of his research over the last 30 years. This Web site has a searchable database of recent research findings.

http://pbis.org. The Technical Assistance Center on Positive Behavioral Interventions and Supports (PBIS) has been established by the Office of Special Education Programs, U.S. Department of Education, to give schools capacity-building information and technical assistance for identifying, adapting, and sustaining effective schoolwide disciplinary practices.

www.uiowa.edu/%7Ecenteach/resources/ideas/term-paper-download.html. This paper, entitled "Downloadable Term Papers: What's a Teacher to Do?" gives a good overview of online papers and offers concrete suggestions for teachers interested in preventing this kind of cheating.

PRINTED MATERIALS

Cizek, G. J. (2003). *Detecting and preventing classroom cheating*. Thousand Oaks, CA: Corwin Press.

Henderson, J. Q. (1981). A behavioral approach to stealing: A proposal for treatment based on 10 cases. *Journal of Behavior Therapy & Experimental Psychiatry, 12*(3), 231–236.

Whitley, B. E., Jr., & Keith-Spiegel, P. (2002). *Academic dishonesty: An educator's guide*. Mahwah, NJ: Erlbaum.

CHAPTER 4

LOW SELF-EFFICACY AND MOTIVATIONAL ISSUES

Although all students are "motivated," they may not always be motivated to perform in the academic tasks assigned. In fact, Steinberg (1996) found that, even when excluding dropouts, 40 to 60 percent of secondary students studied are more disengaged than engaged in their academic work.

Concern over the lack of motivation among students has spurned a number of explanatory theories and suggestions. One model, the value/expectancy theory (Feather, 1982), has been supported empirically when applied to academic performance (Wigfield & Eccles, 2000) and offers counselors a useful framework for considering reasons behind students' lack of motivation as well as direction for possible interventions. According to this theory, the effort people are willing to expend in performing a particular task is the product of (1) the degree to which they value the rewards they anticipate from successfully completing a task and (2) the degree to which they expect to be able to perform the task successfully.

Using the value/expectancy theory as a framework, one could assume that a student, although capable of engaging in an academic activity, will choose not to if the activity is of low interest and low value to that student. Further, students for whom the material is valued and relevant may still exhibit low motivation to engage in the work if they believe that it is unlikely that they will be successful.

Research in this area of expectancy, or self-efficacy, suggests that feelings of efficacy can motivate students to attempt tasks (e.g., Bandura, 1993; Seifer, 2004; Schunk, 1995). Students with low self-efficacy generally demonstrate low academic motivation and have difficulty persisting at tasks (Schunk, 1991). Motivation appears to be enhanced when students feel a sense of autonomy, competence, and meaning within a classroom and perceive they are making progress (Seifert, 2004).

OVERVIEW

The studies found in this chapter emphasize these two components of motivation: value and expectancy. As will be noted, the studies demonstrate the value of contingency management as a means of increasing task value, as well as the importance of goal setting and feedback to enhance expectancy (Table 4.1). Also, the study by Duhon and colleagues (2004) demonstrates the value of assessing the specific form of deficit, either skill or performance, as the first step to developing an intervention program.

TABLE 4.1 Overview of Studies Presented

TARGET PROBLEM	REFERENCE	K–6	6–9	9–12	OTHER SPECIFICATIONS
The use of contingency contracting and goal setting for increasing and maintaining academic performance	Kelly & Stokes (1984)	N	N	Y	Employed A-B design to assess effectiveness
Poor academic achievement, using goal setting and contingency contracting	Duhon et al. (2004)	N	Y	N	Demonstrates the importance of tailoring intervention to either skill or performance deficit
Increased academic achievement, using feedback and goal setting	Oppenheimer (2001)	N	N	Y	Case study of a freshman undergraduate class
Small group counseling protocol to improve academic performance of low motivated, at-risk student	Boutwell & Myrick (1992)	Y	N	N	Employed a pre-post test design

SAMPLE INTERVENTIONS

Goal Setting for Academic Improvement

Author: Mary Lou Kelley and Trevor F. Stokes

Précis: Demonstrates the use of contingency contracting and goal setting for increasing and maintaining academic performance.

Introduction

The use of reward contingencies to promote academic motivation and achievement has been described extensively in the literature (Cameron & Pierce, 1994, 1996; Kohn, 1996; Lepper, Keavney, & Drake, 1996). The current study, although somewhat dated, provides evidence of the utility of reward contingencies, especially when employed with goal-setting and self-efficacy strategies.

Research on self-efficacy (e.g., Schunk, 1991; Bandura, 1988) has found a link between goal setting and self-efficacy. This research demonstrates that when teachers give students a goal or help them to identify their own goals for an activity there is an initial increase in self-efficacy for that activity. Further, as students work toward the goal and receive feedback on their progress, self-efficacy is enhanced. The current study utilized both contingency contracting (as a transition vehicle) and self-managed goal setting as a way of improving student productivity.

Intervention

The study engaged 8 students (aged 16 to 21) who attended an occupational education program half of the day and spent the other half preparing for their general equivalency diploma. The specific focus was on the students' completion of their academic skill workbook assignments.

In the first phase (baseline), the students were paid for completed assignments. During the contracting phase, the students were paid up to $6.00 daily for correct workbook items. The teacher and the student would set reasonable work goals, and the student would earn a bonus of $13.50 for meeting all daily goals in a given week. This bonus was pro-rated for students who met their goals four or fewer days. In the early contracting phase, teachers would push for a 10-percent increase in performance over baseline, with increments of 5 to 10 percent each week. During the goal-setting phase, students set their own daily and weekly standards and were paid as during the contracting phase.

The authors noted an increase in students' academic performance with the contingency contracting and goal setting when compared to baseline. Data reflecting the quantity of work completed by each student in a self-paced textbook served as both the pre- and post-measures of production.

Reflection

As previously suggested, goal setting enhances goal commitment and self-efficacy. The current study further supports this notion by demonstrating that contracting that involved the discussion, explanation, and negotiation of goals helped the students not only set appropriate goals for self-management, but also resulted in increased attention to correct workbook answers and motivation to academic performance. The obvious limitation and concern for the approach employed in the study is the reliance on money as reinforcement. For application within a public school setting, one would have to find a more "natural" reinforcer as a substitute for money. Even when reinforcers are used, fading needs to be implemented so that the use of artificial or atypical reinforcement can be removed and replaced with the general sense of satisfaction that comes with goal achievement. Such a modification of the research, however, should be "tested" for effectiveness.

Source: Kelly, M. L., & Stokes, T. F. (1984). Student-teacher contracting with goal-setting for maintenance. *Behavior Modification, 8,* 223–244.

SAMPLE INTERVENTIONS

Poor Performance: Skill or Motivation?

Authors: Gary Duhon, Noell George, Joseph Witt, Jennifer Freeland, Brad Dufrene, and Donna Gilbertson

Précis: The use of goal setting or rewards to increase academic engagement.

Introduction

Following upon the value/expectancy theory of motivation, a number of researchers have pointed out the importance of making a distinction between those students who are skilled and not exhibiting those skills versus those who lack the competency to perform said skills (see Noell et al., 2000). With such a distinction in mind, counselors would do well to first attempt to assess the deficit (either in skill or performance motivation) that serves as the basis for poor performance. It would follow that for those students exhibiting skill deficits, goal-setting interventions may be necessary. For those students for whom the issue is performance deficit, the use of contingency management may be an effective strategy. The current study demonstrates the utility of such an approach in designing intervention programs as a function of assessing whether the deficit is in the area of skill or performance.

Intervention

Participants included four general-education students referred by their teacher for poor academic performance. All participants were African American males who ranged in age from 8 to 10 years.

Treatments targeting both skill enhancement and motivation were developed and provided for each student. The skill-based treatment focused on improving student performance by providing presession practice, guided advanced organization, or an instructional prosthetic. The performance-deficit treatments focused on goal setting and rewards for achieving goals. All sessions were 10 minutes in length, with one session conducted per day for each subject.

The authors reported that for two students rewards were effective in the brief assessment, suggesting a performance-deficit hypothesis, and for two students they were not, suggesting a skill-deficit hypothesis. In all cases, the intervention approach suggested by the initial brief analysis was supported in the extended analysis.

Reflection

The value of the current study is in the support it provides for a two-factor model or organizational scheme for understanding a student's poor academic performance. The brief assessment described provides a tool for tailoring a specific intervention (i.e., either skill focused or performance focused) to the unique needs of any one student.

Source: Duhon, G. J., Noell, G. H., Witt, J. C., Freeland, J. T., Dufrene, B. A., & Gilbertson, D. N. (2004). Identifying academic skill and performance deficits: The experimental analysis of brief assessments of academic skills. *School Psychology Review, 33*(2), 429–443.

SAMPLE INTERVENTIONS

Goal Setting and Self-Assessment

Author: Robert Oppenheimer

Précis: The use of a model of change involving self-assessment, goal setting, and positive feedback.

Introduction

Research has demonstrated the motivational value of specific, moderately difficult and accepted goals on increased performance (e.g., Latham & Locke, 1979; Latham & Baldes, 1975; Locke & Latham, 1990). The current study advanced this line of research by focusing on a process that would help students move beyond simply setting goals to accepting them and actually committing to implementing them. The intervention model was based on one developed by Kurt Lewin (1951) in which there is first a level of disruption in normal behavior (disequilibrium or unfreezing); a change; and then a process of stabilization, or refreezing.

Intervention

The case study involved students in an undergraduate course in organizational behavior. A midterm evaluation of students' in-class contributions served as the initial unfreezing point. Students were generally disappointed with their grades and thus were open to (motivated to) change. Students were administered a midterm self-assessment and improvement plan. Using a 5-point scale (1 = very pleased, 5 = very displeased), students assessed the degree to which they were satisfied with their participation, raising questions in class on issues that were unclear to them, and reviewing material after class. They were also asked to rank on a 4-point scale how important each of these areas was to them, with 1 being most important and 4 being least important. The questions were asked so that the students would focus on what was important to them, with the objective of increasing their commitment to taking specific action in the areas they identified as important. The next step involved having the students identify specific steps they would take to increase their satisfaction in each of the performance areas. One week later, students were asked to identify what they had done that was helpful and what, if anything, they would do differently. This question was intended to serve as a self-assessment and self-administered feedback mechanism. The instructor also provided supportive feedback to those showing improvement. Follow-up data were collected using similar procedures, one week and one month after this initial planning. The data suggested that students' grades and participation in class had improved, and the students reported that it was helpful to have a written plan in at least one of the four areas.

Reflection

Although the case study presents a very practical, concrete application of one model of change (Lewin, 1951), it also provides a good illustration of the limitations of a case study in which no experimental controls are employed. The absence of a control drastically restricts the degree to which one can conclude that the specific intervention was responsible for the noted changes in student performance. As noted by the author, it is unclear whether improvement was attributable to the questionnaire and discussions about its usefulness or evaluative feedback in the form of grades.

Although the concept of goal setting as a method of increasing student motivation has been supported by others (see Latham & Locke, 1979; Latham & Baldes, 1975; Locke & Latham, 1990), further research is needed on the conditions that facilitate acceptance and ownership of goals.

Source: Oppenheimer, R. J. (2001). Increasing student motivation and facilitating learning. *College Teaching, 49*(3), 96–99.

DETAILED INTERVENTION

The "Go For It" Club

Introduction

Following upon research on motivation and goal setting and based on the reality of resource and time limitations for providing extensive individual counseling, the authors created a small group counseling protocol in hopes of improving the academic performance of low-motivated, at-risk students.

Method

The students included within the study were selected due to failing grades as indicated on their progress reports or report cards. Students were grouped according to grade level (third, fourth, and fifth grade) and attended weekly grade-level meetings. The authors reported on three separate pretest, posttest studies demonstrating the effectiveness of this approach, with improvement in student achievement for 76 to 83 percent of the students attending.

Intervention

The intervention strategy involved a series of weekly grade-level "club" meetings. Each club was composed of 6 to 10 students. Thirty-minute club meetings were held once a week in the counselor's office. Although groups typically met for six weeks, the exact number varied based on the nature of the group and the level of support needed. The meetings were structured around specific skills and attitudes necessary for success in school.

The first meeting involved an introduction to the group and the process to be employed. Participants were informed that as members of the club they would meet once a week for fun activities and games and that prizes could be earned if the participants received a good grade in their "Go For It" (GFI) subject (i.e., an area of academic weakness).

The teacher of each student's GFI class provided a grade for the student. Students picked a "prize" from one of four boxes (D-, C-, B-, or A-level achievement) based on their performance in the GFI class. Students were also asked to grade their personal GFI efforts each day. Finally, the students are informed that a party would be held at the end of the six-week period to celebrate "those who went for it and made it" and that all students who obtained at least a D in their GFI on their final report card would be able to attend. The first session ends with a "Go For It" cheer.

Future sessions focused on providing students with helpful hints and suggestions for school success. Although the activities varied according by counselor and group, all activities were targeted at increasing members' awareness of their responsibility for their own goals and outcomes and each attempted to provide motivation and/or skill suggestions. Sessions included activities such as:

- *Rhythm sticks.* A stick is passed from one person to another until the music stops. The person holding the stick says the name of his or her GFI subject and offers one thing that he or she is doing to improve performance in the GFI subject. Group members also share stories of times when they felt successful in school or when they found it best to do homework or study for tests.
- *Eggstra Special Egg Hunt.* Students engage in an egg hunt using plastic eggs. Each egg contains a statement related to academic performance (e.g., "I will do my homework before watching T.V."). Students share the statements they find in the eggs.
- *List making.* Members identify classroom behaviors associated with academic success.

Brief meetings (about 10 minutes) were held each Friday to process weekly grade reports, review teacher comments, and collect prizes. Prizes included such things as small trinket toys, pencils, fancy erasers, marbles, and so on.

In addition to the reinforcement received in the form of prizes, a "Go For It" cheer—"Go for it, go for it, hey, hey, hey! (child's name), you're on your way"—was said for each student who had improved his or her weekly grade. Finally, a graduation party is scheduled at the end of the intervention where students receive a certificate of recognition.

Reflection

The authors reported that this intervention resulted in improvement in academic performance for 78 to 83 percent of those students attending the various groups. Students who failed to show improvement were later identified as having significant learning and emotional disabilities that required special attention.

The intervention appears well suited for elementary school students who are free from significant cognitive or emotional impediments to learning. The supportive nature of the group; the verbal encouragement provided by the counselor, staff, teacher, and even principal; and the prizes appeared to serve as positive reinforcement for the students' increased motivation and effort. A question that was not addressed was the degree to which the improvements were sustained once the students "graduated" from the club. The issue of generalization or transfer of effect back to the classroom should be considered by counselors employing this strategy.

Source: Boutwell, D. A., & Myrick, R. D. (1992). The Go For It club. *Elementary School Guidance & Counseling, 27*(1), 65–73.

FROM THE FIELD

The suggestions that follow are in line with the value/expectancy model identified at the beginning of the chapter. As with previous "From the Field" suggestions, these reflect the practical suggestions of those working in the field and not the experimental findings of controlled research.

Increasing Value

- De-emphasize competition, focus on mastery.
- Make tasks challenging, but within reach.
- Encourage self-expression: Encourage students to share experiences, feelings, and opinions.
- Make assignments reflective of students' culture and experience.
- Design assignments in ways to encourage positive peer interactions.
- Use cooperative, crossed-age, groupings.
- Elicit creative expression through the use of art and music.
- Make assignments relevant; help students see how the knowledge and skills can be applied in the real world.
- Provide tasks that create cognitive dissonance. A moderate amount of incongruity stimulates curiosity.

Increasing Self-Efficacy

- Set realistic, short-term, concrete goals that are achievable, yet challenging.
- Provide students with immediate feedback regarding their performance.
- Have students monitor their progress and encourage self-reinforcement.
- Inform students about peer performance increased their belief that the goals were attainable and increased self-efficacy.
- Have students set their own goals, being as specific and concrete as possible (e.g., I will do all eight homework problems, neatly).
- Assign tasks (e.g., organizing task materials, assisting another student, etc.) that allow students to experience and demonstrate competence.
- Reinforce persistence and effort.
- Teach needed learning strategies and stress modeling of successful peers.
- Stack the deck by making assignments moderately challenging so that unmotivated students experience success. Link new work to recent successes.

Management

- Implement a system of contingency contracting to reinforce assignment and task completion and active class participation. Use the smallest, most natural reinforcers available and plan on fading reinforcement out as increased performance and success becomes their own reinforcement.
- Work with students and parents to employ the Premack principle, an operant process of using a higher-probability behavior to act as a reinforcer for a

lower-probability behavior. An example would be allowing for play, game involvement, or television watching only after completion of homework or assignments.

- Seat undermotivated students near peers who could provide positive modeling.
- Reinforce students' active involvement in class with verbal praise.
- Ask students what rewards would increase their motivation to perform in class and employ these as reinforcers contingent on academic performance.
- Help students concentrate on tasks, rather than on fear of failure.
- Help students identify role models that could be used as a template in a "how would _______ approach this" strategy for self-direction and motivation.
- Have students make one positive self-talk statement daily about school and their ability to succeed.
- Have students make collages or drawings that reflect how things would change in school and at home and how they would feel about these changes once they completed their assignments.
- Help students identify failure as function of insufficient effort or ineffective strategies rather than lack of ability.

REFERENCES

Bandura, A. (1988) *Self-regulation of motivation and action through goal systems.* In V. Hamilton & G. H. Bower (Eds.), *Cognitive perspectives on emotion and motivation* (pp. 3761). New York: Kluwer Academic/Plenum Publishers.

Bandura, A. (1993). Perceived self-efficacy in cognitive development and functioning. *Educational Psychologist, 28*(2), 117–148.

Boutwell, D. A., & Myrick, R. D. (1992). The Go For It club. *Elementary School Guidance & Counseling, 27*(1), 65–73.

Cameron, J., & Pierce, W. D. (1994). Reinforcement, reward, and intrinsic motivation: A meta-analysis. *Review of Educational Research, 64,* 363–423.

Cameron, J., & Pierce, W. D. (1996). The debate about rewards and intrinsic motivation: Protests and accusations do not alter the results. *Review of Educational Research, 66,* 39–51.

Duhon, G. J., Noell, G. H., Witt, J. C., Freeland, J. T., Dufrene, B. A., Gilbertson, D. N. (2004). Identifying academic skill and performance deficits: The experimental analysis of brief assessments of academic skills. *School Psychology Review, 33*(2), 429–443.

Feather, N. (Ed.). (1982). *Expectations and actions.* Hillsdale, NJ: Erlbaum.

Kelly, M. L., & Stokes, T. F. (1984). Student-teacher contracting with goal-setting for maintenance. *Behavior Modification, 8,* 223–244.

Kohn, A. (1996). By all available means: Cameron and Pierce's defense of extrinsic motivators. *Review of Educational Research, 66,* 1–4.

Latham, G. P., & Baldes, J. J. (1975). The "practical significance" of Locke's theory of goal setting. *Journal of Applied Psychology, 60,* 122–124.

Latham, G. P., & Locke, E. (1979). Goal setting—a motivational technique that works. *Organizational Dynamics, 8*(2), 68–80.

Lepper, M. R., Keavney, M., & Drake, M. (1996). Intrinsic motivation and extrinsic rewards: A commentary on Cameron and Pierce's claim that rewards do not undermine intrinsic motivation. *Review of Educational Research, 66,* 5–32.

Lewin, K. (1951). *Field theory in social science.* New York: Harper and Row.

Locke, E. A., & Latham, G. P. (1990). *A theory of goal setting and task performance.* Upper Saddle River, NJ: Prentice Hall.

Noell, G. H., Roane, H. S., VanDerHeyden, A. M., Whitmarsh, E. L., & Gatti, S. L. (2000). Programming for the generalization of communication to the classroom following assessment and training outside of the classroom. *School Psychology Review, 29*(3), 429–453.

Oppenheimer, R. J. (2001). Increasing student motivation and facilitating learning. *College Teaching, 49*(3), 96–99.

Ryan, R. M., & Deci, E. L. (2000). Self-determination theory and the facilitation of intrinsic motivation, social development, and well-being. *American Psychologist, 55,* 68–78.

Schunk, D. H. (1985). Participation in goal setting: Effects on self-efficacy and skills of learning disabled children. *Journal of Special Education, 19,* 307–317.

Schunk, D. H. (1990, April). Perceptions of efficacy and classroom motivation. Paper presented at the annual meeting of the American Educational Research Association, Boston, MA.

Schunk, D. H. (2003). Self-efficacy for reading and writing: Influence of modeling, goal setting and self-evaluation. *Reading & Writing Quarterly, 19*(2), 159–173.

Seifert, T. L. (2004). Understanding student motivation. *Educational Research, 46*(2), 137–150.

Steinberg, L. (1996). *Beyond the classroom: Why school reform has failed and what parents need to do.* New York: Simon & Schuster.

Wigfield, A., & Eccles, J. S. (2000). Expectancy-value theory of achievement motivation. *Contemporary Educational Psychology, 25,* 68–81.

ADDITIONAL RESOURCES

INTERNET

www.eric.ed.gov/ericdigests/ed346558.html. The ERIC Clearinghouse on Educational Management provides ideas for making the school environment one where academic success and the motivation to learn are expected and rewarded.

www.educationplanet.com/search/Education/Teacher_Resources/Teaching_Methods_and_Strategies/Student_Motivation. Education Planet provides easy access to articles, resources materials, and suggestions on numerous topics relevant to today's teacher. This particular link takes the reader to resources for motivating students within the classroom.

http://db.education-world.com/perl/browse?cat_id=6166. Education World is a rich resource for teachers. The Web site provides numerous articles and ideas for motivating students within the classroom.

PRINTED MATERIALS

Alderman, M. K. (1999). *Motivation for achievement: Possibilities for teaching and learning.* Mahwah, NJ: Erlbaum.

Ehly, S., & Topping, K. (1998). *Peer-assisted learning.* Mahwah, NJ: Erlbaum.

Pajares, F., & Urdan, T. (Eds.). (2005). *Adolescence and education, Volume V: Self-efficacy beliefs of adolescents.* Greenwich, CT: Information Age Publishing.

Tauber, T. (1997). *Self-fulfilling prophecy: A practical guide to its use in education.* Westport, CT: Praeger.

CHAPTER 5

TASK COMPLETION AND HOMEWORK ISSUES

Homework, although a focus of much debate and discussion among educators in the past, has received increased emphasis as an integral part of raising education standards. Teachers use homework as a way for students to complete unfinished work or, more typically, to practice and reinforce classwork. The value of homework for high school students is supported by research that has consistently shown a positive correlation between time spent on homework and achievement (Cooper & Valentine, 2001). Parents of young elementary children identify other, more abstract benefits of homework, such as the emphasis on the development of qualities such as responsibility, self-regulation, and time management (Warton, 1998; Xu & Corno, 1998). Despite these benefits, the truth of the matter is that many children fail to complete their homework or complete assignments with low rates of accuracy. Research has demonstrated that U.S. students have higher negative attitudes toward homework compared to their peers in other countries (e.g., Chen & Stevenson, 1989; Hong et al., 2000).

Quite often homework tasks go unfinished because they are either too difficult to complete or simply boring (Bryan, Nelson, & Mathur, 1995). Students, both those with learning disabilities and their nondisabled peers, report homework to be unimportant and that they simply forget to complete it (Gajria & Salend, 1995). In the absence of supervision and with the inability to sustain attention and motivation, many students simply find alternative ways to spend their after-school hours with the result being a failure to complete homework. This most likely results in decreased student preparation and achievement.

OVERVIEW

Because the academic development of the student is a central concern for the school counselor, it is important that the school counselor develop programs and strategies for assisting students in their development of the attitudes, knowledge, and skills that contribute to academic achievement. By extension, this means the completion of homework. However, research that supports effective strategies for improving rates of homework and task completion center on applications within the classroom by teachers or at home by parents. Of the following interventions, three involve direct teacher involvement (Table5.1). It is important for counselors to understand these techniques and employ them in their role as consultant to the classroom teacher.

TABLE 5.1 Overview of Studies Presented

TARGET PROBLEM	REFERENCE	K–6	6–9	9–12	OTHER SPECIFICATIONS
Increasing homework completion through multidimensional interventions	Hall (2003)	N	Y	N	Case study, intervention implemented by teacher
Increased homework completion	Bryan & Sullivan-Burstein (1998)	Y	Y	N	Factorial multivariate analysis of variance contrasting two treatments and three levels of student populations
Homework completion	Hinton & Kern (1999)	Y	N	N	Used a reversal design to assess effect of intervention
Homework completion	Miller & Kelley (1994)	Y	N	N	A combined multiple baseline and reversal (ABAB) design involving four parent–child dyads

SAMPLE INTERVENTIONS

Use of Learning Stations to Increase Self-Control for Homework Completion

Author: Arlene M. Hall

Précis: The use of a learning station to improve students' self-control in order to complete homework.

Introduction

Students report that they often fail to complete assignments, including homework, or do so with a low rate of accuracy, because assignments are either too difficult or too boring (Bryan, Nelson, & Mathur, 1995). The author employed a learning station that contained components to alleviate boredom and foster self-focus, leading to increased self-control. Students were stimulated through color, music, and movement; a mirror was used to increase self-focus.

The learning station (Hall & Zentall, 2000) was a freestanding three-sided panel. Each panel was covered with green contact paper. The left panel contained a turquoise pocket that held log sheets and a purple pocket with activity choice cards. The middle panel had a square mirror. The right panel had a yellow pocket for completed log sheets, a royal blue pocket for pencils, and a red pocket with an audiotape. The cassette tape had recorded videogame music from Sonic the Hedgehog Boom (Nilson, 1993). The music was played in 15-minute intervals separated by 5 minutes of blank tape.

Intervention

The author observed math homework completion and accuracy for three seventh graders. The students were trained in the use of the learning station in their homes. The log sheets in the learning station contained the following instructions:

1. Set up your learning station.
2. Get your materials out.
3. Log your start time.
4. Start the tape and begin work.
5. When the music stops, write down the number of problems you completed during that period.
6. Choose an activity break from the choice pocket.
7. List the number of the chosen activity next to the X, do it!
8. When the music starts, return to work. Do this until your math homework is complete.

9. When you have finished, log the end time.
10. Ask one of your parents to sign the log.

The author reported increased homework completion rates for all three students. During baseline, student completion rates were 20, 25, and 94 percent. During the intervention, completion rates increased to 69, 92, and 100 percent, respectively. Accuracy percentages during baseline were 15, 25, and 74 percent; during intervention, these increased to 54, 64, and 80 percent, respectively.

Reflection

The data reflected an improvement in both completion and accuracy rates. It is difficult to determine from the study which of the many components of the learning station contributed to the successful outcome and helped students increase their sense of self-control. As noted, the program provides numerous possible interventions, including increased organization (steps 1 and 2), self-monitoring (steps 3, 5, 7, and 9), parental involvement (step 10), and reinforcement strategies (step 6). Future research may better determine the specific degree to which each of these elements contributes to the successful outcome of this intervention. In the meantime, the approach appears to provide a creative way of improving student task completion.

Source: Hall, A. M. (2003). The use of a Learning Station to increase self-control for homework completion. *The Behavior Analyst Today, 4*(2), 124–126.

SAMPLE INTERVENTIONS

Reinforcements and Real-Life Homework

Authors: Tanis Bryan and Karen Sullivan-Burstein

Précis: Demonstrates the effect of reinforcement and the assignment of real-life homework on homework completion rates.

Introduction

A wealth of data shows that positive reinforcements increase targeted behaviors, including homework completion (e.g., Patzelt, 1991). The current study is unique in that it focuses on the nature of the task rather than on student characteristics. In a response to the often-heard student complaint that homework is dull and boring (Bryan, Nelson & Mathur, 1995), the authors attempted to increase homework completion rates by adjusting the personal relevance of homework assignments.

The current study compares the relative effectiveness of reinforcement against two other conditions: employment of real-life homework and the utilization of reward and real-life homework. Real-life homework assignments were those designed to help students make a link between schoolwork and ordinary activities in their home lives.

Intervention

The study employed 11 teachers (4 primary grade, 5 intermediate grade, and 2 learning disabilities teachers). The students (n = 123) were identified by their teachers as demonstrating erratic homework completion and/or inaccurate completion on 25 percent of assignments or more. An 11-week intervention program was implemented that consisted of (1) baseline data collection (2 weeks); (2) the use of reinforcement for completed homework (3 weeks); (3) the assignment of real-life homework (3 weeks); and (4) the use of reinforcement and real-life assignments as intervention (3 weeks.) Each teacher provided students with reinforcement each Friday if assignments had been completed for that week.

The authors reported significant increases in homework completion (math and spelling), as well as improvement in math and spelling test performance.

Reflection

It appears that increased relevance leads to increased involvement, at least when it comes to homework. The success and relative simplicity of this approach makes it a useful tool in the counselor's tool box, especially as the counselor works in the role of teacher-consultant.

Source: Bryan, T., & Sullivan-Burstein, K. (1998). Teacher-selected strategies for improving homework completion. *Remedial & Special Education, 19*(5), 263–276.

SAMPLE INTERVENTIONS

Personalizing Homework

Authors: L. Michelle Hinton and Lee Kern

Précis: Incorporated topics of student interest into homework assignments in order to improve completion rates.

Introduction

The study reports on the use of an antecedent-control strategy as a means of increasing homework completion. The approach focused on altering stimuli that are discriminative for desirable or undesirable behavior. This study attempted to alter the reinforcing properties of a nonpreferred activity (i.e., homework) by integrating topics of high interest to students.

Intervention

The authors employed a reversal design to evaluate the effects of the intervention in which homework completion was the dependent measure. The study involved 22 fifth-grade students from an inner-city middle school. Following baseline, students were informed that if they completed their homework, the next homework assignment would include their names. That is, the teacher would modify the assignment's content so that scenarios used in mathematics word problems would pertain to the students within the class. Specifically, the teacher would incorporate the names and familiar community activities and locations of those students who had completed the previous homework assignment.

The mean homework completion rate moved from 58 percent at baseline to 96 percent with intervention and returned to levels near baseline (61 percent) when the intervention was removed, only to return to 93 percent when the intervention was reinstated. The authors concluded that the results demonstrate the efficacy of an antecedent-intervention approach.

Reflection

The study provides not only what appears to be an effective intervention applicable to an entire class, but it also shows the potential benefit of employing nonpunitive interventions. Questions regarding the generalizability of this technique to other schools and classrooms, and even to non-math-related classes within the same school, need to be investigated further. Also, the brief period over which the study was conducted (12 school days) calls for further study of the long-term effects of such an intervention. Finally, although the intervention does not require specialized materials, it does require the cooperation and collaboration of the teacher. The development of personalized homework assignments may be time-consuming, because each assignment must be individually prepared. Thus, the level of success would be highly dependent on the cooperation and full involvement of the classroom teacher.

Source: Hinton, L. M., & Kern, L. (1999). Increasing homework completion by incorporating student interests. *Journal of Positive Behavior Interventions, 1*(4), 231–234.

DETAILED INTERVENTION

The Use of Goal Setting and Contingency Contracting

Introduction

The study examined the effects of goal setting and contingency contracting on homework performance. A number of studies have shown the utility of contingency management (e.g., Harris & Sherman, 1974; Goldberg, Merbaum, Even, Getz, & Safir, 1981) in improving the quality and quantity of homework performance. In addition, others (e.g., Miller & Kelley, 1992) have suggested that goal setting may ameliorate children's homework difficulty. The present study was designed to assess the efficacy of both goal setting and contingency contracting for increasing homework completion.

Method

The authors employed a combined multiple baseline and reversal (ABAB) design involving four parent–child dyads in which the child exhibited substantial homework problems. The children included an 11-year-old sixth grader (male), an 8-year-old fourth grader (female), an 11-year-old fifth grader (female), and a 10-year-old fifth grader (male). The following information was recorded: the existence of homework problems as measured by a homework-problem checklist (Anesko, Schoiock, Ramirez, & Levine, 1987), the accuracy of completed homework, and on-task behavior during homework time. During baseline, parents and children approached homework as usual.

Interventions

Following the baseline period, the parents received training in goal-setting procedures. The parents were taught the rationale behind the intervention program of goal setting and contingency contracting. Parents were taught using printed materials, practice, and performance feedback on how to negotiate with their children on goal setting.

Parents explained the treatment procedure to their children and began the initial goal-setting procedure in the presence of the researchers. The researchers provided performance feedback to the family, especially if it appeared that the goals they were setting were either too difficult or too easy.

Parents and children discussed the materials needed to complete homework assignments (e.g., text, workbooks, etc.), and each night the parent–child team would assess if all materials had been brought home.

Parents and the children were taught to divide homework assignments into specific small goals. Both parent and child would suggest a goal and then record a compromise goal (e.g., complete three problems in five minutes). The goals were meant to be achievable, yet challenging. Goals were renegotiated each week. If the goals for a particular week were not achieved, they were incorporated into the goal list of the following week. Students received weekly rewards if homework goals were achieved. Rewards varied from child to child and were adjusted weekly by parents and the child in order to maintain their reinforcing value. Rewards included items, such as stickers and snacks, and privileges, such as staying up later than usual or having sleepovers. Sanctions, such as loss of a bedtime snack or application of early bedtime, were imposed if the student failed to bring home needed materials. All four students showed an increase in work accuracy.

Reflection

The fact that all four students demonstrated increased homework accuracy is an important finding. As noted by the other researchers (Gorges & Elliot, 1995; Harris & Sherman, 1974), homework time and the accuracy of completed homework promotes positive classroom performance. Further, the utilization of goal setting as an intervention strategy has found extensive support (as noted in Chapter 4) for increasing motivation to achieve and now as an intervention for homework completion.

The procedure described in this study appears particularly beneficial for home application because it engages parental involvement with homework. Researchers have noted the importance of parental involvement and communication between parent and teacher with regard to homework requirements (e.g., Hoover-Dempsey, Bassler, & Burrow, 1995; Kay, Fitzgerald, Paradee, & Mellencamp, 1994). The involvement of parents as joint goal setters and contingency managers offers parents a mechanism for providing specific, timely, and, most often, positive feedback.

Further, the use of goal structuring and the requirement for the children to monitor their own behavior would appear to be an important step toward self-control and self-efficacy. However, one must be careful in generalizing the findings of studies based on small sample sizes to other settings and individuals. As such, counselors would do well to monitor the effect of these techniques when using them with students in their own school setting.

Source: Miller, D. L., & Kelley, M. L. (1994). The use of goal setting and contingency contracting for improving children's homework performance. *Journal of Applied Behavior Analysis, 27,* 73–84.

FROM THE FIELD

What follows are practical suggestions employed by counselors in the field. These suggestions reflect the experience and anecdotal reporting of counselors engaged in school counseling and have not been tested using experimental design. As personal suggestions, they need to be employed with caution and their impact monitored.

Working with Parents and Students

- Inform parents of the homework policy, including the amount of time a student should devote to homework, criteria for assessment, late policies, and so on.
- Do periodic checks with parents to assess their perceptions on the appropriateness, level, amount, and effectiveness of assignments.
- Make sure parents and students understand their roles and responsibilities as they pertain to homework requirements, expectations, time allotment, usefulness, and grading policy.
- Provide parents with feedback as to students' performance on homework assignments.
- Use homework planners or calendars so students and parents can keep track of homework expectations and completion dates.

Working with Teachers: Tasks and Task Assignments

- Homework should be interesting. Assign homework that is interesting and valuable.
- Survey students to identify areas of interest and activities in which they are engaged. Incorporate these into homework assignments.
- Focus homework on definite concepts or problems.
- Questions should be posed in a way that provides the background information necessary to respond to the teacher's questioning the next day.
- Be sure to explain homework and even practice or provide examples if necessary.
- Homework should be arranged to reinforce previously taught materials. It should not be used as simple, mindless practice.
- Provide a minimum set of assignments to all students but offer enrichment activities for high-achieving students desiring to do more.
- Do not assign homework if it is not to be checked and used as a vehicle through which a teacher can provide prompt, corrective feedback.
- Categorize homework as to its nature and purpose: practice, preview, review, discovery, application, problem solving, and creativity.
- Do not give or use homework as punishment; do not release students from homework as a reward.

- Be sure to assign homework that allows for student success.
- Begin homework in class using activities that stimulate curiosity and interest.

Working with Students

- Help the student get organized. Set up a time for checking that assignments are listed and that all needed materials are available at home.
- For behavioral interventions to be effective, the student needs to know what specifically he or she must do and what the contingencies will be.
- Review assignments and, if needed, help the student to break assignments down into small, achievable steps.
- Help the student to chart homework completion as well as success within class. It is important for the student to see the connection between homework and in-class performance.
- Be sure to employ verbal encouragement, notes home, and "pats on the back" for completed homework.
- Develop homework groups and chart individual performance. Encourage group achievement through group contingency.
- Negotiate realistic short-term (two days, one week) homework goals.
- Model positive, realistic attributions to the student. Use statements such as "You earned a B on the assignment because YOU took your time, followed directions, and set small goals."
- Review the processes and techniques the student employed for successfully completing the homework. Reinforce the student's behavior and success.
- Connect the student with a homework pal, who can serve as a resource for reminding the student as to what needs to be done, suggesting how to attack it, and providing verbal support.
- Help the student reduce tension and anxiety around assignments. Teach the student to take assignments in small steps, with frequent breaks. Employ breathing-relaxation and refocusing strategies and provide self-reinforcement for successful efforts.

REFERENCES

Anesko, K. M., Schoiock, G., Ramirez, R., & Levine, F. M. (1987). The homework problem checklist: Assessing children's homework difficulties. *Behavioral Assessment, 9*, 179–185.

Bryan, T., & Sullivan-Burstein, K. (1998). Teacher-selected strategies for improving homework completion. *Remedial & Special Education, 19*(5), 263–276.

Bryan, T., Nelson, C., & Mathur, S. (1995). Doing homework: Perspectives of primary students in mainstream, resource, and self-contained classrooms. *Learning Disabilities Research and Practice, 10*, 85–90.

Chen, C., & Stevenson, H. W. (1989). Homework: A cross-cultural examination. *Child Development, 60*, 551–561.

Cooper, H., & Valentine, J. C. (2001). Homework: Symposium. *Educational Psychologists, 36*(3), 143–221.

Epstein, M. H., Polloway, E. A., & Foley, R. M. (1993). Homework: A comparison of teachers' and parents' perceptions of the problems experienced by students identified as having behavioral disorders, learning disabilities, or no disabilities. *RASE: Remedial & Special Education, 14*(5), 40–50.

Etzioni, A. (1984). Self-discipline, schools, and the business community. Chamber of Commerce of the United States, Washington, DC. National Chamber Foundation (BBB22740), Washington, DC, ERIC Document Reproduction Services No. UD 023853).

Gajria, M., & Salend, S. J. (1995). Homework practices of students with and without learning disabilities: A comparison. *Journal of Learning Disabilities, 28*(5), 291–297.

Goldenberg, C. (1989). Parents' effects on academic grouping for reading. Three case studies. *American Educational Research Journal, 26,* 329–352.

Gorges, T. C., & Elliott, S. N. (1995). Homework: Parent and student involvement and their effects on academic performance. *Canadian Journal of School Psychology, 11*(1), 18–31.

Hall, A. M. (2003). The use of a Learning Station to increase self-control for homework completion. *The Behavior Analyst Today, 4*(2), 124–126.

Hall, A. M., & Zentall, S. S. (2000). The effects of a learning station on the completion and accuracy of math homework for middle school students. *Journal of Behavioral Education, 10*(2–3), 123–137.

Harris, V. W., & Sherman, J. A. (1974). Homework assignments, consequences, and classroom performance in social studies and mathematics. *Journal of Applied Behavior Analysis, 7,* 505–519.

Hinton, L. M., & Kern, L. (1999). Increasing homework completion by incorporating student interests. *Journal of Positive Behavior Interventions, 1*(4), 231–234.

Hong, E., Topham, A., Carter, S., Wozniak, E., Tomoff, J., & Lee, K. (2000). A cross-cultural examination of the kinds of homework children prefer. *Journal of Research and Development in Education, 34,* 28–39.

Hoover-Dempsey, K. V., Bassler, O., & Burrow, R. (1995). Parents' reported involvement in students' homework: Strategies and practices. *Elementary School Journal, 95,* 435–450.

Kay, P. J., Fitzgerald, M., Paradee, C., & Mellencamp, A. (1994). Making homework work at home: The parent's perspective. *Journal of Learning Disabilities, 27,* 550–561.

Miller, D. L., & Kelley, M. L. (1992). Interventions for improving homework performance. A critical review. *School Psychology Quarterly, 6,* 174–185.

Miller, D. L., & Kelley, M. L. (1994). The use of goal setting and contingency contracting for improving children's homework performance. *Journal of Applied Behavior Analysis, 27,* 73–84.

Nilson, J. (1993). A glitch or a gulf? *Commonweal, 120*(4), 6–9.

Patzelt, K. E. (1991). Increasing homework completion through positive reinforcement. Disabilities and Gifted Education (EC300985) (ERIC Document Reproduction Services No. ED 343306).

Warton, P. M. (1998). Mothers' views about homework in the early years of school. *Australian Journal of Early Childhood, 23*(1), 35–39.

Xu, J., & Corno, L. Case studies of families doing third-grade homework. *Teachers College Record, 100*(2), 402–437.

ADDITIONAL RESOURCES

INTERNET

www.kidinfo.com/. The Kid Info Web site is a homework help resource for teachers, students, and parents that provides suggestions, materials, and additional resources.

http://cybersleuth-kids.com/. CyberSleuth-Kids is an Internet search guide for K–12 students, providing information and hints by subject area.

http://school.discovery.com/students/. The School Discovery Web site provides more than 700 links to sites that will help students with homework.

PRINTED MATERIALS

Christenson, S. L., & Conoley, J. C. (Eds.). (1992). *Home–school collaboration: Enhancing children's academic and social competence*. Silver Springs, MD: National Association of School Psychologists.

Epstein, J. L., Coates, L., Salinas, K. C., Sanders, M. G., & Simon, B. S. (1997). *School, family, and community partnerships: Your handbook for action*. Thousand Oaks, CA; Corwin.

Gajria, M., & Salend, S. J. (1995). Homework practices of students with and without learning disabilities: A comparison. *Journal of Learning Disabilities, 28*(5), 291–296.

Hong, E., & Milgram, R. M. (2000). *Homework: Motivation and learning preference*. Westport, CT: Greenwood.

SECTION 2

ASSISTING STUDENTS WITH INTERPERSONAL RELATIONSHIPS

While the "business" of school is the facilitation of academic development, the reality is that learning happens within a social context. For many children and teens, functioning effectively with their peers and the adults in their life is a challenge. The following chapters present intervention strategies that have demonstrated effectiveness in helping children with issues of shyness, social anxiety, violence, aggression, bullying, defiance, non-compliance, conduct problems, antisocial behavior, sexual behavior, and prejudice.

CHAPTER 6

SOCIAL WITHDRAWAL, SHYNESS, AND SOCIAL ANXIETY

Although it is not unusual to find a student who at one time or another has experienced some form of social anxiety, for most such an experience is transitory (Carducci, 1999). Similarly, not all students need to be outgoing and extroverted. In fact, many who are labeled as "shy" are quite social within smaller arenas. This chapter was not written for those students for whom social anxiety is transient nor for those who choose to be less extroverted. The chapter and the interventions described are intended for those students for whom social anxiety is not only pervasive, but that is so intense that it results in impaired interpersonal relationships and academic performance (Bruch & Cheek, 1995).

Shy students who are negatively impacted by their own social anxiety may go unnoticed. Unlike the class clown or the generally disruptive student, the shy student tends to engage in significantly less social misbehavior than other children (Sanson et al., 1996). Shy students attempt to physically and psychologically pull back from social attention, and thus do little to draw attention—positive or negative—to themselves. Although such withdrawal is protective, it is also self-punitive in that it isolates the student from peer interaction, thus further impeding social development.

Research supports the notion that even moderate levels of social anxiety are associated with significant functional impairment and distress for the individuals (e.g., Dell'Osso et al., 2003). Shy children tend to be perceived as shy, unfriendly, and untalented; they tend to feel lonely and have low self-esteem and exhibit academic impairment, substance abuse, and higher than average levels of gastrointestinal problems (Chung & Evans, 2000; Jones & Carpenter, 1986; Ginsburg, La Greca, & Silverman, 1998). Further, this pattern of social withdrawal, social anxiety, and shyness may continue into adolescence and adulthood (Prior, Smart, Sanson, & Oberklaid, 2000). In addition to social disruptions, socially anxious children and adolescents are at risk for poor academic performance (Beidel, 1991), substance abuse (Pine, Cohen, Gurley, Brook, & Ma, 1998), and depression (Inderbitzen-Nolan & Walters, 2000).

A number of interventions have been found to be effective in ameliorating social anxiety, withdrawal, and shyness. Early research has demonstrated the effect of modeling on children's social assertiveness (Christoff et al., 1985). Behavioral treatments such as exposure therapy (Lowenstein, 1983); contingency management (Bandura, Jeffery, & Wright, 1974); and social-skills training (Christoff et al., 1985) have also been found to be effective. Others have successfully employed peer mediated or "peer helper" strategies (e.g., Morris, Messer, & Gross, 1995). In cases of severe social withdrawal, the use of medication including selective serotonin reuptake inhibitors (SSRIs) (e.g., Federof & Taylor, 2001) has proven effective.

School-based treatment programs appear to be particularly well suited to addressing social anxiety issues, because school is the context in which socially anxious students most often experience their greatest concerns and challenges (Hofmann et al., 1999).

The interventions presented in this chapter (Table 6.1) are transferable to school settings. They are but a few examples of effective intervention strategies used with children exhibiting shyness and social withdrawal. The interventions presented employ cognitive-behavioral strategies, with additional attention given to the development of social skills.

TABLE 6.1 Overview of Studies Presented

TARGET PROBLEM	REFERENCE	K–6	6–9	9–12	OTHER SPECIFICATIONS
Social anxiety	Beidel, Turner, & Morris (2000)	Y	Y	N	Random control group design
Shyness	Christopher, Hansen, & MacMillian (1991)	Y	N	N	Use of peer support and models
Social anxiety and social withdrawal	Groenewold & Du-Fay (1987)	Y	N	N	Case study of female fourth grader
Shyness	Christoff, Scott, Kelley, Schlundt, Baer, & Kelly (1985)	N	Y	Y	Male and female students

SAMPLE INTERVENTIONS

Social-Effectiveness Therapy

Authors: Deborah C. Beidel, Samuel M. Turner, and Traacy L. Morris

Précis: Reports on the application of Social Effectiveness Therapy for Children (SET-C).

Introduction

In the past, shyness and other forms of social anxiety disorder (SAD) have been treated with a variety of cognitive-behavioral techniques. Social Effectiveness Therapy for Children (SET-C) is a comprehensive, multifaceted behavioral treatment program. The program involves education-exposure-group and behavioral rehearsal facets.

Intervention

The authors examined the efficacy of SET-C in the treatment of childhood social anxiety disorder. Employing a random, control group design, the authors randomly assigned 67 students (aged 8 to 12) diagnosed with SAD to either SET-C (the experimental condition) or to "Test-busters," a control group that experienced a program on study habits.

Those engaged in the 12 weeks of SET-C treatment experienced the following:

- One session that provided the students with information on SAD and gave them an overview of the SET-C program.
- Twelve weeks of 60-minute individual sessions involving in vivo exposure exercises designed to address the students' unique pattern of social fears.
- Weekly group sessions (60 minutes) in which four to five students would work on friendship-making and communication skills.
- A peer-generalization activity (90 minutes) that involved engaging students in unstructured group activities (e.g., bowling, skating, pizza parties) where they could employ their new skills.

The authors reported statistically and clinically significant improvement in social skills and a reduction in social anxiety for those engaged in the SET-C program.

Reflection

The study is noteworthy in that it is one of the few to employ random assignment to treatment and an active, but nonspecific, control group (i.e., the study-skills group). A concern, however, may be that the population targeted exhibited social anxiety disorder, not shyness. For some, this is less of a concern because shyness and related behavior appear to be associated closely with social anxiety disorder and social phobia (Bruch & Cheek, 1995). Thus, generalization from the study population to a shy population may be appropriate.

The major limitation of this approach when viewed from the perspective of the school counselor is the amount of time and energy required of the counselor. The study was designed and conducted in a specialized anxiety clinic in which weekly 60-minute individual and group sessions were feasible. The frequency and duration of this intervention may not be possible for those working with caseloads of 300 or more students in a system expecting time-limited interventions.

Source: Beidel, D. C., Turner, S. M, & Morris, T. L. (2000). Behavioral treatment of social phobia. *Journal of Consulting and Clinical Psychology, 68,* 1072–1080.

SAMPLE INTERVENTIONS

Peer Pairing

Authors: Jeanette Christopher, David Hansen, & Virginia MacMillan

Précis: Use of peer pairing as treatment of shyness.

Introduction

It has been suggested that peer pairing—the assignment of a socially active peer to assist a shy peer in social settings—can promote the generalization and maintenance of prosocial behaviors (Vaughn & Lancelota, 1991). The technique described within this study involves the strategic pairing of children who exhibit social difficulties with well-liked, socially skilled peers. With the peer helper as an aide, the shy student is provided opportunities to engage in joint-task activities. The rationale for such peer intervention is that because children belong to their own "societies" with their unique rules and norms, a peer may be more of an expert on social etiquette and nuance in that "society" than an adult would. It has also been suggested that because peers serve as major socialization agents in a child's natural development, their involvement in therapy may foster generalization of the trained social behaviors.

Intervention

The authors employed a peer-helper intervention to increase the number of prosocial interactions and social status of three socially withdrawn, elementary-aged boys. Teachers identified two socially adept peer helpers (males) who were to interact with each of the withdrawn boys during morning recess. The peer helpers were trained over the course of two 30-minute sessions to:

- Initiate and maintain interactions.
- React supportively when the withdrawn child exhibited negative behavior.
- Structure play activities that the two of them could do during recess.

Using a time-series design, the authors found an increase in the frequency of prosocial behaviors that were initiated by each of the three students as compared to baseline recordings. In follow-up, the authors found that the gains persisted for five months after treatment ended.

Reflection

As described, the technique appears to be an effective approach for assisting shy, withdrawn students to increase and maintain prosocial behaviors. The "naturalness" of the intervention—that is, inviting the shy, withdrawn child to participate in a social setting with a peer—appears congruent with the mission and philosophy of an elementary school. However, a couple of things must be considered with regard to the generalizability of this approach.

First, it is essential to choose a peer helper who is socially competent and of high social status so that the peer's interaction with the socially withdrawn child is effective but does not damage the peer's own social status. Second, a limitation of this intervention is that although it helps the shy, withdrawn child to become more engaging, it does not provide opportunity for the child to learn ways to respond to negative peer reactions or to resist avoidance or escape strategies when anxious. Finally, the reader should view the findings with caution, given the small sample and lack of experimental control. Counselors should maintain a close eye and use assessment procedures when employing peers as agents of change. It is important to monitor all positive and negative changes observed in both the shy student and the peer helper that may result from the pairing.

Source: Christopher, J. S., Hansen, D. J., & MacMillian, V. M. (1991). Effectiveness of a peer-helper intervention to increase children's social interactions: Generalization, maintenance, and social validity. *Behavior Modification, 15*, 22–50.

SAMPLE INTERVENTIONS

Cognitive Restructuring Strategy: A Case Study

Author: G. Frank Groenewold and Der Du-Fay

Précis: A case study using self-instructional training as a cognitive restructuring strategy for elementary-aged children.

Introduction

Self-instructional training is a cognitive restructuring strategy whereby students are taught to replace negative, maladaptive self-statements with positive, self-enhancing statements. This technique has been used with numerous populations, including schizophrenics, impulsive individuals, and social isolates.

Intervention

The case involved a fourth-grade female who exhibited evidence of social anxiety disorder and social withdrawal. The intervention used in this case study—Self-Instructional Training—employs fundamental cognitive therapy tenets. The process involves:

1. The counselor performing a task while speaking the instructions aloud (cognitive modeling)
2. The student performing the same task under the direction of the counselor's instruction (overt, external guidance)
3. The student performing the task while speaking the instructions aloud (overt, self-guidance)
4. The student whispering the instructions while working through the task (faded, overt self-guidance)
5. The student performing the task while guiding his or her performance via private speech (covert self-instruction)

In this case, the counselor modeled the self-talk and provided written and behavioral homework assignments. In sessions, the student practiced behaviors such as walking with head up, sitting straight, and maintaining eye contact and rehearsed self-verbalizations such as, "When someone is talking, I must look at the person and listen. There, I can do it! Great!" These verbalizations were created using the student's own words and were practiced overtly and then covertly following the sequence described.

Anecdotal reports from the student's teacher suggested that improvements were observed in both academic performance (especially active participation in class) and increased social inclusion and interaction with peers.

Reflection

The technique described in this case study has extensive support in the literature pointing to its effectiveness when applied to other populations (e.g., schizophrenics, impulsives, and adult social isolates). The current study extends the utility of this intervention process to elementary-aged students exhibiting social anxiety and withdrawal. The technique appears to be one suitable for the school counselor in that it can be employed in a format of short training sessions. As with all such case studies, the lack of experimental control makes any conclusions about treatment and outcome connection very difficult. As such, counselors employing this approach need to carefully monitor the progress and apparent impact of the self-instructional training.

Source: Groenewold, G. F., & Du-Fay, D. (1987). Self-instructional training: A case study. *Elementary School Guidance and Counseling, 22*(2), 117–123.

DETAILED INTERVENTION

Social-Skills Training for Shy Adolescents

Introduction

The very fact that one of the developmental tasks for early adolescence is the establishment of same- and opposite-sex relationships and the navigation through interpersonal problems highlights the need for effective interventions when working with shy, socially withdrawn students. The authors of this study conceptualize effective social functioning in terms of two competencies: social skills and problem-solving ability. They posit that in order to be effective in interpersonal relationships adolescents must have the behavioral social skills needed to initiate and maintain social interaction, as well as possess the social problem-solving skills needed to help them plan ways to meet and interact with others and generate effective methods of resolving interpersonal conflicts that may arise. The study reports on the effect of a group-training procedure targeted to improve these skill sets. Specifically, the study investigated the effect of social problem-solving and conversational skills training on shy adolescents' social interactions.

Method

The study involved four females and two males, ages 12 to 14 years. The students were selected based on school staff recommendation. Students were identified as having few friends, not engaging in social or extracurricular activities, and generally presenting as "loners." The authors employed a multiple baseline design in which group problem-solving and social-skills training sessions were presented sequentially across time. Skill acquisition was assessed during four baseline sessions and at the end of each training session. Data were collected on the students' ability to problem solve and to maintain a five-minute conversation with a peer.

Interventions

Phase I involved training in problem-solving skills. This phase involved four group sessions in which the following occurred:

- Rationale for acquiring problem-solving skills was provided along with an outline of the components of effective problem solving. The students were trained to:

  - Recognize a situation as a problem.
  - Define the problem completely.
  - Generate multiple solutions.

  - Evaluate the possible consequences (negative and positive) of each solution.
  - Determine the best solution.
  - Develop a plan for implementation.

- The group was provided simulated social situations and asked to apply effective problem-solving skills. Situations included:

  - Joining a group conversation
  - Initiating conversation with a peer
  - Inviting a peer to participate in a mutual activity
  - Making a request of an adult

- In subsequent sessions, students would review the components of problem solving and report how they would apply the skills to a range of interpersonal problems.
- Students were assigned a worksheet on which they applied their skills to an interpersonal problem of their choice. These were discussed in sessions.

Phase II involved conversational skills training. These four sessions consisted of social-skills training that included the presentation of a specific topic to improve conversational skills along with modeling of the skill and rehearsal by the students. Students role-played skill use and received corrective feedback. Following each session, students were assigned homework to practice the skills covered that day. The skills included:

- Listening skills
- Talking about oneself, disclosure
- Initiating conversations
- Making requests of others

Reflection

The authors reported that the group-training procedures were effective in improving the subjects' social problem-solving skills and behavioral skills needed for effective peer conversation. Further, their data suggest that the treatment effected positive changes in self-esteem and the number of interactions the subjects engaged in with peers, parents, and teachers.

Although the use of social-skills training as intervention for shyness is neither new nor novel, the current investigation distinguishes itself in that unlike previous social-skills training models that used highly structured practice scenarios, the authors employed extended, unstructured conversations between pairs of adolescents as a form of behavior rehearsal. This interaction format more realistically approximated typical conversations between adolescents and is felt to have increased the generalizability of the training. Another valuable element of this intervention was its use of the group format for skill training. Not only does the peer group provide a realistic, normalized arena for skill rehearsal, but it is a cost-effective way of serving multiple clients.

Although the study provides support for the utility of social-skills and social problem-solving training of shy adolescents, the small sample size may limit the ease and degree to which this technique can successfully be applied to other populations. As such, practitioners are cautioned to consider the demographics and developmental needs of the students for whom this technique will be employed and to closely monitor the impact of the sessions on each of the students.

Source: Christoff, K. A., Scott, W. O. N., Kelley, M. L., Schlundt, D., Baer, G., & Kelly, J. A. (1985). Social skills and social problem solving training for shy young adolescents. *Behavior Therapy, 16,* 468–477.

FROM THE FIELD

The studies presented provide an array of interventions that may be useful for the school counselor working with children exhibiting social anxiety, social withdrawal, and shyness. The recommendations to follow reflect current practices of school counselors acquired by way of survey and literature review. It is important to emphasize that the recommendations are simply that—recommendations by practicing counselors. These suggestions have not been tested experimentally for validity and thus need to be applied with caution.

Working with Students

- Hold private rehearsal sessions with the student in which the student can practice various social skills, such as making social introductions, sharing or self-disclosure, asking for information, and so on.
- Include the student in a group counseling session. Be sure to pick others who model appropriate communication skills and who are not threatening or overbearing.
- Role-play situations from the classroom, but have the student act as if he or she were the teacher, the best student, the funniest student, and so on.
- Have extremely shy students practice communicating through a hand puppet, doll, or action figure.
- Have the student practice communicating by telephone (real or simulated).
- Identify points of interest (e.g., music, art, writing, sports) and pair the student up with a member of a school group engaged in that activity. Encourage the student to join that group.
- Develop a reward system to reinforce the student whenever the student initiates social contacts or engages in activities with peers.
- Identify a least threatening "friend" to invite for an overnight.
- Use "Skillstreaming: The Adolescent Kit" (available through Childswork/Childsplay, LLC) to teach the student positive social skills.
- Encourage the student to use art and music vehicles for expressing his or her feelings and interests.
- Involve the student in cross-age tutoring.
- Enlist the help of peers to draw out the withdrawn child and involve the child in group activities and play.

Working with Teachers

- Only call on the student to recite or respond when you have prior knowledge that the student knows the materials exceptionally well.
- Have the student serve as the recorder for small group discussions.
- Have the student carry messages to other teachers, administrators, or the guidance office at first in written format, but eventually replace with requests that the student has to share verbally.

- Pair the student with a "social star" in the class. The "star" should be chosen because she or he provides good modeling and social reinforcement for the contributions of the shy student.
- Identify a student who likes the child and allow them to sit together.
- Seat the student among friendly classmates.
- Assign the withdrawn child to collect and/or distribute papers, treats, materials, and so on.
- If taking a poll (e.g., how many children will be going to the game), have the withdrawn child do the head count and report (verbally) to the teacher.

REFERENCES

Bandura, A., Jeffery, R., & Wright, C. L. (1974). Efficacy of participant modeling as a function of response introduction aids. *Journal of Abnormal Psychology, 83,* 56–64.

Beidel, D. C. (1991). Social phobia and overanxious disorder in school age children. *Journal of the American Academy of Child and Adolescent Psychiatry, 30,* 545–552.

Beidel, D. C., Turner, S. M., & Morris, T. L. (2000). Behavioral treatment of social phobia. *Journal of Consulting and Clinical Psychology, 68,* 1072–1080.

Bruch, M. A., & Cheek, J. M. (1995). Developmental factors in childhood and adolescent shyness. In R. G. Heimberg, M. R. Liebowitz, D. A. Hope, & F. R. Schneier (Eds.), *Social phobia: diagnosis, assessment and treatments* (pp. 163–181). New York: Guilford.

Carducci, B. J. (1999). *Shyness: A bold new approach: The latest scientific findings, plus practical steps for finding your comfort zone.* New York: Harper Collins.

Christoff, K. A., Scott, W. O. N., Kelley, M. L., Schlundt, D., Baer, G., & Kelly, J. A. (1985). Social skills and social problem-solving training for shy young adolescents. *Behavior Therapy, 16,* 468–477.

Christopher, J. S., Hansen, D. J., & MacMillian, V. M. (1991). Effectiveness of a peer-helper intervention to increase children's social interactions: Generalization, maintenance, and social validity. *Behavior Modification, 15,* 22–50.

Chung, J. Y., & Evans, M. A. (2000). Shyness and symptoms of illness in young children. *Canadian Journal of Behavioural Science, 32,* 49–57.

Crozier, W. R. (2000). Shyness and social relationships: continuity and change. In W. R. Crozier (Ed.), *Shyness: Development, consolidation and change* (pp. 1–21). London: Routledge.

Dell'Osso, L., Rucci, P., Ciapparelli, A., Vivarelli, L., Carlini, M., Ramacciotti, C., & Cassano, G. B. (2003). Social anxiety spectrum. *European Archives of Psychiatry & Clinical Neuroscience, 253*(6), 286–291.

Federoof, I. C., & Taylor, S. (2001). Psychological and pharmacological treatment of social phobia: A meta-analysis. *Journal of Clinical Psychopharmacology, 21,* 311–324.

Ginsburg, G. S., LaGreca, A. M., & Silverman, W. K. (1998). Social anxiety in children with anxiety disorders: Relation with social and emotional functioning. *Journal of Abnormal Child Psychology, 26,* 175–185.

Groenewold, G. F., & Du-Fay, D. (1987). Self-instructional training: A case study. *Elementary School Guidance and Counseling, 22*(2), 117–123.

Hofmann, S. G., Albano, A. M., Heimberg, R. G., Tracey, S., Chorpita, B. F., & Barlow, D. H. (1999). Subtypes of social phobia in adolescents. *Depression and Anxiety, 9,* 15–18.

Inderbitzen-Nolan, H. M., & Walters, K. S. (2000). Social anxiety scale for adolescents: Normative data and further evidence of construct validity. *Journal of Clinical Child Psychology, 29,* 360–371.

Jones, W. J., & Carpenter, B. N. (1986). Shyness, social behavior, and relationships. In W. H. Jones, J. M. Cheek, & S. R. Briggs (Eds.), *Shyness: perspectives on research and treatment* (pp. 227–238). New York: Plenum.

Lowenstein, L. (1983). Treatment of extreme shyness by implosive counseling and conditioning approaches. *Association of Educational Psychologists, 6,* 64–69.

Morris, T. L., Messer, S. C., & Gross, A. M. (1995). Enhancement of social interaction and status of neglected children: A peer-pairing approach. *Journal of Clinical Child Psychology, 24,* 11–20.

Pine, D. S., Cohen, P., Gurley, D., Brook, J., & Ma, Y. (1998). The risk for early-adult anxiety and depressive disorders in adolescents with anxiety and depressive disorders. *Archives of General Psychiatry, 55,* 56–64.

Prior, M., Smart, D., Sanson, A., & Oberklaid, F. (2000). Does shy inhibited temperament in childhood lead to anxiety problems in adolescence? *Journal of the American Academy of Child and Adolescent Psychiatry, 39,* 461–468.

Sanson, A., Pedlow, R., Cann, W., Prior, M, & Oberklaid, F. (1996). Shyness ratings: Stability and correlates in early childhood. *International Journal of Behavioral Development, 19,* 705–724.

Vaughn, S., & Lancelotta, G. (1991). Teaching interpersonal social skills to low accepted students: Peer-pairing versus no peer-pairing. *Journal of School Psychology, 28,* 181–188.

ADDITIONAL RESOURCES

INTERNET

www.shyness.com/shyness-institute.html. The Shyness Institute is a nonprofit research corporation founded in 1994 that is dedicated to research regarding shyness, social anxiety, and related anxiety disorders. Its Web site is a good source for research and useful literature.

http://kidshealth.org/kid/feeling/thought/shy.html. This KidsHealth Web site provides child-friendly information, resources, and activities geared to helping the student understand shyness and begin working with it. A companion site for teens is http://kidshealth.org/teen/your_mind/emotions/shyness.html.

http://dir.yahoo.com/Health/Diseases_and_Conditions/Shyness/. The Yahoo! Health Directory is a good resource for professional articles as well as rapid links to support forums and additional resources.

www.proedinc.com/store/index.php?mode=product_detail&id=0365. The "ACCEPTS Program" offers a complete curriculum for teaching effective social skills to students at the middle- and high-school levels. The program teaches peer-to-peer skills, skills for relating to adults, and self-management skills.

PRINTED MATERIALS

Carducci, B. (2003). *The shyness breakthrough: A no-stress plan to help your shy child warm up, open up and join the fun*. New York: Rodale.

Crozier, W. R., & Alden, L. E. (Eds.). (2001). *International handbook of social anxiety: Concepts, research, and interventions relating to the self and shyness*. Chichester: Wiley.

Gilroy, B. D. (2001). Using magic therapeutically with children. In H. G. Kadusun and C. E. Schaefer (Eds.), *101 more favorite play therapy techniques* (pp. 429–438). Northvale, NJ: Jason Aronson, Inc.

CHAPTER 7

VIOLENCE: AGGRESSION AND BULLYING

A review of the national news will quickly alert us to the fact that we live in a world and time in which violence, aggression, and destructive behavior abound. These behaviors are neither restricted to off-school sites nor do they occur only in adult populations. According to the U.S. Census Bureau (2001), from 1985 to 1998 the number of cases for violent offenses handled by juvenile courts increased by 54 percent. The picture painted by researchers suggests that over 35 percent of students in grades 9 through 12 had been part of a physical fight in the previous month and 8 percent of high school students were threatened or injured with a weapon on school grounds (Anderson, 2001; Kann et al., 2000). In the samples studied, over 17 percent of students in grades 9 through 12 admitted to carrying a weapon (e.g., gun, knife, or club), and close to 7 percent reported bringing a weapon to school (Kann et al., 2000). Finally, based on the data reported by these authors, homicide was the third leading cause of death among young people 10 to 14 years of age and the second leading cause of death for those 15 to 19 years of age (Tolan, 2001). Violence is clearly part of our society, and it is affecting our youth on a large scale.

One form of violence, bullying, has received a lot of attention of late. Research on the topic of bullying demonstrates an increased frequency of bullying in our schools and its devastating impact on victims (Olweus, 1993, 1994; Nansel et al., 2001). Bullies are highly aggressive to both peers and adults and tend to be somewhat impulsive, with a strong need to dominate (Olweus, 1994). Some believe that bullying is part of a more general antisocial, conduct-disordered developmental pattern that points to children at risk (Olweus, 1994). Because of the at-risk behavior exhibited by bullies and the feelings of depression and loneliness experienced by the victims of bullying (Hawker & Boulton, 2000), early intervention is essential.

OVERVIEW

Clearly the problem of violence in our schools is a major national concern (Margolin & Gordis, 2000). Government agencies; professional organizations, such as the American School Counseling Association and the American Psychological Association; and local schools have begun taking steps to better understand the nature of aggression, violence, and bullying in our schools and to develop prevention and intervention programs. The studies found in this chapter outline interventions that employ individual counseling and small-group and schoolwide interventions (Table 7.1).

TABLE 7.1 Overview of Studies Presented

TARGET PROBLEM	REFERENCE	K–6	6–9	9–12	OTHER SPECIFICATIONS
Anger and aggression	Lochman (1992)	Y	Y	N	Matched control group study demonstrating long-term effectiveness
Reducing attribution of hostile intent	Hudley & Graham (1993)	Y	N	N	Control group design
Bullying	Olweus (1991)	Y	Y	N	Systemwide programming
Anger control	Larson (1992)	N	Y	N	Control group design

SAMPLE INTERVENTIONS

Group CBT for Aggressive Boys

Author: John E. Lochman

Précis: Investigation of the long-term effects of an anger coping program.

Introduction

Aggression in preadolescents has been identified as a risk factor for future drug use, higher levels of conduct disorder, and adult criminality. As such, preadolescent children exhibiting aggressive tendencies are an important at-risk group that should be targeted for prevention and intervention programming. Some researchers have suggested that cognitive-behavioral therapy (CBT) is a promising intervention approach with children with aggressive behavioral problems (e.g., Lochman, 1990). The current study extends this research to investigate the long-term maintenance of treatment gains following CBT.

Intervention

The study followed up on previous work done by the author (see Lochman, 1985; Lochman, Burch, & Curry, 1984; Lochman & Curry, 1986) in which pre-post intervention results demonstrated the effectiveness of CBT when compared to control groups of untreated aggressive students and nonaggressive students. For the current study, 145 students were selected from a pool of 354 boys who had been identified by teachers and peers as aggressive. The subjects for this study were all males and came from the fourth, fifth, and sixth grades. The study presented here examined the original treatment group from these prior studies. Participants met for weekly group sessions over the course of four to five months. Each session lasted 45 to 60 minutes and focused on:

- Establishing group rules and reinforcement contingent on abiding by group rules
- Using self-statements to inhibit impulsive behaviors and to screen out distractions from several motor, memory, and social tasks
- Identifying problems and children's perspectives and intentions in pictured and actual social-problem situations
- Generating a variety of solutions and consequences to these solutions for pictured and actual social situations
- Viewing modeling videotapes of children who become aware of physiological arousal and use of self-statements (e.g., "Stop! Think! What should I do?") and social problem solving to cope with anger
- Having the children plan and make their own videotapes using inhibitory self-statements and social problem solving with problems they have encountered

- Using discussion, role-playing, and dialoguing to develop children's social problem-solving skills with their current and recent anger arousal problems

The author reported that the CBT intervention with aggressive boys produced long-lasting effects when compared to an aggressive untreated comparison group. Three years after the end of the intervention, those high-risk boys who received the intervention displayed lower levels of substance use than did the comparison group. The treated boys had higher levels of self-esteem and problem-solving skills than the untreated controlled group.

Reflection

The study is included within this text because of its unique focus; that is, it is a follow-up study investigating the long-term effects of an intervention. All too often, the focus of outcome research is on post-treatment change, and follow up is not included. This study, which incorporated a matched group, control group design provides evidence of both the initial effectiveness of treatment as well as its long-term prevention value. One disappointing outcome was that there was no significant overall effect found in terms of the adolescents' classroom behavior at follow up. However, a subset of the study who received a second booster intervention during the school year did demonstrate significant positive changes. It would appear that as counselors we need to employ strategies that not only demonstrate initial results, but that we follow up on these interventions even after initial changes have been observed. For long-term outcomes it appears that interventions need to be of longer duration and more intensive.

Source: Lochman, J. E. (1992). Cognitive-behavioral intervention with aggressive boys: Three-year follow up and preventive effects. *Journal of Consulting and Clinical Psychology, 60*(3), 426–432.

SAMPLE INTERVENTIONS

Changing Attribution of Hostile Intent

Authors: Cynthia Hudley and Sandra Graham

Précis: Changing students' tendency to attribute hostile intentions to peers following peer provocations of ambiguous cause.

Introduction

Research has demonstrated that aggressive boys often exhibit a marked attributional bias to perceive their peers as acting with hostile intentions. Those researching this attributional bias assume a cognition-to-behavior linkage. That is, when we judge others as responsible for negative outcomes, we may conclude that an injustice has been done that needs to be righted, which in turn results in the emotional response of anger and aggressive behavior. It is further assumed that the cognition accompanying such an emotional response is a judgment of "ought," "should have," or "could have." This study assumed that if biased attributions instigate a motivational sequence resulting in aggression, then modifying or changing this attributional bias should, in turn, reduce students' anger and aggressive actions.

Intervention

The authors selected 101 aggressive and nonaggressive African American elementary school boys and assigned them to an attributional intervention group, an attention training program, or a no-treatment control group. The authors employed a random, control group design with pre- and post-test measurement of three categories of dependent variables: (1) judgment of intent and feelings of anger and aggressive behavior in response to both hypothetical and actual peer provocation; (2) teacher ratings of aggressive behavior; and (3) the number of formal referrals for school disciplinary action.

The attributional treatment was a 12-lesson cognitive intervention. The focus of the training was on teaching the student *not* to infer hostile peer intent in negative social encounters. The subjects were taught the concepts of intent and ambiguity in interpersonal interactions and given practice in identifying intent, distinguishing intended from unintended outcomes, and deciding on how to respond given attributional uncertainty. Specifically, the program was designed as follows:

- In lessons 2 through 6, students engaged in role-play, discussion, and interactive games targeted at helping the students identify intentionality and to discriminate between situations of prosocial, accidental, hostile, and ambiguous peer intent.

- Lessons 7 through 9 were designed to help the students make attributions to nonhostile intent when experiencing ambiguous negative social encounters.
- Lessons 10 and 11 employed written vignettes to practice generating attributions to nonhostile intent and to identify when and how to enact a nonhostile response.

When compared to their control-group counterparts, aggressive students in the attribution retraining program showed a marked reduction in both the intentional bias to presumed hostile intent and their reliance on aggressive behavior.

Reflection

The study provides support for the importance of cognitive change for aggressive students. Further, the nature of the "training" would appear to be culturally compatible to most school settings, and thus appears to be a viable group intervention strategy for school counselors. It should be noted, however, that for the study all situations where either hypothetical and/or simulated. The question remains whether students will be able to generalize their skills to a real-life setting and negative social encounter. The other limitation noted by the authors is that although effectiveness was demonstrated through group comparison, not all individuals in the treatment group benefited equally from the attributional treatment. Therefore, counselors employing this technique need to monitor individual student's feelings and behaviors in order to identify those in need of additional or alternative intervention.

Source: Hudley, C., & Graham, S. (1993). An attributional intervention to reduce peer-directed aggression among African American boys. *Child Development, 64*, 124–138.

SAMPLE INTERVENTIONS

Bullying: A School-based Intervention

Author: Dan Olweus

Précis: Reducing the incidence of bullying in school through an educational program geared for parents, students, and school staff.

INTRODUCTION

Dan Olweus has developed a multilevel, systems-focused approach to bullying. As a result of an incident of bullying that resulted in several students committing suicide, the Ministry of Education in Norway instituted a nationwide program against bullying. Through a nationwide effort, data were collected that profiled bullies and the extent of victimization in Norway. As a result of these data, a systemwide intervention program was developed with the goal of reducing existing bullying and preventing future problems with bullying.

Intervention

The program was designed to establish firm limits to unacceptable behavior, applying sanctions in a nonhostile, nonphysical manner. The primary goal of this intervention was to create a warm school environment in which the social norm was strongly nonhostile and nonbullying.

The program consisted of five components:

1. In an attempt to increase awareness of the problem, a booklet describing the problems and specific interventions was distributed to school personnel.
2. In order to increase parental involvement, folders containing information and advice to parents of bullies and victims of bullying were created.
3. Video illustrations of bullying were employed as teaching tools to educate students on bullying and its effects and to help develop clear rules against bullying.
4. Support for victims was established, and students provided information (via an anonymous questionnaire) on their experiences with bullying in the school.
5. The final component was introduced 15 months after the initiation of the program. This involved a two-hour meeting with the staff to provide feedback on the level of the problem, the basic principles introduced, and the overall reaction of the school to the program.

A study of the program's effectiveness in 42 primary and junior high schools (grades 4–7) in Norway using pre- and post-test questionnaires on the frequency of bullying revealed that 8 months after the program's implementation bullying had decreased. Further, data based on assessment 20 months after implementation suggested that bullying continued to decrease. Additional data suggested that other antisocial behaviors such as theft, vandalism, and truancy were also reduced.

Reflection

The study is impressive in the size of sample and extensive impact reported. The focus on "education" and establishing a warm, nonviolent school environment required few additional resources or the introduction of alien programming.

A couple of caveats need to be stated, however. The authors note that although bullying was reduced in this quasi-experiment (pre-post testing, self-report), it was not eliminated. It is possible that even when the climate—social context—is changed and is not supportive of aggressive behavior, some students may resist social pressure and continue to employ aggression as a coping mechanism. As such, it is important for counselors to recognize that in some cases additional, individual forms of intervention may be needed. A second caution is that this study was performed in a context other than that of an American school system. Support by the Norwegian government, along with the values of that nation, must be considered when attempting to generalize the program outside of Norway.

Source: Olweus, D. (1991). Bully/victim problems among schoolchildren: Basic facts and effects of a school based intervention program. In D. J. Pepler & K. H. Rubin (Eds.), *The development and treatment of childhood aggression* (pp. 411–448). Hillsdale, NJ: Erlbaum.

DETAILED INTERVENTION

Think First!

Introduction

The authors attempted to employ an in-class intervention for students exhibiting high levels of anger and aggression. The authors felt that schools needed a systematic and effective method to intervene with these students within the general school population as opposed to the more typical way of responding, which most often resulted in removing these students from the mainstream. The study reports on an anger–aggression management curriculum applied in the classroom setting that employs cognitive-behavioral principles and techniques.

Method

The study targeted 48 students (both genders) at an urban middle school. The group targeted for treatment was a racially integrated classroom of 22 males and females. A placebo control group was also employed. Numerous measures of anger and aggression were used as dependent measures (e.g., Children's Inventory of Anger, the Jesness Inventory, and a teacher-scored measure of aggressive behavior). Data were also obtained from teacher-initiated incident referral forms (IRFs). These were single-page deportment reports used by school staff to refer incidences of student aggression or disruptive behavior to an administrator. In addition to the pre- and post-test assessments on standardized measures, a baseline based on IRFs was established prior to treatment.

Interventions

The treatment group received anger-control and problem-solving training (the "Think First Program"); the control group received a group-discussion placebo intervention. Both groups met twice a week for 10 weeks. Each session lasted approximately 50 minutes. The intervention, the "Think First Program," focused on teaching students the following: a functional analysis of angry behavior, a self-instructional method of anger-aggression control, and a procedure for applying the self-instruction procedures to problem solving. The intervention employed modeling (both live and prerecorded videotape) as well as role-play procedures. In addition, operant procedures utilizing a token-exchange system were employed as added inducement to complete self-monitoring homework assignments and to encourage attendance.

The outline of the 10 treatment sessions follows:

- Session 1: Group members were taught to conceptualize incidences of angry aggression in terms of antecedent, behavior, and consequence. Videotaped models were employed to demonstrate concepts. A self-monitoring process employing a "hassle log" was explained and the token system for completing the hassle log was introduced.

- Session 2: Students learned to recognize their own physiological and cognitive arousal cues. Again, video models of peer-aged groups discussing anger cues and deep breathing strategies were presented and students role-played anger-reduction techniques (deep breathing).
- Session 3: The concept of "triggers" (anger-provoking stimuli) was introduced. Students were taught (using videotaped models) to identify external cues (e.g., being called a name) and internal cues (e.g., self-statements about the external trigger).
- Session 4: Using incidents from the students' hassle logs, students rehearsed overt, out-loud self-instructions (i.e., reminders) as self-instruction and control. Students practiced timing and fading to covert self-instruction.
- Sessions 5 and 6: Continued self-instruction role-playing from the hassle log. Group members videotaped themselves modeling the technique.
- Session 7: The practice of self-instruction as reinforcement for successful anger control or as self-coaching following failure was explained and rehearsed.
- Session 8: Focus expanded to include training in problem-solving skills.
- Session 9: Group members were taught to clearly define problems (avoid broad or narrow definitions) and to practice taking multiple perspectives. Again, model and rehearsal took place.
- Session 10: In the final session, the students learned and practiced evaluating the consequences of choosing an identified alternative response.

Using a 2×3 repeated measures ANOVA, the post-treatment data indicated a statistically significant decrease in incident referrals for the treatment group, which appeared more clinically significant when compared to the increase in referrals for the control group over the same period.

Reflection

The data collected from this study suggests that the 10-week program was effective in reducing misconduct referrals; however, the authors noted that the intervention did not appear to significantly effect changes in students' post-test scores on the Children's Inventory of Anger or the Jesness Inventory. The authors concluded that this perhaps suggests that a more comprehensive prevention curriculum addressing not just anger-aggressive behavior, but also orientation to delinquent subculture values, may be needed.

The program's structured format and applicability within a classroom setting makes the intervention one that should prove valuable to the school counselor. The use of video models requires the availability of on-site equipment and a willingness on the part of the students, or their cohorts, to serve as "actors." The use of familiar actors, however, could increase both the interest and modeling effect of the video.

As with all interventions, it is essential that the counselor employ both outcome-assessment strategies as well as formative, process evaluation. Following each session with a brief evaluation tool may provide insight in the formulation or reformulation of the next session.

Source: Larson, J. D. (1992). Anger and aggression management techniques through the Think First curriculum. *Journal of Offender Rehabilitation, 18* (1–2), 101–117.

FROM THE FIELD

The following suggestions reflect the experience and anecdotal reporting of counselors engaged in school counseling and have not been tested using an experimental design. As personal suggestions, they need to be employed with caution and their impact monitored.

Working with Students

- Teach alternative, nonaggressive responses to problems.
- Restrict access to instruments of aggression.
- Present classroom guidance lessons in conflict resolution techniques.
- Establish trust and rapport with students and convey your understanding of their frustrations and your desire to help.
- Teach students to use "I messages."
- Teach students to identify their feelings and express their wants in calm tones.
- Teach the frustrated student the simple technique of counting to 10 or using breathing as a relaxation tool prior to responding.
- Help the student to identify situations, people, and events that act as triggers and then help them develop strategies to remove these triggers and/or modify their reaction to them.

Working with School Personnel

- Restrain from public displays of verbal and physical aggression, reduce the modeling effect.
- Engage the students in the curriculum, structuring it to promote success and academic achievement.
- Employ more cooperative modes of instruction.
- Employ deescalating forms of intervention when conflict occurs.
- Remain calm and controlled and use a comforting voice when conflict occurs.
- With increasing aggressiveness on the part of the student, increase your levels of empathy and reflection.
- Allow the student to "save face."
- Model appropriate behavior. Children imitate what they see and experience. Aggressive discipline will result in aggressive behavior in children toward other children and even the parent.
- Intervene immediately. When a student becomes aggressive toward others or his or her own body, have a time-out period before discussing the behavior and alternative behaviors.
- Focus your attention on the hurt child. Even negative attention will reinforce aggressive behavior. Put the aggressor in time out, walk away, and comfort the hurt child.

- Use role-play. Make a list of scenarios and ways to ask for things; for example, to borrow a pencil, see a book, and so on. Discuss different possible responses or refer to the list every time the student uses aggression.

Working with the System

- Develop programs that address the experience of social inequity within the school.
- Review methods of discipline and control within the school. Are they coercive? Do they model aggression? Violence as a means of reducing aggression is counterproductive.
- Establish a culture of nonaggression (see Olweus, 1993).
- Review placement criteria to ensure that students are at the optimal level of challenge and not frustrated with ongoing failure.
- Provide a mechanism for an aggressive child to remove him- or herself to a place of safety.
- Involve parents in supporting nonaggressive conflict resolution strategies at home.

REFERENCES

Anderson, R. N. (2001). Deaths: Leading causes for 1999. *National Vital Statistics Reports, 49*(11).

Hawker, D. S. J., & Boulton, M. J. (2000). Twenty years' research on peer victimization and psychosocial maladjustment: A meta-analytic review of cross-sectional studies. *Journal of Child Psychology and Psychiatry, 41*, 441–455.

Hudley, C., & Graham, S. (1993). An attributional intervention to reduce peer-directed aggression among African-American boys. *Child Development, 64*, 124–138.

Kann, L., Kinchen, S. A., Williams, B. I., Ross, J. G., Lowry, R., Grunbaum, J. A., & Kolbe, L. J. (2000). Youth risk behavior surveillance: United States, 1999. *Morbidity and Mortality Weekly Report, 49*, 1–96.

Larson, J. D. (1992). Anger and aggression management techniques through the Think First curriculum. *Journal of Offender Rehabilitation, 18* (1–2), 101–117.

Lochman, J. E. (1985). Effects of different treatment lengths in cognitive behavioral interventions with aggressive boys. *Child Psychiatry & Human Development, 16*(1), 45–56.

Lochman, J. E. (1990). Modification of childhood aggression. In M. Hersen & R. M. Eisler (Eds.). *Progress in behavior modification*, Vol. 25 (pp. 47–85). Thousand Oaks, CA: Sage.

Lochman, J. E. (1992). Cognitive-behavioral intervention with aggressive boys: Three-year follow up and preventive effects. *Journal of Consulting and Clinical Psychology, 60*(3), 426–432.

Lochman, J. E., & Curry, J. F. (1986) Effects of social problem-solving training and self-instruction training with aggressive boys. *Journal of Clinical Child Psychology, 15*(2), 159–164.

Lochman, J. E., Burch, P. R., & Curry, J. F. (1984). Treatment and generalization effects of cognitive-behavioral and goal-setting interventions with aggressive boys. *Journal of Consulting & Clinical Psychology, 52*(5), 915–916.

Margolin, G., & Gordis, E. B. (2000). The effects of family and community violence on children. *Annual Review of Psychology, 51*, 445–479.

Nansel, T. R., Overpeck, M., Pilla, R. S., Ruan, W. J., Simons-Morton, B., & Scheidt, P. (2001). Bullying behaviors among U.S. youth. *Journal of the American Medical Association, 285*(16), 2094–2100.

Olweus, D. (1991). Bully/victim problems among schoolchildren: Basic facts and effects of a school based intervention program. In D. J. Pepler & K. H. Rubin (Eds.), *The development and treatment of childhood aggression* (pp. 411–448). Hillsdale, NJ: Erlbaum.

Olweus, D. (1993). *Bullying at school: What we know and what we can do.* Cambridge, MA: Blackwell.

Olweus, D. (1994). Bullying at school: Basic facts and effects of a school based intervention program. *Journal of Child Psychology and Psychiatry, 35,* 1171–1190.

Tolan, P. H. (2001). Emerging themes and challenges in understanding youth violence involvement. *Journal of Clinical Child Psychology, 30,* 233–239.

United States Census Bureau. www.census.gov/

ADDITIONAL RESOURCES

INTERNET

www.clemson.edu/olweus/content.html. The Olweus Bullying Prevention Program is a comprehensive, schoolwide program designed for use in elementary, middle, and junior high schools. Its goals are to reduce and prevent bullying problems among schoolchildren and to improve peer relations at school. The program has been found to reduce bullying among children, improve the social climate of classrooms, and reduce related antisocial behaviors, such as vandalism and truancy.

www.stopbullyingnow.hrsa.gov/index.asp. This Web site, entitled "Take a Stand. Lend a Hand. Stop Bullying Now!" was developed by the U.S. Department of Health and Human Services, the Health Resources and Services Administration, and the Maternal and Child Health Bureau. It provides excellent material for both adults and children.

www.naspcenter.org/factsheets/socialskills_fs.html. This Web site, which is sponsored by the National Association of School Psychologists, provides information and recommendations on social-skill training as a tool for promoting positive behavior, academic success, and school safety.

www.dontlaugh.org/curricula/. This is the download site for the "Don't Laugh At Me" (DLAM) curricula for use by school superintendents, principals, and other educators who are helping to choose schools in which the DLAM curriculum will be disseminated. The site offers materials for counselors, teachers, and other school personnel for reducing bullying in schools.

PRINTED MATERIALS

Koplow, L. (2002). *Schools that heal.* New York: Teachers College Press.

Larson, J., & Lochman, J. E. (2002). *Helping school children cope with anger: A cognitive-behavioral intervention.* New York: Guilford Press.

Lochman, J., Salekin, E., Randall, T., & Haaga, D. A. F. (2003). Prevention and intervention with aggressive and disruptive children: Next steps in behavioral intervention research. *Behavior Therapy, 34*(4); 413–419.

Espelage, D. L., & Swearer, S. M. (Eds.). (2004). *Bullying in American schools.* Mahwah, NJ: Erlbaum.

CHAPTER 8

NONCOMPLIANCE, DEFIANCE, AND OPPOSITIONAL BEHAVIOR

Even the most seasoned and caring educators will often find their emotions and mental health stretched to the limit by the child who defiantly refuses to follow classroom rules or complete assigned tasks. Noncompliance and defiance are certainly neither benign nor trivial considerations. When a student's level of negativistic, defiant, disobedient, and hostile behavior toward authority figures becomes a recurrent pattern, it may be categorized as Oppositional Defiant Disorder (ODD) (APA, 2000). Students exhibiting such a pattern are often described as having temper outbursts, exhibiting persistent stubbornness and unwillingness to compromise or negotiate with adults or peers, and being generally resistant to direction. These students typically test limits and may employ verbal and minor physical aggression.

Although ODD children and adolescents who have been diagnosed with Conduct Disorder (see Chapter 9) exhibit ODD symptoms (Mash & Wolfe, 2002), ODD does not invariably result in more serious conduct problems (Erk, 2004).

Even when these disruptive behaviors fail to reach levels that significantly impair the student's social or academic function, they present practical problems for teachers and may serve as an early warning sign of developing antisocial behavior (Loeber et al., 1993). Classroom disruptions and defiance of teacher authority bring the instructional process to a grinding halt, and sadly, quite often, teacher responses to such defiance exacerbate the problem.

Teachers often respond to disobedience and defiance by increasing their control and imposing demands for compliance, threatening punishment, and issuing ultimatums. These emotionally charged confrontations often model aggression for the student and result in ill-conceived interventions (Richmond, 2002). In other situations, a teacher may attempt to adjust work and routines to accommodate the student. This adjustment may in fact reinforce the student's use of disruption and defiance as a means of getting what he or she wants.

The school counselor is in the position to assist the classroom teacher with strategies that not only reduce defiant behavior, but do so in an efficient and economical way so as to return the classroom focus to task and instruction. Research has demonstrated the effectiveness of parent-training interventions (see Breston & Eyberg, 1998), problem-solving training (e.g., Kazdin, Siegel, & Bass, 1992), and more multidimensional cognitive-behavioral interventions (e.g., Greene & Ablon, 2004) when working with the defiant and oppositional child. However, as with all interventions, it is important to remember that the effective treatment will be one that is responsive to a comprehensive assessment and understanding of the factors contributing, in this case, to the student's defiant, resistant, oppositional behavior (Greene, Ablon, & Goring, 2003).

OVERVIEW

The following interventions appear to be effective for individual and classroom-wide utilization and serve as valuable additions to the counselor's toolbox of intervention methods, especially when consulting with the classroom teacher (Table 8.1).

TABLE 8.1 Overview of Studies Presented

TARGET PROBLEM	REFERENCE	K–6	6–9	9–12	OTHER SPECIFICATIONS
Aggressive and oppositional behaviors	Muris, Meesters, Vincken, & Eijkelenboom (2005)	Y	Y	N	Cross-over design and standardized group intervention
Noncompliance	Fields (2004)	Y	N	N	Uses teacher training as the intervention process
Defiance	Kiselica (1988)	N	N	Y	Case study of ninth-grade student
Noncompliance	Olmi, Sevier, & Nastasi (1997)	Y	N	N	Case study of preschool student with developmental disabilities

SAMPLE INTERVENTIONS

Reducing Oppositional and Aggressive Behavior: Social-Cognitive Group Intervention

Authors: Peter Muris, Cor Meesters, Manon Vincken, and Anneke Eijkelenboom

Précis: A cross-over study to test the effectiveness of a self-control program in reducing aggressive and oppositional behavior.

Introduction

The authors cite research supporting the value of social-cognitive self-control programs for children exhibiting disruptive behavior disorders. This research typically employed clinical populations. The current study extended this research to the school setting.

Intervention

The intervention was applied to 42 students aged 9 to 12 years who were identified as exhibiting oppositional behaviors in school. A cross-over design was used in which one group of children was first treated with the social-cognitive program during phase 1 and then assigned to a follow-up (waiting) period during phase 2. The order of treatment for the other group was reversed.

The intervention was a standardized group intervention program for four to six students developed by Van Manen (2001). The program focuses on correcting faulty social-information processing and takes place over 11 weeks, with each session lasting 70 to 90 minutes.

The authors reported that the social-cognitive intervention yielded statistically significant reductions in problematic behavior and an increase of social-cognitive skills. Follow-up assessment indicated that the intervention effects were retained over a three-month period.

Reflection

This study was included in the text because it demonstrates an eloquent design for counselors to consider when assessing the effectiveness of their own interventions. Additionally, the study provides support for the value of cognitive interventions to help students correct information-processing deficits and distortions as a means of reducing oppositional defiant behaviors.

The study's use of the cross-over design provided good control over threats to internal validity. One of the major limitations of the study is the generalizability of the findings to American schools. The study and the standardized group intervention were designed and employed with students from the Netherlands. Questions of the degree to which there may be a culture-by-treatment effect remain unanswered, and thus the ability to generalize these findings to U.S. schools is limited. Counselors employing this intervention need to carefully monitor the impact of the interventions on the students involved.

Source: Muris, P., Meesters, C., Vincken, M., & Eijkelenboom, A. (2005). Reducing children's aggressive and oppositional behaviors in the schools: Preliminary results on the effectiveness of social-cognitive group intervention program. *Child & Family Behavior Therapy, 27*(1), 17–32.

SAMPLE INTERVENTIONS

Facing Defiance—Avoiding the Power Struggle

Author: Barry Fields

Précis: The use of a classroom management strategy targeted at reducing noncompliance and defiance within the classroom.

Introduction

The authors noted that teachers traditionally respond to defiance and noncompliance in nonprofessional ways, often escalating controlling behaviors, which in turn aggravates the situation. The authors noted that student behaviors, such as noncompliance and defiance, are often perceived as personal affronts and challenge a teachers' sense of authority and control in the classroom. With this perception, teachers become emotionally charged and respond with ill-conceived forms of intervention, often disciplinary action. The authors present a more effective, less power-struggle-oriented strategy for classroom management and intervention called the *defensive management strategy*. The strategy attempts to avoid coercive, aggressive, emotional, and irrational responses to challenging behaviors, with a focus on the prevention of power struggles. Teachers are instructed to employ early detection, deflection, and defusion in response to noncompliance and defiance.

Intervention

The defensive management strategy was tested with 30 primary-grade teachers who were completing postgraduate study at a regional Australian university. Pre- and post-assessment using a teacher efficacy scale and a frequency measure of discipline referrals served as the dependent measures. The teachers received a print-based package of materials explaining the rational and the steps for implementing the defensive management program. The program entailed:

- Preparation: Baseline data collection of teacher observations and recording of incidents.
- Positive contact: The teacher employs preemptive positive contact with the problem-behavior student.
- Warning signs: Teacher attends to signs of disengagement or agitation.
- Emotional control: Teacher is helped to recognize and control the physical signs of stress and tension in response to student challenges.
- Defuse: Teacher is taught to respond in ways designed to deescalate exchanges through listening to the student, acknowledging feelings, using calm speech, and other techniques.

- Reconnect: Teacher initiates positive exchange shortly after the incident has been diffused and encourages student to formulate a plan to avoid this behavior in the future.

The strategy has been described in detail by Fields (2003).

Results indicate that teachers who completed the program improved their efficacy and reduced the use of disciplinary referral.

Reflection

The program, as outlined, appears to be based on solid classroom management principles. The counselor, working as consultant to the classroom teacher, can employ this program to assist teachers to identify their own emotional and behavioral reactions to the stress of defiance. This early identification, along with the application of cognitive-behavioral strategies to relax and reduce ego involvement, allows for the implementation of the techniques described within the defensive management program. With this added calm and the expanded methods of management at their command, teachers relied less on coercive, escalating approaches to responding to the defiant, oppositional student. The nature of this intervention, with its utilization of printed material, lends itself to group presentation, and thus could be presented by counselors as a teacher in-service program.

Source: Fields, B. (2004). Breaking the cycle of office referrals and suspensions: Defensive Management. *Educational Psychology in Practice, 20*(2), 103–116.

SAMPLE INTERVENTIONS

Student Self-Analysis on Monitoring of Behavior

Author: Mark S. Kiselica

Précis: The use of student self-analysis of events before, during, and after incidents of defiance as a way of reducing such behavior.

Introduction

The program outlined in this study attempted to facilitate a student's ownership of cognitive-behavioral interventions by having the student analyze conditions eliciting and supporting misconduct. The study focused on a 15-year-old, ninth-grade male student.

Intervention

The counselor employed cognitive reframing and alternative response training as intervention strategies. However, significant to this study was the counselor's use of a "Before, During, and After Program" (BDA) as a self-monitoring strategy to increase the student's understanding of his behavior and methods he could use to modify his reactions. Over the course of 16 sessions (twice a week for 8 weeks), the counselor helped the student gather data on his thoughts, feelings, and behaviors that occurred before, during, and after each event. The goal of the data recording was to assist the student to see the relationship between his angry thoughts and his aggressive behavior. The student would identify an event and then would list questions and answers—for example, "What was I thinking before I became angry"—that would help him identify the thought–behavior connection. Next, the student would attempt to identify what he did once he became angry, which was written in a section of the data card marked "during." Finally, the student would describe what happened to him and others afterward.

The counselor and student would review these data and attempt to devise alternative ways of thinking and behaving to these and similar provocative events. In the intervention sessions, the student would rewrite the BDA on the back of his data card. He would answer questions such as "What could I say to avoid becoming angry when criticized?" or "How could I act other than punching when I become angry?" and, finally, "How would I feel and what would happen to me if I used these alternative responses?" The student continued to chart his behavior and employ the BDA approach for two months, with the result being that his aggressive incidents reduced from a baseline frequency rate of 15 incidents to zero incidents by the seventh week. The author reports that at one-year follow-up the student was no longer viewed as a problem.

Reflection

Although this study is somewhat dated (1988), it illustrates a successful cognitive behavioral intervention with an oppositional teen. The value of the study is in its illumination of the value of reframing therapeutic language into that which is easily understood and embraced by the student. The use of BDA cards and graphs provided a concrete focus of the intervention and empowered the student to better understand those factors contributing to his acting out and to develop alternative, self-directed strategies for behavior. In this case. the approach allowed the student to control the direction he would take, as opposed to having an adult tell him how he should change.

The major concern, of course, is that this was a case study of one student and that the baseline data were gathered for only a week-long period. As such, counselors employing such a BDA approach may wish to closely monitor the validity and reliability of the student self-monitoring.

Source: Kiselica, M. S. (1988). Helping an aggressive adolescent through the "before, during, and after program." *The School Counselor, 35*, 299–306.

DETAILED INTERVENTION

Time-In/Time-Out

Introduction

Numerous behavioral strategies have been incorporated into the management of oppositional, defiant, and resistant students. The technique investigated by the authors of this study for reducing noncompliant behavior was "time-out." Time-out, that is, removing the student from reinforcing events, has been used with students exhibiting various behavioral disorders. The authors note that the use of time-out should be considered as part of a larger treatment approach, one including the creation of a time-in rich environment, because the relative reinforcing properties of the time-in serve as the major determinant of the effectiveness of time-out.

The current study reported on the use of time-in (physical touch and verbal praise in response to appropriate behavior) and time-out to arrest inappropriate and noncompliant behavior of a preschooler. The preschooler was a 4-year-old African American child with speech and language disabilities. The child had an extensive history of noncompliance and acting-out behaviors. The authors noted that after three 90-minute sessions of intervention training, compliance rates increased from an archival base rate of 9 percent to a mean session rate in the range of 97 to 100 percent. Compliance rates stayed well into the 90-percent range even at 40-week follow-up.

Method

The study reported on a simple-phase single-case design in which parent and teacher reports were used to estimate archival baseline rates of targeted behavior. The student's compliance rate after the first time he was presented with teacher or parent instruction was estimated to be approximately 9 percent. Noncompliance, which was defined as not following teacher-presented instructions within five seconds of presentation, was selected as the target for intervention. The intervention included time-in and time-out procedures.

Intervention

The intervention included time-in procedures that involved the use of contingent touch and verbal praise each time the student complied with the adult-presented instruction. The time-in process was supplied on a near-continuous basis for those occasions when the student followed the teacher-presented instruction. When the student failed to comply within a five-second window, time-out (placement in a location for a brief period of time devoid of adult attention) was employed.

The intervention program was implemented for three 90-minute sessions. Implementation was eventually transferred to the classroom teacher as a means of generalizing the process. The specifics of the time-out program included the following:

1. The child was instructed by the teacher to begin or cease an action. The student was given five seconds to begin following the instruction.
2. If the student failed to begin to alter his behavior within five seconds, the child was placed in a spot two to three feet away from the site of the activity, with as little physical guidance as necessary. The student was instructed: "You did not follow my instruction, time-out."
3. When the child was in time-out, he was not visually attended to nor touched or spoken to.
4. When the child became quiet (not making unnecessary sounds or motor movement), a three-to-five-second contingent release period began.
5. After the contingent release period, the child was directed "You are quiet, out of time-out."
6. Upon exiting time-out, the original instruction was repeated. This was followed by time-in if the child complied.

Reflection

Behavioral procedures have been used to modify various forms of disruptive behavior across both clinical and nonclinical populations. Time-out is a specific application of behavior modification that has proven effective for use with a wide range of populations.

As with any reductive procedure, the use of time-out may result in increased aggression, withdrawal, or escape behavior wherein the child refuses to go to time-out. The authors hoped to address this element by incorporating a positive component to the process, that is, easy re-access to time-in. The apparent effectiveness (see caveat below) of the program, along with its ease of implementation (i.e., no need for special materials or long, extensive training) would appear to make this intervention a useful one for the counselor's repertoire.

The phrase "apparent effectiveness" is used to denote the fact that the nonreversal, noncontrol nature of the experiment limits the degree to which one can absolutely conclude a treatment effect. However, the long-standing history of the student's noncompliance and the immediate and radical shift in levels of compliance following the introduction of the treatment provides strong intuitive support for the treatment's effectiveness. A further limitation to the design is that it does not allow for a clear identification of which element of the treatment, that is, time-out or time-in, was accountable for the noted changes.

Finally, a general caveat needs to be offered. Time-out procedures may be one of the most familiar intervention strategies targeted to reducing undesirable behavior. They also may be the most misused operant strategy. When using time-out, the following guidelines and caveats should be considered:

- Students should understand the reason for time-out and the rules governing placement and removal from time-out.
- Students should not be sent to time-out in anger or as a means of humiliation. Directives to time-out should be given in a firm, calm voice with as few words as possible.
- Going to time-out is *not* negotiable. Don't get into a large debate over whether the infraction constitutes a valid reason for time-out. Simply remind the student that the more they delay entering the time-out, the more time they will spend there.
- Time-out should not be used for extended periods of time. As a rule of thumb, use no more than 1 minute per year of age and never more than 15 minutes.
- Be sure the time-out area is safe and humane.
- Be sure the time-out area is nonreinforcing (no toys, games, distractions, or other students).
- Finally, use time-out with a reentry (time-in) program, whereby the student's appropriate behavior can be reinforced and increased in frequency.

Source: Olmi, D. J., Sevier, R. C., & Nastasi, D. F. (1997). Time-in/time-out as a response to noncompliance and inappropriate behavior with students with developmental disabilities: Two case studies. *Psychology in the Schools, 34*(1), 31–39.

FROM THE FIELD

The following suggestions reflect the experience and anecdotal reporting of counselors working both in direct service with students and indirectly with teachers. These strategies have not been tested using an experimental design. As personal suggestions, they need to be employed with caution and their impact monitored.

Working with Students

- Try to confer one on one with the student. Attempt to "listen" for the student's sources of resistance and demonstrate a caring, nonconfrontational attitude.
- Convey to the student your belief that his or her needs do matter.
- Assist the student to find a goal, a purpose, for his or her participation in this class.
- Try to identify ways to engage the student, perhaps in an active leadership role, as a way of increasing the value of the class for that student.
- Help the student develop alternative, more socially appropriate ways of sharing his or her resistance to an assignment. Reframe the resistance as the student's attempt to make assignments or material more personally relevant and engage the student in reshaping the assignment to bring this personal value to the front.
- Consider using more cooperative learning exercises—the social engagement of peers (vs. adult authority) may serve as social pressure for compliance.
- Assist all students in learning to attack issues—not people—when working in small groups.
- Have the resistant student work with more socially mature students who can model conflict resolution and cooperation.
- Teach the student conflict resolution strategies of a win-win nature.
- Teach the student to employ assertive skills, such as the use of "I statements," as a way of communicating dissatisfaction.

Working with Teacher: Tasks and Task Assignment

- Avoid public confrontation, ridicule, or criticism as much as possible.
- Review assignments to make sure they are within the student's capabilities and that the expectations are clear.
- Do not use tests or assignments that are intended to "catch" the students or punish them.
- When confronting the student, avoid engaging in emotional debate; simply state the rule or task to be followed, your expectations, and consequences for failure to perform. Do not engage in long debates or discussion of tangential issues.
- Try not to take resistance, defiance, or even verbal attacks personally. Use the traffic cop model: "Sir, did you see you ran the red light? I'm sorry but here's your ticket." Walk away.

- If another faculty member has had more success with a particular student in the past, use this person as a resource and an ally. Perhaps meet with the student and this teacher to problem solve.
- Try to avoid sharply worded directives (e.g., "Lori, PUT that down . . . NOW!").
- Incorporate the Premack principle by having the student complete a behavior before being allowed to engage in a more desirable activity.
- When directing an ODD child, provide a choice between two acceptable alternatives (e.g., "It's time now to take our seats," "Tina would you like to read first or second?").

REFERENCES

American Psychiatric Association (2000). *Diagnostic and statistical manual of mental disorders*, 4th ed., text revision. Washington, DC: Author.

Breston, E. V., & Eyberg, S. M. (1998). Effective psychosocial treatment of conduct-disordered children and adolescents: 29 years, 82 studies, and 5,272 kids. *Journal of Clinical Child Psychology, 27*(2), 180–189.

Erk, R. E. (2004). *Counseling treatment for children and adolescents with DSM-IV-TR disorders*. Upper Saddle River, NJ: Pearson.

Fields, B. A. (2003). Managing noncompliance and defiance through defensive management. Paper presented at the State Conference of the Australian Association of Special Education & Association of Special Education Administrators of Queensland, Toowoomba, University of Southern Queensland.

Fields, B. (2004). Breaking the cycle of office referrals and suspensions: Defensive Management. *Educational Psychology in Practice, 20*(2), 103–116.

Greene, R. W., Ablon, J. S., & Goring, J. C. (2003). A transactional model of oppositional behavior: Underpinnings of the collaborative problem-solving approach. *Journal of Psychosomatic Research, 55*(1), 67–75.

Greene, R. W., Ablon, J. S., Goring, J. C., Fazio, V., & Morse, L. R. (2004). Treatment of Oppositional Defiant Disorder in children and adolescents. In P. M. Barrett & T. H. Ollendick (Eds.). *Handbook of interventions that work with children and adolescents* (pp. 369–394). West Sussex, England: John Wiley & Sons, Ltd.

Kazdin, A. E., Siegel, T. C., & Bass, D. (1992). Cognitive problem-solving skills training and parent-management training in the treatment of antisocial behavior in children. *Journal of Consulting and Clinical Psychology, 60*(5), 733–747.

Kiselica, M. S. (1988). Helping an aggressive adolescent through the "before, during, and after program." *The School Counselor, 35*, 299–306.

Loeber, R., Wung, P., Keenan, K., Girous, B., Stouthamer-Loeber, M., Van Kammen, W. B., & Maughan, B. (1993). Developmental pathways in disruptive child behavior. *Development and Psychopathology, 5*, 103–133.

Mash, E. J., & Wolfe, D. A. (2002). *Abnormal child psychology*. Belmont, CA: Wadsworth.

Muris, P., Meesters, C., Vincken, M., & Eijkelenboom, A. (2005). Reducing children's aggressive and oppositional behaviors in the schools: Preliminary results on the effectiveness of social-cognitive group intervention program. *Child & Family Behavior Therapy, 27*(1), 17–32.

Olmi, D. J., Sevier, R. C., & Nastasi, D. F. (1997). Time-in/time-out as a response to noncompliance and inappropriate behavior with students with developmental disabilities: Two case studies. *Psychology in the Schools, 34*(1), 31–39.

Richmond, C. (2002). Searching for balance: A collective case study of 10 secondary teachers' behavior management language. Unpublished doctoral thesis, University of New England, Armindale.

Van Manen, T. G. (2001). *Zelf-controle. Een social-cognitief interventieprogramma voor kinderen met agressief en oppositioneel gedrag (Self-control. A social-cognitive intervention program for children with aggressive and oppositional behavior).* Houten/Diegem: Bohn Stafleu Van Loghum.

ADDITIONAL RESOURCES

INTERNET

www.colorado.edu/cspv/blueprints. Web site developed by the Center for the Study and Prevention of Violence at the University of Colorado at Boulder. Provides a database, resource guides, and information on well-evaluated intervention programs.

www.4teachers.org/4teachers/profd/motivtrack.shtml. Classroom management tracks are resource sites developed by educators. The information provided is practical and comes from the experience of those within the classroom.

www.mentalhealth.com/dis/p20-ch05.html. A good resource on oppositional defiant disorders. Provides diagnostic and early identification information, intervention strategies, reading materials, and Internet links.

PRINT MATERIALS

Greenberg, M. T., & Kusche, C. A. (1998). Preventive interventions for school-age deaf children: The PATHS curriculum. *Journal of Deaf Studies and Deaf Education, 3,* 49–63.

Greenberg, M. T., Kusché, C., & Mihalic, S. F. (1998). *Blueprints for violence prevention, book 10: Promoting alternative thinking strategies (PATHS).* Boulder, CO: Center for the Study and Prevention of Violence.

Kavale, K. A., Forness, S. R., & Walker, H. M. (1999). Interventions for oppositional defiant disorder and conduct disorder in the schools. In H. C. Quay & A. E. Hogan (Eds.), *Handbook of disruptive behavior disorders* (pp. 441–454). Dordrecht, Netherlands: Kluwer Academic Publishers.

Riley, D. A. (1997). *The defiant child: A Parent's guide to oppositional defiant disorder.* Dallas, TX: Taylor Trade Publishing.

CHAPTER 9

CONDUCT PROBLEMS AND ANTISOCIAL BEHAVIOR

A broad range of behaviors can be grouped under the heading of "conduct problems." As a "spectrum disorder," conduct problems may present themselves as minor annoying behaviors or as more serious forms such as physical aggression, destructiveness, and stealing. However, when the behavior is presented as a repetitive and persistent pattern in which the basic rights of others or major age-appropriate societal norms or rules are violated, it qualifies as *conduct disorder* (APA, 2000). For a child to be diagnosed with conduct disorder, the child must have demonstrated repeated violation of rules, age-appropriate societal norms, or the rights of others over the course of at least 12 months as evidenced by three or more behaviors reflecting aggression against people or animals (e.g., bullying, physical cruelty to people or animals, extortion, mugging); property destruction; or lying, theft, and/or a serious rule violation.

The prevalence of conduct disorder appears to have increased over the course of the past decade (Mash & Wolfe, 2002). Actual statistics on its prevalence vary depending on the population sampled (e.g., clinical vs. nonclinical; urban vs. suburban).

It is important to note that conduct problems have been reported as being stable over time (e.g., Loeber et al., 2000) and that early conduct disorder behavior appears to be related to a range of adverse psychological and social-emotional outcomes, including aggressiveness and antisocial behavior (Brame, Nagin, & Tremblay, 2001; Loeber & Farrington, 2000). As such, it would appear that early identification and treatment are essential. The school counselor is in a unique situation to assist in these intervention efforts.

Numerous approaches have been employed in the treatment of conduct problems (e.g., Hill & Maughan, 2001), with many utilizing family-based interventions (e.g., Patterson, Reid, & Dishion, 1992); multicomponent interventions (e.g., Kazdin, 2001); and community-based programs, including residential programs (e.g., Larzelere et al., 2001). Recent evidence suggests that prevention strategies are effective in reducing antisocial behavior. Readers interested in these prevention strategies should visit the Web site for the Center for the Study and Prevention of Violence (www.colorado.edu/cspv/index.html).

OVERVIEW

Although no one modality of intervention will be effective for every student with conduct problems, the studies presented with this chapter provide a broad-spectrum view that will expand the intervention options available to the school counselor. The following interventions target pre-K through high school students. The interventions range from individual direct service counseling and teacher-implemented programs to large, systemwide prevention programs (Table 9.1).

TABLE 9.1 Overview of Studies Presented

TARGET PROBLEM	REFERENCE	K–6	6–9	9–12	OTHER SPECIFICATIONS
Reducing risk for development of conduct disorders	Ialongo, Poduska, Werthamer, & Kellam (2001)	Y	N	N	Randomized block design
Early onset conduct disorder	Webster-Stratton & Hammond (1997)	Y	N	N	Random control group design
Expressed anger in student with conduct disorder	Dykman (2001)	N	N	Y	Single subject, pre-post test design with eight students
Prevention of antisocial behavior of at-risk students	Conduct Problems Prevention Research Group (1999)	Y	Y	Y	Large sample, controlled study using varied geographic settings and cultural groupings

SAMPLE INTERVENTIONS

First-Grade Prevention Program

Authors: Nick Ialongo, Jeanne Paduska, Lisa Werthamer, and Sheppard Kellam

Précis: Reports on the impact of a classroom-centered intervention designed to reduce the risk of later conduct problems by enhancing teachers' behavior management of first graders.

Introduction

Evidence suggests that without early intervention, conduct problems in young children can become crystallized behavior patterns with a resultant spiral of academic problems, school drop-out, substance abuse, delinquency, and violence (Snyder, 2001). Although the antecedents of conduct problems may be apparent as early as first grade, the authors note that relatively few randomized controlled studies of universal preventive interventions aimed at these early antecedents have been developed. The current study reported on the distal impact of classroom-centered interventions.

Intervention

The classroom-centered intervention consisted of three components: (1) curriculum enhancement (designed to enhance critical thinking, listening, comprehension. and social problem-solving skills); (2) enhanced behavior management practices (the use of the "Good Behavior" game whereby classroom groups are reinforced for "good behavior"); and (3) backup strategies for children who are not performing adequately. A randomized block design was used, with schools serving as the blocking factor. Three first-grade classrooms in each of nine urban elementary schools were randomly assigned to one of the two intervention conditions or a control condition. The results suggested that the intervention had a significant impact on early risk behaviors for future antisocial behavior through the second-grade follow up. Further, in analysis of distal impact (sixth grade), the treatment classes showed significantly fewer teacher-reported conduct problems, school suspensions, or referrals for mental health services.

Reflection

The current study suggests that immediate and appropriate intervention at the first-grade level can significantly reduce the appearance of conduct problems in the future (five years later). With national surveys suggesting that the prevalence of aggressive conduct problems in preschool and young school-aged children may be as high as 25 percent (Snyder, 2001), early intervention strategies are imperative. Further, given the connection between early conduct problems and the later development of more clinically significant conduct and academic problems, it would appear that early interventions should be designed to reduce the immediate difficulty and also to prevent the trajectory of conduct difficulty. The current classroom-centered intervention appears to meet this need with program elements that could be adapted easily to most school settings.

Source: Ialongo, N., Poduska, J., Werthamer, L., Kellam, S. (2001). The distal impact of two first-grade preventive interventions on conduct problems and disorder in early adolescence. *Journal of Emotional and Behavioral Disorders, 9*(3), 146–161.

SAMPLE INTERVENTIONS

Performance-based Intervention—Child Training

Authors: Carolyn Webster-Stratton and Mary Hammond

Précis: A comparison study of child- and parent-training interventions for children manifesting early onset conduct problems.

Introduction

As noted by the authors, many intervention programs have targeted parent training as a way of reducing children's conduct problems. The short- and long-term success of such treatments has been documented. Needless to say, the success of these interventions is contingent on the compliance of the parents in applying the intervention strategies. As a way of reducing reliance on others (i.e., parents), the authors offered an innovative child-training program that targeted antecedent risk factors (i.e., children's deficits in social skills, problem solving, and affect regulation).

Intervention

Families of 97 children ranging in age from 4 to 8 years with early onset conduct problems were randomly assigned to 1 of 4 conditions: a parent-training group; a child-training group; a combined child and parent treatment group; and a wait-list control group. The intervention discussed here is the child-training group.

The children worked with therapists in small groups of five or six. Each child attended 22 sessions, each lasting 2 hours. During the sessions, the children would watch 30 minutes of noncontinuous videotaped programs (i.e., 10 to 12 vignettes of modeled skills per session). After each vignette, the therapist led a discussion of the taped interaction, eliciting the children's reactions, ideas, and questions. The video content addressed interpersonal difficulties typically experienced by children with conduct problems: lack of social skills and conflict resolution skills, loneliness and negative attribution, an inability to empathize or to understand another perspective, and problems at school. The videotape vignettes depicted children using stress-reduction strategies, problem solving, and alternative responses to bothersome situations. Results indicated significant improvement in problem solving and conflict management skills and significant reduction in child conduct problems at home.

Reflection

The interactive videotape modeling employed in this intervention is based on a model that encourages the child to discuss the use of positive social skills in different situations. Working in small groups allowed for collaboration among the students as well as the opportunity to practice these skills. It is clear that the intervention was effective; and effects were maintained at a one-year follow-up. However, the resources required to create the needed materials (video vignettes) and run the two-hour group training sessions may prove prohibitive to many school counselors. Despite the significant resources required, the performance-based, small-group approach described in the study appears to have value (even if modified in duration and intensity) and may be a useful tool for school counselors. But as with any intervention, modification of the specific steps in the procedure should be done with caution and the impact of the program will need to be evaluated.

Source: Webster-Stratton, C., & Hammond, M. (1997). Treating children with early onset conduct problems: A comparison of child and parent training interventions. *Journal of Consulting and Clinical Psychology, 65*(1), 93–109.

SAMPLE INTERVENTIONS

Decreasing Expression of Anger with CBT

Author: Bruce Dykfman

Précis: School-based cognitive-behavioral program treating expressed anger in adolescents with conduct disorders.

Introduction

Adolescents with conduct disorder present with deficits in interpersonal development and limited awareness of the social perspectives of others. Social-cognitive approaches to aggression posit that it is this very limitation in one's level of interpersonal understanding and problem solving that results in the aggressive behavior typical of those with a conduct disorder. From this perspective, the aggressive person is one who misreads social situations and perceives threats and provocations where none exist. Social-cognitive intervention strategies, therefore, focus on the development of interpersonal understanding, problem-solving skills, and the development of perspective taking.

The current study examined the effectiveness of a school-based cognitive-behavioral intervention program targeted at decreasing expressions of anger by students previously diagnosed with early childhood onset conduct disorder.

Intervention

A single-subject, pretest-posttest design was used to assess treatment efficacy for 8 students ages 14 to 16. Treatment consisted of 24 one-hour sessions consisting of cognitive-behavioral counseling over an 8-week period. The counselor paired students together whereby one member of the pair was somewhat older, more mature, and showed fewer symptoms. The counselor had each pair discuss situations where they felt others precipitated their feelings of anger. Role-play and role reversals were used to assist students understand the perspectives of others. The counselor also helped the students engage in reciprocal problem solving by encouraging each pair to (1) identify a problem, (2) consider possible options and outcomes, (3) choose a strategy, and (4) plan on how to evaluate the outcome. The author noted significant changes from pretest levels of anger expression and anger control.

Reflection

The current study suggests that students receiving cognitive-behavioral intervention based on social-cognitive understanding and dialectical behavioral problem solving are able to reduce the inappropriate expressions of anger and maintain control of angry feelings. These results seem hopeful for school counselors working with students exhibiting situational and state anger.

The single case study design limits the generalization of these findings to other students, other developmental levels, and other settings. Counselors employing this strategy need to carefully monitor the effects of the intervention with their particular students.

Source: Dykman, B. (2001). Cognitive behavior treatment of expressed anger in adolescents with conduct disorders. *Education, 121*(2), 298–300.

DETAILED INTERVENTION

Fast Track

Introduction

The Fast Track program is a comprehensive multisite program targeted at preventing serious and persistent antisocial behavior among high-risk children. The Fast Track design is based on empirical findings of longitudinal research conducted by the Conduct Problems Prevention Research Group (CPPRG, 1992). This model assumes that antisocial behavior is caused by multiple factors, such as neuropsychological deficits that undermine executive functioning, parenting styles, the presence of maternal substance abuse, nutritional deprivation, physical abuse, and lack of stimulation. The model also assumes that contextual factors, such as family poverty, family instability, negative school experiences, particularly problematic peer relations, and academic difficulties, contribute to the development of antisocial conduct problems. The Fast Track program identifies risk factors to target in prevention and suggests the kinds of competencies that must be enhanced to move high-risk children into more adaptive developmental trajectories.

Method

High-risk schools at four sites were selected based on crime and poverty statistics of the neighborhoods they served. Within each site, the schools were divided into two sets matched for demographics (i.e., size, percentage who received free or reduced lunch, and ethnic composition). The sets were randomly assigned to intervention and control conditions. Multiple assessment methods, including ratings, interviews, peer nominations, and home and school observations were employed using multiple informants (i.e., children, parents, teachers, peers, and interviewers). Data were collected on aggressive and oppositional behaviors, level of authority acceptance, and classroom adaptation, along with other behavioral problems.

Because part of the intervention (described below) involved a school-based intervention, entire schools ($n = 54$) were assigned to either the intervention or the control condition. The intervention condition involved 445 children in 191 classrooms. The control condition had 446 children in 210 classrooms.

Results following the first year of intervention implementation showed that the intervention-group children, relative to the children in the control condition, progressed significantly in their acquisition of almost all of the skills deemed to be critical protective factors by the developmental model. They improved in both emotional and social-coping skills, and they made distinct progress with basic word-attack skills for reading. Skill improvements were accompanied by more positive peer relations at school, as well as better language arts grades. Parents in the intervention condition, relative to the control condition, demonstrated more warmth and positive involvement, more appropriate and consistent discipline, more positive school involvement, and less harsh discipline. Intervention-group parents also reported greater positive changes in their parenting behavior and parenting satisfaction and self-efficacy. Finally, the authors noted some of the indexes of child behavior problems indicated initial effects on the reduction of disruptive and aggressive behavior problems among what was a highly disruptive and aggressive group of children in the intervention condition.

Intervention

The Fast Track program was designed to address the major deficits that lead to subsequent school failure, rejection by peers and increased aggression toward them, and disruptive and defiant behavior toward authority. Fast Track is designed to extend across the school years from first through tenth grade, although the current study focused only on the impact of Fast Track at the first-grade level. Fast Track uses a "unified model of prevention" consisting of both universal and selective components. The first-grade intervention was composed of seven integrated programs [the PATHS (Promoting Alternative THinking Strategies) curriculum, parent groups, child social-skills training groups, parent–child sharing time, home visiting, child peer pairing, and academic tutoring]. These components took place in the school, during two-hour extracurricular "enrichment programs" involving both parents and children, and in the home.

Universal Intervention

First-grade classroom teachers were trained to deliver an adapted version of the PATHS curriculum (Kusche & Greenberg, 1994). The teacher-implemented curriculum served as the universal (school-based) component of the intervention. Teachers implemented the classroom-level program throughout the year, teaching an average of two to three lessons per week covering four skill domains: (1) skills for emotional understanding and communication (i.e., recognizing and labeling emotions), (2) friendship skills (i.e., participation, cooperation, fair play, and negotiation), (3) self-control skills (i.e., behavioral inhibition and arousal modulation), and (4) social problem-solving skills (i.e., problem identification, response generation, response evaluation, and anticipatory planning).

Selective Interventions

In addition to PATHS, the intervention included parent groups; child social-skills training groups; and academic tutoring during a weekly, two-hour enrichment program held at the school building on Saturdays or weekday evenings.

Primary content areas of the parent-group curriculum included (1) establishing a positive family–school relationship and supporting child adjustment to school, (2) building parental self-control, (3) promoting developmentally appropriate expectations for the child's behavior, and (4) improving parenting skills to improve parent–child interaction and decrease disruptive behavior. Training techniques included instruction, modeling, discussion, and role-playing (See McMahon, Slough, & CPPRG, 1996, for further details about the parent-focused intervention components).

To help generalize the learning to the home environment, home visits (every other week) by Fast Track staff were implemented to (1) develop trusting relationships with the entire family system; (2) promote generalization of newly acquired parenting skills to the home; (3) promote parental support for the child's school adjustment; and (4) promote parental problem solving, coping, and goal setting as a means of dealing with the many stressful life events (e.g., marital conflict, substance use, social isolation, and housing issues) that these families often experience.

Academic support involved individual tutoring by paraprofessional tutors to promote reading skills.

Reflection

The results of the study indicated the early effectiveness of the Fast Track intervention in terms of the children's social cognition, academic performance, peer relations, and aggressive-disruptive behaviors, as well as parenting behavior and parents' social cognitions. The intervention is impressive both in terms of both impact and the extensiveness of its design.

An important design feature of the Fast Track study was its implementation in four culturally and geographically diverse communities. This variation permitted the authors to evaluate the program with a large, diverse sample of children and families and to examine program impact by gender, ethnicity, and child and family characteristics. The apparent generalizability of the findings is especially important to note. At least in its early phases, the intervention seems equally effective for both boys and girls, with African American and European American children and parents, across urban and rural sites, and across three cohorts.

The long-range goal of this prevention is to reduce adolescent delinquency, substance abuse, risky sexual practices, school failure, and psychological disorders. The logic of the design is that building competency, reducing stressors, and moderating contextual factors that promote deviance are keys to the ultimate success of these children. Clearly, additional research is needed to assess the extent to which changes in these risk factors may account for changes in child antisocial behavior and contribute over time to more adaptive child developmental trajectories.

Source: Conduct Problems Prevention Research Group. (1999). Initial impact of the Fast Track prevention trial for conduct problems: I. The high-risk sample. *Journal of Consulting and Clinical Psychology, 67*(5), 631–647.

FROM THE FIELD

Working with Students

- Use overcorrection. Confront the child in every situation where he or she is violating school rules.
- A student exhibiting destructive behaviors, including fire-setting, needs to be monitored closely. Start a project, such as building a model, to help the student find satisfaction and attention through productivity and care.
- Use time-out every time the student exhibits aggression or violates a rule.
- Reinforce all prosocial and nonaggressive behaviors exhibited by the student.
- When the student is using pencils, school materials, and other items for aggressive/destructive purposes, the items should be removed and returned contingent on the demonstration of acceptable classroom behavior.
- Increase the student's involvement in extracurricular (peer interaction) activities.
- Confront all antisocial behavior and attitudes, highlighting the consequences of such behaviors and attitudes.
- Teach mediation strategies such as relaxation, stop-look-listen and think, and so on.
- Provide play and art materials to enable the student to express feelings of anger and frustration.
- Have the student read a story to a younger student or assist in helping the younger student clean up his or her cubby and praise the student for prosocial behavior.
- Construct a behavior modification system of consistent rules and clear positive and response-cost consequences.

Working with Teachers

- Teachers should resist focusing on inappropriate behavior, but rather focus on desirable replacement behavior.
- Provide the student with opportunities to practice and reinforce appropriate behavior.
- Employ humor as a way of diffusing the student's anger and avoid escalation.
- Target specific prosocial behaviors (e.g., taking turns, working with others, demonstrating positive verbal and nonverbal interactions) and provide practice.
- Pair the student with a strong, socially appropriate model.

REFERENCES

American Psychiatric Association. (2000). *Diagnostic and statistical manual of mental disorders* (4th ed., Text Revision). Washington, DC: Author.

Brame, B., Nagin, D. S., & Tremblay, R. E. (2001). Developmental trajectories of physical aggression from school entry to late adolescence. *Journal of Child Psychology and Psychiatry, 42*, 503–512.

Conduct Problems Prevention Research Group. (1992). A developmental and clinical model for the prevention of conduct disorder: The Fast Track program. *Development and Psychopathology, 4*, 509–527.

Conduct Problems Prevention Research Group. (1999). Initial impact of the Fast Track prevention trial for conduct problems: I. The high-risk sample. *Journal of Consulting and Clinical Psychology, 67*(5), 631–647.

Dykman, B. (2001). Cognitive behavior treatment of expressed anger in adolescents with conduct disorders. *Education, 121*(2), 298–300.

Hill, J., & Maughan, B. (2001). *Conduct disorders in childhood and adolescence*. Cambridge, UK: Cambridge University Press.

Ialongo, N., Poduska, J., Werthamer, L., Kellam, S. (2001). The distal impact of two first-grade preventive interventions on conduct problems and disorder in early adolescence. *Journal of Emotional and Behavioral Disorders, 9*(3), 146–161.

Kazdin, A. E. (2001). Treatment of conduct disorder. In J. Hill & B. Maughan (Eds.), *Conduct disorders in childhood and adolescence* (pp. 408–448). Cambridge, UK: Cambridge University Press.

Kusche, C. A., & Greenberg, M. T. (1994). *The PATHS curriculum*. Seattle, WA: Developmental Research and Programs.

Larzelere, R. E., Dinges, K., Schmidt, M. D., Spellman, D. F., Criste, T. R., & Connell, P. (2001). Outcomes of residential treatment: A study of the adolescent clients of Girls and Boys Town. *Child and Youth Care Forum, 30*, 175–185.

Loeber, R., & Farrington, D. P. (2000). Young children who commit crime: Epidemiology, developmental origins, risk factors, early interventions and policy implications. *Development and Psychopathology, 12*, 737–762.

Loeber, R., Burke, J. D., Lahey, B. B., Winters, A., & Zera, M. (2000). Oppositional defiant and conduct disorder: A review of the past 10 years. Part I. *Journal of the American Academy of Child and Adolescent Psychiatry, 34*, 499–509.

Mash, E. J., & Wolfe, D. A. (2002). *Abnormal child psychology*. Belmont, CA: Wadsworth.

McMahon, R. J., Slough, N., & Conduct Problems Prevention Research Group. (1996). Family-based intervention in the Fast Track program. In R. D. Peters & R. J. McMahon (Eds.), *Preventing childhood disorders, substance abuse, and delinquency* (pp. 90–110). Thousand Oaks, CA: Sage.

Patterson, G. R., Reid, J. B. & Dishion, T. J. (1992). *Antisocial boys*. Eugene, OR: Castalia.

Snyder, H. (2001). Epidemiology of official offending. In R. Loeber & D. P. Farrington (Eds.), *Child delinquents: Development, intervention, and service needs* (pp. 25–46). Thousand Oaks, CA: Sage.

Webster-Stratton, C., & Hammond, M. (1997). Treating children with early onset conduct problems: A comparison of child and parent training interventions. *Journal of Consulting and Clinical Psychology, 65*(1), 93–109.

ADDITIONAL RESOURCES

INTERNET

www.colorado.edu/cspv/index.html. Web site for The Center for the Study and Prevention of Violence. This site is an excellent source for research literature and resources on the causes and prevention of violence. It provides direct information services to the public by offering topical searches on customized databases.

teenswithproblems.com. Good source of literature on parenting teens with conduct and oppositional defiant disorder.

www.aacap.org/clinical/CONDCT~1.HTM. Web site for the American Academic of Child and Adolescent Psychiatry. Good article on the diagnosis and treatment of conduct disorders in adolescents.

PRINTED MATERIALS

Peters, R. D., & McMahon, R. J. (Eds.). (1996). *Preventing childhood disorders, substance abuse, and delinquency*. Thousand Oaks, CA: Sage.

Quay, H. C., & Hogan, A. E. (1999). *Handbook of disruptive behavior disorders*. Dordrecht, Netherlands: Kluwer Academic Publishers.

Shapiro, L. E. (1995). *The very angry day that Amy didn't have*. Plainview, NY: Childsworth/Childsplay, LLC.

Webster-Stratton, C., & Herbert, M. (1994). Strategies for helping parents of children with conduct disorders. In M. Hersen & R. M. Eisler (Eds.), *Progress in behavior modification*, Vol. 29 (pp. 121–142). Belmont, CA: Brooks/Cole.

CHAPTER 10

SEXUAL BEHAVIOR

Sexual feelings and sexual behaviors are clearly part of the normal developmental process. Sexual behavior in children—including curiosity, interest, and experimentation—is progressive over time. Sometimes, however, sexual behaviors occur in situations or in forms that are socially inappropriate (e.g., public masturbation), potentially harmful (e.g., risky sexual behavior), or that may signal other, more serious problems (e.g., sexual abuse).

RISKY BEHAVIOR

Research suggests that preteens and teens not only are becoming sexually active at increasing rates, but also they are engaging in sexually risky activities. Students may engage in sexual behaviors that place them at risk for consequences more dangerous than peer rejection and humiliation. For example, more than 15 million new instances of sexually transmitted diseases (STDs) are reported annually in the United States, nearly one-fourth among teens aged 15 to 19, and in 2000 an estimated 822,000 pregnancies occurred among U.S. teens aged 15 to 19 (Cubbin, Santelli, Brindis, & Braveman, 2005). Although these statistics pointing to the at-risk sexual behavior of U.S. teens is alarming, research now indicates that certain at-risk behaviors, such as coerced oral sexual activity, mutual masturbation, and sexual intercourse, are being reported by elementary school counselors among children as early as first grade (Aspen Publishers, 2001).

INAPPROPRIATE BEHAVIOR

Although instances of public masturbation may be infrequent, when they do occur, especially within the classroom, they serve as a major disruption and place the child at risk for rejection and humiliation. Compulsive, public masturbation or extreme genital preoccupation may reflect immaturity, developmental delay, or evidence of sexual victimization. In either case, it is important not just to assist the student in identifying what is appropriate and inappropriate behavior, but to also assist them in coping more successfully with stress, negative feelings, or previous traumatic experiences.

INDICATION OF ABUSE

Unusual sexual behavior and/or intense preoccupation with sex in children may indicate sexual abuse (Hillman & Solek-Tefft, 1988; Gough, Kelly, & Scott, 1993). Although these behaviors may be indicators of other problems a student may be experiencing, it is important that the school counselor be aware of the possibility of abuse and reach out to these students and not simply focus on the elimination of the behavior. An article written by Susan Hackbarth James (1999) offers excellent suggestions as to how counselors can recognize and interview students when they suspect sexual abuse.

OVERVIEW

Schools are an important arena for fostering the social development of our youth. School counselors and school personnel are in a unique position to assist students in understanding and managing their developing sexuality. Knowledge and development of the skills necessary to manage sexual feelings, make informed decisions, and avoid risky sexual activities is essential. The school counselor can promote healthy sexual development through the roles of consultation, direct service counseling, and coordination with other professionals. The following interventions will support such efforts (see Table 10.1).

TABLE 10.1 Overview of Studies Presented

TARGET PROBLEM	REFERENCE	K–6	6–9	9–12	OTHER SPECIFICATIONS
Reducing public masturbation	Janzen & Peacock (1977)	Y	Y	N	Case study, time-series design, 9-year-old female
Reducing at-risk sexual behaviors	Coyle, Birby, Marin, Gomez, & Gregorich (2004)	Y	Y	N	Randomized controlled trial design involving 19 ethnically diverse public middle schools (grades 6 to 8) to test the effectiveness of a 3-year program
Afrocentric pregnancy prevention program	Dixon, Schoonmaker, & Philliber (2000)	N	Y	Y	Nonrandomized control group design involving 65 African American females aged 14 to 19 living in low-income neighborhoods
Abstinence-only prevention program	Blake, Simkin, Ledsky, Perkins, & Calabrese (2001)	Y	Y	N	Random control group design involving a large sample size (n = 351)

SAMPLE INTERVENTIONS

Behavioral Management of Public Masturbation

Authors: William B. Janzen and Renee Peacock

Précis: Describes the use of fading procedures within a behavioral management contract with a 9-year-old girl who masturbated in the classroom.

Introduction

Little research has been conducted concerning the treatment of compulsive masturbation. Various behavioral strategies, including alternative response training and the use of coercive strategies, have been employed with varying degrees of success. Many of the strategies (e.g., shaping) require extensive involvement on the part of the teacher, which is not realistic, or even appropriate. The current study employed a behavioral management contract with the details implemented on a fading basis. The program placed minimal demands on the child during the initial phases of treatment; demands increased with the passage of time.

Intervention

Baseline data revealed that the subject engaged in masturbation 90 percent of the day, discontinuing the activity only during recess and lunch. The treatment consisted of four phases. Phase I took place during the first and second week. During the first week, the student was told to refrain from masturbatory activity for the first hour of the school day, with one warning. Television watching was made contingent upon successful inhibition. During the second week, the child was not allowed any warnings in order to be successful. In Phase 2, reinforcement was contingent on nonmasturbatory activity for the first two hours of the day. After five days, this process was expanded (Phase 3) to inhibition of masturbatory activity from 8 A.M. to noon. Phase 4, the final phase, made reinforcement contingent upon inhibition of masturbatory activity for the entire school day. The authors reported that with the exception of one time during Phase 1, the client met the criterion each day of the program, and the student successfully eliminated all masturbatory activity during the school day.

Reflection

Although behavioral management contracting has a long history of use and effectiveness with a variety of behaviors, the current case highlights the functional value of employing fading as an effective adjunct to reinforcement programs. The current case required less involvement on the part of the teacher then would typical shaping approaches, which increased the likelihood of teacher compliance.

A concern with any procedure that removes a previous "functional" behavior is the possibility of the development of symptom substitution. The authors noted that the student did not initiate masturbation at home nor did she develop any maladaptive behaviors at school.

Source: Janzen, W. B., & Peacock, R. (1977). Treatment of public masturbation by behavioral management. *American Journal of Psychotherapy, 32*(2), 300–306.

SAMPLE INTERVENTIONS

Draw the Line/Respect the Line: Middle School Prevention Programming

Authors: Karin K. Coyle, Douglas, B. Birby, Barbara V. Marin, Cynthia A. Gomez, and Steven E. Gregorich

Précis: The long-term effectiveness of a theoretical curriculum designed to reduce sexual risk behaviors among middle school adolescents.

Introduction

Sexually transmitted diseases (including HIV) and pregnancy among teens are increasingly serious problems. Nearly 4 million new STD cases each year are reported among adolescents (U.S. Dept. of Health and Human Services, 2000).

Although prevention programs targeted at reducing risky sexual practices among teens have been shown to be effective (Kirby, 2001), the authors of this study suggest that it is important to target younger students with prevention messages before they begin having risky sexual intercourse.

Intervention

The authors employed a randomized controlled trial involving 19 ethnically diverse public middle schools to test the effectiveness of a 3-year, school-based HIV, other STD, and pregnancy prevention program for youths in sixth, seventh, and eighth grades.

The Draw the Line/Respect the Line intervention is a 20-session curriculum based on social cognitive theory and social inoculation theory. The goal of the program is to help students develop their personal sexual limits and practice the skills needed to maintain those limits even when they are challenged. The sixth-grade curriculum included five lessons that featured limit setting and refusal skills in nonsexual situations (e.g., pressures to steal, lie, or use drugs). The seventh-grade curriculum included eight lessons that addressed determining personal limits regarding sexual intercourse, understanding the consequences of unplanned sexual intercourse (including STDs and pregnancy), using intra- and interpersonal skills (identifying risky situations and refusal skills) to maintain limits, and respecting others' limits. The eighth-grade curriculum included seven lessons and featured an HIV-infected speaker; a condom demonstration and a brief activity on other methods of protection; and practice of refusal skills in dating contexts. The lessons were sequential, with later lessons building on concepts from earlier ones. Lessons were interactive and used a variety of instructional strategies (e.g., small and large group discussions, paired and small-group skill practice, stories, individual activities).

The results indicated that male youths exposed to the 3-year, 20-lesson curriculum delayed sexual initiation compared with peers who received regular sex education. A 1-year follow up demonstrated that the males who received the intervention were significantly less likely than their peers to report having any sexual activity in the previous 12 months. However, a similar delay in sexual initiation was not found in the females who participated in the study. The authors offer possible explanations for this gender difference.

Reflection

The Draw the Line/Respect the Line curriculum produced several positive and programmatically important behavioral effects among boys in the cohort, but not among girls. One factor offered by the authors to explain this apparent lack of effect for the females in the study was that the females were influenced by older boyfriends with whom they were having sex, and the program did not prepare the girls on how to counter pressure from older partners. Clearly, the effect on the boys should not be discounted nor minimized; however, additional research is needed to better understand factors influencing girls' decisions to engage in sexual intercourse so that more effective interventions can be developed.

Source: Coyle, K. K., Birby, D. B., Marin, B. V., Gomez, C. A., & Gregorich, S. E. (2004). Draw the Line/Respect the Line: A randomized trial of a middle school intervention to reduce sexual risk behaviors. *American Journal of Public Health, 94*(5), 843–851.

SAMPLE INTERVENTIONS

Culturally Sensitive Pregnancy-Reduction Program

Authors: Angela Coleman Dixon, Christopher T. Schoonmaker, and William W. Philliber

Précis: A study examining the effects of an Afrocentric pregnancy prevention program on African American adolescent females.

Introduction

African American females aged 15 to 17 are more likely than their white counterparts to have sexual intercourse since menarche and to have engaged in their first sexual experience (intercourse) without the use of effective contraception (National Center for Health Statistics, 1997). As a result, the pregnancy rate among African American teenagers is almost double that of white females aged 15 to 19 (Alan Guttmacher Institute, 1999).

Educational programs that use an Afrocentric approach appear to be effective in changing the behaviors of African American teenagers. The current program "A Journey Toward Womanhood," is a 13-week pregnancy-prevention program explicitly designed for teenage girls of African descent.

Intervention

The study employed a nonrandomized control group design that included 65 African American females aged 14 to 19 living in low-income neighborhoods. Thirty-three of the females participated in the treatment program, 32 did not.

The girls in the program met for 13 weeks in small groups (no more than 10 participants) for 4 hours once a week. The foci for the group meetings were as follows:

- **Weeks 1–4: Reaching for Success**. The first four sessions explored self-definition and the importance of seeing oneself as a unique individual. Participants explored culture, with an emphasis on the role of women in history. They examined aspects of different countries, critiqued current media images, shared self-descriptions, viewed historical documentaries, and explored diversity.
- **Weeks 5–7: Developing Inner Health for Outer Beauty**. The second phase focused on diet and nutrition, exercise and fitness, holistic well-being, peer pressure, sexual health, and healthy relationships. Participants toured a Planned Parenthood clinic, met with a teen mother (who provided insights into the challenges of being a young single parent), and attended a forum with African American teenage males who were taking part in a local rite-of-passage program.

- **Week 8: Progressing with Finesse, Dignity, and Pride**. Participants engaged in role-playing and affirmations to develop skills in public speaking, job interviewing, and interpersonal communication. This, in turn, increased their social skills, self-confidence, dignity, and pride.
- **Week 9: Field Trip**. Participants went on an out-of-town field trip, fostering group bonding, widening their perspective, developing social skills, and learning planning techniques.
- **Weeks 10–13: Knowing the Tools for Survival**. The focus for these sessions was on encouraging self-sufficiency. Activities include sewing a unique cultural garment, hosting a luncheon to honor parents and friends, budgeting, investing, saving money, and job hunting. Entrepreneurship and economic stability are encouraged, and teen pregnancy is discouraged.

The authors reported that of the 26 members in the treatment group who had not had sexual intercourse before they began the program, only 24 percent had experienced intercourse by the time of the survey, as compared to 69 percent of the nonparticipants. Further, participants who did engage in sexual intercourse were less likely than nonparticipants to engage in unprotected intercourse. As a result, pregnancies were more than twice as frequent among nonparticipants than among participants. It appears the program reduces pregnancy both by delaying the initiation of sexual intercourse and by increasing the use of contraceptives among those who are sexually experienced.

Reflection

The small sample size, the self-selection to treatment, and the absence of a randomized control group are significant limitations to this study. What is unique and worth noting, however, is the tailoring of the program to specific cultural values of the participants rather than attempting to employ a "one size fits all" program. For those working with African American students, the elements included in this program that focused on (1) the development of cultural heritage and pride, (2) the fostering of independence and self-determination, (3) and the development of an increased awareness of how their future will be brighter if they avoid early pregnancy would appear to be useful elements to include in any such prevention program.

Source: Dixon, A. C., Schoonmaker, C. T., & Philliber, W. W. (2000). A journey toward womanhood: Effects of an Afrocentric approach to pregnancy prevention among African-American adolescent females. *Adolescence, 35*(139), 425–429.

DETAILED INTERVENTION

Reducing Sexual Risk-Taking Behaviors

Introduction

School personnel and parents concerned with early adolescent sexual risk-taking behaviors have looked for systemwide forms of intervention and prevention. The Center for Adolescent Reproductive Health at Grady Memorial Hospital developed a skills-based curriculum, Managing the Pressures Before Marriage (MPM), that has proven effective (see Howard, 1985). Because research has demonstrated that the quality of parent–child relationships and communications about sex and sexuality appear to be strong determinants of adolescent sexual behavior, the current authors developed an intervention/prevention program that augmented the MPM curriculum with five homework assignments geared to increase parental participation and reinforce the MPM curriculum.

Method

A school-based abstinence-only curriculum was implemented among 351 middle school students. Students were assigned at random to receive either classroom instruction alone or classroom instruction enhanced by five homework assignments. The assignments were designed to be completed by the students and their parents. The authors employed a pretest-posttest design with a survey of multiple determinants of sexual onset and risk-related behaviors as the dependent measure.

Interventions

The MPM curriculum consists of five one-hour sessions led by pairs of trained youth leaders. The program addresses the risks associated with early sexual involvement, social pressures, and pressures placed on adolescents by the media to become sexually active. The program employs class discussion, group activities, videos, and role-playing, as well as skill training and rehearsal.

Program Components

The five sessions focused on the following:

- **Session 1**: Session focused on risks of early sexual involvement and helped students explore reasons why some teens choose to have sex and why some choose to wait.
- **Session 2**: Students were taught how to resist social pressures that can lead to early sexual involvement.
- **Session 3**: Students identified peer pressures that can affect sexual behavior in teenagers. Students worked to determine their own limits for physically expressing affection.

- **Session 4**: Students were taught assertive responses to help them resist pressure to engage in sex.
- **Session 5**: Session involved reinforcement of the material learned in previous sessions.

Parent–Child Homework Assignments

The five homework assignments were designed to educate parents about the changes and pressures faced by middle school students; facilitate quality parent–child communication about sex and sexuality; assist parents in teaching their children how to avoid or resist peer pressure to become sexually active; and teach parents and children about how they can successfully identify and reduce the risks of pregnancy, HIV, and other STDs. The homework assignments were structured as follows:

- **Homework Assignment 1**: The first assignment incorporated ice-breaker activities, including ground rules for conversation, a stages of life chart that described issues arising at different developmental milestones, and a make-a-wish activity.
- **Homework Assignment 2**: This assignment reinforced the second MPM session. It included a parent-interview activity; a reasons-to-wait activity; a worksheet on facts and myths about HIV, STDs, and pregnancy; and a "Messages in the Media" activity.
- **Homework Assignment 3**: The third assignment dealt with media pressures and how to deal with them. Activities included a "Messages in the Media" activity; a "Reasons for Having Sex" activity; and a "Ways to Handle Internal Pressures" activity.
- **Homework Assignment 4**: The fourth assignment included activities on "What are my strengths?" "Choosing Best Friends," "Resisting Peer Pressures," and "Dealing with Peer Pressure to Have Sex."
- **Homework Assignment 5**: The final homework assignment was about resisting pressures on a date. It included the following activities: "Dating: Deciding Who You Will Go Out With," "Dealing with Pressures to Have Sex," and "Resisting Dating Pressures."

A more detailed description of these activities can be found in the appendix of the original article.

Using an analysis of covariance controlling for baseline scores, adolescents receiving the enhanced curriculum (i.e., with homework) reported greater self-efficacy for refusing high-risk behaviors than did those who received the classroom instruction only. The enhanced curriculum group also expressed less intention to have sex before finishing high school and more frequent parent–child communications about prevention and sexual consequences.

Reflection

The effectiveness of school-based abstinence-only curriculums has been mixed. In spite of the limited consistent findings of effectiveness, substantial amounts of federal dollars are being spent on abstinence education programs. Therefore, it is important to identify programs that show promise in producing positive outcomes. The current study has attempted to increase the efficacy of one education program through the inclusion of parent–child homework.

The curriculum model employed is based on social inoculation theory, which emphasizes behavioral rehearsal to "immunize" students by practicing resistance to future peer pressures to engage in risky behavior. The emphasis of a social-cognitive learning approach appears suitable for the classroom setting. Further, the inclusion of parental involvement in the planning and implementation of the program would appear to attain the sanctioning needed for the implementation of such a program.

Although the data suggest that the enhanced curriculum was effective in modifying students' attitudes, a major limitation to the study was that no long-term follow up was done to observe whether the immediately reported attitude shifts were maintained and translated into behavioral decisions. Another limitation is the fact that the group studied was suburban middle school students, which makes it difficult to project to the efficacy of such a program with urban and highly ethnically diverse populations. Finally, and perhaps most significantly, was the fact that the study reflected a possible self-selection bias. Homework was not completed by all the students in the enhanced curriculum. It is unknown if those students who did complete homework were those already at a lower risk for risky behavior or those who had higher levels of parent–student communication prior to the intervention.

Although these caveats are important, the simplicity of the program, its relative brevity, and the apparent supportive findings makes this program one worth considering.

Source: Blake, S. M., Simkin, L., Ledsky, R., Perkins, C., & Calabrese, J. M. (2001). Effects of a parent–child communications intervention on young adolescents' risk for early onset of sexual intercourse. *Family Planning Perspectives, 33*(2), 52–61.

FROM THE FIELD

The following suggestions reflect direct service counseling strategies and consultation targets for application with teachers. These suggestions are based on the experience and anecdotal reporting of counselors engaged in school counseling; they have not been tested using experimental design. As personal suggestions, they need to be employed with caution and their impact monitored.

Masturbation: Working with Students

- Attend to any signs of possible sexual abuse and make a referral when and where appropriate.
- Refer the child for a medical exam to rule out skin conditions such as eczema.
- Help the student with methods to increase awareness of this activity and to employ alternative response training.

Risky Sexual Behavior: Working with Students

- Provide assertiveness training.
- Peer pack: Agreements made between adolescents to support each other in resisting peer pressure.
- Use social rehearsal to help students resist peer pressure.
- Educate parents and students about the impact of risky sexual behaviors.

Masturbation and Sexual Activity: Working with Teachers

- Privately correct the child and inform him or her about acceptable behavior. Redirect the child to another task rather than publicly attending to masturbation.
- Engage the child in activities that require the use of his or her hands, such as modeling, finger painting, keyboard activities, etc.
- Arrange classrooms so that children are visible, unable to hide behind bookcases, cubbies, in activity areas, and so on.
- Supervise students at all times—on the playground, moving to and from restrooms, on buses, etc.
- Help teachers become aware of inappropriate student behaviors and help them to listen to student questions and concerns and respond appropriately.

Prevention Programming

- Provide teacher in-service training on normal sexual development and symptoms of sexual abuse.
- Develop a library of materials for use by parents to facilitate discussion of sexual feelings, concerns, and so on with their children.

- Provide parent workshops on sexual development and the symptoms of sexual abuse.
- Provide developmental guidance programs to increase students' awareness of at-risk behaviors and provide them with the tools (communication, behavior) to say no and protect themselves.

REFERENCES

Alan Guttmacher Institute. (1999). *Teenage pregnancy: Overall trends and state-by-state information.* New York: The Alan Guttmacher Institute.

Aspen Publishers, Inc. (2001). Early, inappropriate sexual activity: A safety issue for elementary schools? *Inside School Safety, 6*(1), 7–9.

Blake, S. M., Simkin, L., Ledsky, R., Perkins, C., & Calabrese, J. M. (2001). Effects of a parent–child communications intervention on young adolescents' risk for early onset of sexual intercourse. *Family Planning Perspectives, 33*(2), 52–61.

Coyle, K. K., Birby, D. B., Marin, B. V., Gomez, C. A., & Gregorich, S. E. (2004). Draw the Line/Respect the Line: A randomized trial of a middle school intervention to reduce sexual risk behaviors. *American Journal of Public Health, 94*(5), 843–851.

Cubbin, C., Santelli, J., Brindis, C. D., & Braveman, P. (2005). Neighborhood context and sexual behaviors among adolescents: Findings from the National Longitudinal Study of Adolescent Health. *Perspectives on Sexual and Reproductive Health, 37*(3), 125–134.

Department of Health and Human Services, Division of STD Prevention. (1999). *Sexually transmitted disease surveillance, 1998.* Atlanta: Centers for Disease Control and Prevention.

Dixon, A. C., Schoonmaker, C. T., & Philliber, W. W. (2000). A journey toward womanhood: Effects of an Afrocentric approach to pregnancy prevention among African-American adolescent females. *Adolescence, 35*(139), 425–429.

Gough, D., Kelly, L., & Scott, S. (1993). The current literature about organized abuse of children. *Child Abuse Review, 2*(4), 281–287.

Hillman, D., & Solek-Tefft, J. (1988). *Spiders and flies: Help for parents and teachers of sexually abused children.* Lexington, MA: Lexington Books, D.C. Heath.

Howard, M. (1985). Postponing sexual involvement among adolescents: An alternative approach to prevention of sexually transmitted diseases. *Journal of Adolescent Health Care, 6*(4), 271–277.

Janzen, W. B., & Peacock, R. (1977). Treatment of public masturbation by behavioral management. *American Journal of Psychotherapy, 32*(2), 300–306.

James, S. H. (1999). School counselor's roles in cases of child sexual behavior. *School Counseling, 2*(3), 211–218.

Kirby, D. (2001). *Emerging answers: Research findings on programs to reduce teen pregnancy.* Washington, DC: National Campaign to Prevent Teen Pregnancy.

National Center for Health Statistics. (1997). *Fertility, family planning, and women's health: New data from the 1995 National Survey of Family Growth.* Hyattsville, MD: National Center for Health Statistics.

U.S. Department of Health and Human Services (DHHS). (2000). *Healthy People 2010: Understanding and improving health.* Washington, DC: U.S. Government Printing Office.

ADDITIONAL RESOURCES

INTERNET

www.focusas.com/SexualBehavior.html. This Web site offers resources, events, speakers, books, and more about adolescent sexual behavior.

www.aboutourkids.org/aboutour/articles/sexual_development_part2.html. This Web site focuses on helping children develop healthy sexual behaviors and attitudes. It offers information on the influences of sexualization in children as well as information on talking to children about sexual issues.

www.sexualityandu.ca/eng/health/SCD/. This site offers definitions, resources, and scenarios regarding sexual behavior in teens and adults. It also offers tips/advice for parents, teachers, and health professionals.

PRINTED MATERIALS

Florsheim, P. (Ed.). (2003). *Adolescent romantic relations and sexual behavior*. Mahwah, NJ: Lawrence Erlbaum.

Martin, K. A. (1996). *Puberty, sexuality, and the self: Girls and boys at adolescence*. Oxford: Routledge.

Sexuality Information and Education Council of the United States. (2004). *Guidelines for comprehensive sexuality education: Kindergarten–12th grade* (3rd ed.). New York: Author.

Young, M., & Young, T. (1994). *Sex can wait: An abstinence-based sexuality curriculum for upper elementary classrooms*. Santa Cruz, CA: ETR Associates.

CHAPTER 11

PREJUDICE AND "ISMS" IN THE SCHOOL

Prejudicial attitudes and beliefs, including the "isms" of racism, classism, and sexism, develop early (Bureau of Justice Assistance, 1999). One in four high school students (grades 10 through 12) have reported being a target of racial or religious bias (Louis Harris and Associates, 1990). According to statistics released in 2002 by the National Education Association, 83.2 percent of gay, lesbian, bisexual, and transgender (GLBT) students reported incidents of targeted name calling, threats, or other forms of verbal harassment during the year 2000.

It should be no surprise that the targets of bias within our schools are the same groups that are targeted for discrimination in society at large (Bloom, 1995). Individuals are often targeted for discrimination and harassment based on their race, ethnicity, religion, or sexual orientation. Such experiences can negatively affect the victimized student's ability to fully participate and benefit from the academic experience (Zirkel, 1999) and may even prove detrimental to the development of a healthy self-identity (Soriano, Soriano, & Jiminez, 1994). Under hostile conditions, survival in school, rather than academic achievement, may be the student's priority.

Whether it is through hate-related graffiti, name calling, sexual taunts, racial slurs, or threatening statements, manifestations of intolerance need to be taken seriously and responded to appropriately. Sadly, these very forms of intolerance are too often overlooked by school personnel (Sherman, 1999). School counselors need to take the lead in creating and implementing programs and interventions that foster increased tolerance and acceptance of difference. Counselors need to be more involved in multicultural awareness training, whether through direct one-on-one counseling, group work, developmental guidance, or staff and parent training and consultation.

OVERVIEW

As noted by Kowalski (2003), extensive literature exists on the development of ethnic prejudice in children, yet there is a real lack of longitudinal or other data suggesting an optimal age to intervene or an ideal mode of intervention to reduce prejudice. The following studies reflect some of the research that supports methods of intervention when confronting the issue of "isms" in the school. The studies presented offer a varied look at the roles and modes of service open to school counselors as they address issues of prejudice within their schools. The interventions presented target racial attitudes, discrimination against students with disabilities, and homophobia (Table 11.1).

TABLE 11.1 Overview of Studies Presented

TARGET PROBLEM	REFERENCE	K–6	6–9	9–12	OTHER SPECIFICATIONS
Modifying racial attitudes	Katz & Zalk (1978)	Y	N	N	Pretest, posttest random control group design
Homophobia	Van de Ven (1995)	N	N	Y	Repeated measures (pretest, posttest, and follow-up), 2 × 2 factorial design with 130 students
Discrimination against people with disabilities	Leyser & Price (1985)	Y	Y	N	Pretest, posttest control group design
Developmental guidance to improve racial attitudes and relations	D'Andrea & Daniels (1995)	Y	N	N	Pretest, posttest analysis of 117 students

SAMPLE INTERVENTIONS

Modifying Racial Attitudes

Authors: Phyllis A. Katz and Sue Rosenberg Zalk

Précis: Modifying negative racial attitudes in white grade school children.

Introduction

The study compared the efficacy of four intervention techniques for modifying negative racial attitudes in 140 white second and fifth graders in two city and suburban schools. The effectiveness of the techniques was reported in previous studies and each appeared appropriate and viable for use within a school setting over a relatively short time period.

Intervention

Using a pretest, posttest matched group design, 160 children identified as having high prejudicial attitudes (on a variety of scales) were randomly assigned to either a treatment or control group. Posttest measures were administered after 2 weeks of treatment and again at a 4- to 6-month follow-up. The four techniques employed were as follows:

- **Group interaction**. For the treatment groups, small groups composed of two white and two black children were assigned the task of assembling a large wooden abstract jigsaw puzzle. Each team was verbally reinforced for completing the task, and a picture of the team and the completed puzzle was taken.
- **Vicarious identification**. Children were asked to listen to a story accompanied by slides and answer questions about it. The story was about a young boy (for males) or girl (for the females) who finds his/her way home from school in the face of adversity. The experimental group saw slides of black characters; the control group was shown the same story but with white characters.
- **Stimulus predifferentiation groups**. In this treatment, children viewed four slides of the same model. The slides varied in several dimensions, such as color of makeup, absence or presence of glasses, the existence of a smile or frown, and the use of two different wigs. The children were taught to recognize and remember the different faces by different names.
- **Conditioning groups**. The children played a game in which they were first shown two blue boxes, one painted with a smile and another with a frown, and were asked to place 10 positive (e.g., candy) and negative (e.g., garbage) pictures in the box they felt the picture belonged. Next, the children were shown a series of 10 black and white animal pictures. They were asked to

select the "right" one. When the children chose a black animal picture, they received a reinforcement. In the final task, they were asked to sort the original 10 positive pictures and 10 negative pictures into these boxes.

The results suggested that each approach resulted in a significant short-term reduction in prejudice, with the vicarious contact and perceptual differentiation strategies proving most effective for both short- and long-term attitudinal shifts.

Reflection

Although each intervention positively affected student racial attitudes in the short term (two-week posttest), the vicarious interaction (i.e., the story technique) was considerably more effective in lowering negative racial attitudes both in the short term and in the longer follow-up (four months). As with any study, concerns about the generalizability of the finding to new settings and samples need to be considered. However, even with this caveat, it appears that the inclusion of positive vicarious interaction (e.g., story telling, illustrations, and examples) may be a useful strategy for counselors and teachers alike. Counselors employing developmental guidance lessons and teachers creating lesson plans may want to consider the inclusion of such positive vicarious interaction stimuli.

Source: Katz, P. A., & Zalk, S. R. (1978). Modification of children's racial attitudes. *Developmental Psychology, 14*(5), 447–461.

SAMPLE INTERVENTIONS

Antihomophobia: A Teaching Module

Author: Paul Van de Ven

Précis: Effect of an antihomophobic teaching unit on hostile attitudes and behavioral intentions.

Introduction

Most of the research on intervention with prejudice has targeted racial and ethnic prejudice, yet antihomosexual prejudice, or homophobia, has profound consequences for gay and lesbian students. Empirical research validating models and approaches for countering homophobia are rare, and where it does exist it often involves college-age students. The current study attempts to address this void by presenting a classroom teaching unit targeted to changing young adolescent attitudes and behaviors toward homosexuals.

Intervention

The study employed a repeated measures (pretest, posttest, and three-month follow-up), 2 × 2 factorial design with 130 students. The treatment represented an information-based, educational intervention aimed at reducing homophobia. The intervention, which was composed of 6 lessons, was designed for use with students in grades 9 through 12 in the Sydney (Australia) Metropolitan Public Schools. Teachers were given a one-day training session on the use of the specific modules. The 6 lessons took a total of 305 minutes of teaching time.

The content focus of the six lessons was as follows:

1. Identify and discuss myths and stereotypes surrounding homosexuality.
2. Inform students about homosexuality and discuss the link between prejudice and violence.
3. Providing examples of gay and lesbian people not fitting the stereotypes.
4. Discuss issues of homophobia and violence reflected in a number of written scenarios and consider the homosexual perspective and acceptable ways of relating to gay and lesbian people.
5. Learn that harassment and violence against homosexuals are criminal offenses and that discrimination against gay and lesbian individuals is also illegal.
6. Reflect on what had been learned and plan actions to be taken to minimize discrimination against lesbian and gay individuals.

Multivariate analyses of variance revealed that participants' anger and behavioral intentions were significantly less homophobic at posttest and follow-up.

Reflection

Because adolescence is a time when students wrestle with questions of identity and sexuality, experiences that challenge "traditional" expectations about gender, sexual orientation, and self-identity may result in anxiety. Offering adolescents an information-based experience may help them to expand their views of gender, sexual orientation, and self-identity, reducing their anxiety and negative attitudes and behaviors toward those who are perceived to be different.

The teaching module presented appears to have resulted in significantly less homophobic anger and fewer negative behavioral intentions. It should be noted, however, that for males, the initial changes reversed to previous levels of homophobia within three months. Such a reversal may indicate the need for more extended programming. Sampling also needs to be considered when interpreting and applying these results. The failure to employ a randomized control group allows for a possible selection effect, and the fact that the study focused on the metropolitan Sidney Australia public schools introduces unique sociocultural variables into the sample and treatment effect.

Source: Van de Ven, P. (1995). Effects on high school students of a teaching module for reducing homophobia. *Basic & Applied Psychology, 17*(1/2), 153–173.

SAMPLE INTERVENTIONS

Attitudes Toward the Handicapped

Authors: Yona Leyser and Steve Price

Précis: Training program designed to improve attitudes of nonhandicapped students toward their handicapped classmates.

Introduction

The practice of inclusion, which supports the right to free and public education for all students, has resulted in children with handicaps being included in mainstream classrooms. Such inclusion, although affording handicapped students with the socio-emotional and educational benefits of interacting with their peers in regular classrooms, has also introduced handicapped students to negative attitudes, prejudice, and bias held by their nonhandicapped classmates.

To combat such negative attitudes, numerous interventions, including direct and indirect (i.e., media) contact with a handicapped person, the provision of educational information, and group discussions, have been employed. The current study tested the effects of a training program that combined these elements and was presented over nine hour-long sessions.

Intervention

The study employed a pretest, posttest control group design. The participants (selected from the school's gifted program) were assigned to either an experimental condition or one of two control conditions. Data were collected using the Attitudes Toward Disabled Persons (ATDP) scale (Yuker, Block, and Young, 1970).

Training included topical presentations, experiences, and discussions that focused on:

1. **Loneliness**. A group discussion after viewing the film *Cipher in the Snow*.
2. **Individual differences**. Each student prepared an individual coat of arms. Group discussion focused on topics of individual differences and needs people have in common.
3. **Learning disabilities**. Students participated in simulation activities and discussion of the implications of perceptual problems in school.
4. **Learning disabilities**. A guest speaker shared his experience and responded to questions.
5. **Self-esteem**. A group discussion followed the viewing of the film *Johnny Lingo* on promoting self-esteem in others.
6. **Physical and sensory handicaps**. Guest speakers (a deaf person, a blind person, and a paraplegic person).

7. **Cooperation**. Activity involved a group simulation entitled "Lutts and Mipps."
8. **Tutorial**. Students were assigned to work with younger students with learning disabilities after having been given guidelines for tutoring.
9. **Reading**. Students chose fictional literature about handicapped individuals and discussed their assignment.

Analyses of variance revealed that a significant shift in positive attitudes (pretest to posttest) occurred for those in the treatment group when compared with members in the control groups.

Reflection

The Education for All Handicapped Children Act, or Public Law 94-142, and the Individuals with Disabilities Education Act (IDEA) were two landmark pieces of legislation. Together, these two acts opened the door to free, public education for all children, regardless of disability. Inclusion of students with disabilities within the regular classroom affords handicapped students the right to experience the benefits of peer modeling and interaction, as well as the opportunity to be a full-fledged member of the school community. However, the actual impact of this inclusion will be, in part, determined by the degree to which those within the setting (both teachers and students) welcome and support the student to the classroom. Clearly, biases and prejudices against those with disabilities continue to exist. The study suggested that negative attitudes toward the disabled can be made more positive by exposing nonhandicapped students to information about disabilities and offering direct and indirect contact with disabled persons.

The program lends itself to application within the school and can be configured as a guidance developmental program. One caution needs to be stated. The study employed students from the school's gifted program as the sample tested. The use of such a narrow sample limits generalizability of this study's findings to other populations. It is important for the school counselor to employ valid design and data collection procedures when employing a new intervention and assessing its impact.

Source: Leyser, Y., & Price, S. (1985). Improving attitudes of gifted children toward the handicapped. *Education, 105*(4), 432–437.

DETAILED INTERVENTION

Developmental Guidance Project Embracing Difference

Introduction

Elementary school counselors have developed and implemented numerous, creative programs aimed at assisting students to develop the cognitive and social skills necessary to be successful within the school. The program described in this study was an extension of the application of a classroom guidance curriculum to address a specific need. The program addressed the interpersonal differences, and resulting conflicts, experienced by students within one school.

As noted by the authors, with the increasing diversification of society, it is important for counselors to implement developmental interventions that promote students' social development in culturally responsive ways. Although programs have been created that foster students' social development, few programs target the specific skills necessary to live peacefully and respectfully with others in a pluralistic society. The current study reports on a program created to do exactly that—to assist students to resolve conflicts that result from negative cultural or ethnic prejudices.

Method

Students were selected from four third-grade classes in a public school in Honolulu. All of the students were from families of low to low-middle socioeconomic background and varied in cultural, ethnic, and racial make-up.

The Social Skills Rating Inventory was used as a pretest and posttest measure. The inventory was used to assess the children's social skills, noting, among other competencies, the degree to which the students exhibited verbally or physically aggressive behaviors toward others and a reluctance to interact with others. Both teacher and student report forms were used in the collection of the data. Pre- and posttest comparisons revealed significant increases in positive behaviors and a reduction in total problem behaviors.

Intervention

The study included 117 third-grade students who participated in a school-based developmental program targeted at helping students to develop the social and interpersonal skills necessary to resolve conflicts that resulted from negative cultural or ethnic prejudices in order to reduce the frequency of fighting exhibited in classrooms and the playground during recess.

The intervention was a 10-session guidance program held once a week in students' homerooms. The content of the sessions was designed to increase positive student-to-student interactions and reduce problem behaviors that these students were experiencing at the school. Sessions included the following activities:

- Session 1: The first session involved setting rules and goals.
- Session 2: Students made name tags and engaged in ice breakers. The session focused on sharing names, favorite foods, songs, places, holidays, and so on. Discussion focused on the various cultural differences associated with the students' responses.
- Session 3: Students were asked to draw a picture of themselves and complete the statement "I am . . . " The focus was on providing positive feedback regarding cultural issues that emerged.
- Session 4: This session introduced concepts of prejudice and stereotyping by assigning labels (good group, bad group) to groups and identifying consequences of belonging to one or the other labeled group (privileges to good group members, restrictions to bad). Students discussed how they feel when they are victims of prejudice/stereotyping.
- Session 5: Students were videotaped as they discussed ways elementary students demonstrate negative prejudices and stereotypes. Students then reviewed their participation in the discussion, commenting on their interactions with other members of the group.
- Session 6: Students played "Multicultural People Bingo." Students were directed to find class members who completed one of the culturally specific statements on their bingo card (e.g., Who is Samoan? Who enjoys sushi?).
- Session 7: Students discussed the meaning of abstract concepts such as "love." They also drew pictures representing these words as demonstrated in their class and school.
- Session 8: Students discussed rainbows and created a poster using the colors of brown, black, white, red, and yellow. Children then placed a photo of themselves near the color that represented their racial background.
- Session 9: Children looked at their own hands and those of their classroom neighbor and responded to questions of differences (size, color, shape) and value ("Do you think any hand is better than another?")
- Session 10: Group leaders identify one thing they have learned and could use when working or playing with others in the class.

Reflection

Counselors and educators are, or should be, at the forefront of efforts to foster cultural sensitivity and tolerance for diversity. As noted in the current study, elementary school counselors are in a position of fostering the development of social attitudes and skills that reflect a respect for diversity. The use of developmental guidance curriculum would appear to be both an appropriate and generally accepted model of counseling intervention within our schools. The intervention described in this study lends itself to helping the students develop the social and interpersonal skills necessary to resolve conflicts that result from negative cultural or ethnic prejudices.

The use of a developmental guidance program is neither new nor unique. In fact, the commonality and general acceptability of this counseling mode makes this intervention particularly valuable for the school counselor. It would appear that the introduction of a 10-week guidance program would meet with less resistance in those schools already familiar with developmental guidance.

It is important to remember, however, that the study employed a self-contained, nonrandomly assigned group design without a control. Thus, caution in interpreting these findings or assuming valid generalization to other settings is necessary. As with all interventions, counselors need to implement designs and strategies that will help them assess the effectiveness of this or any other intervention they employ.

Source: D'Andrea, M., & Daniels, J. (1995). Helping students learn to get along: Assessing the effectiveness of a multicultural developmental guidance project. *Elementary School Guidance & Counseling, 30*(2), 143–155.

FROM THE FIELD

As in previous chapters, suggestions found within the section "From the Field" reflect the experience of those working in the field. As individual recommendations, they need to be employed with caution and their impact monitored.

Working with Students

- Positive contact is essential. Have students buddy younger students of different backgrounds.
- Employ empathy training. Ask students to place themselves in other students' shoes.
- Refer to role models and positive examples from diverse populations.
- Help homophobic teens by helping them expand their definitions of masculine and feminine.
- Students who are homophobic often are having problems understanding and embracing their own sexuality and sense of self. Have students focus on developing their own sense of self.
- Model and encourage students to use feeling language and behavioral descriptions rather than relying on labels and stereotypes when discussing diverse students.
- When working with children who are fearful of those with physical handicaps, it is important to introduce them to students with handicaps and have them investigate the various pieces of equipment the students utilize (e.g., wheelchair, leg brace, oxygen machine, Braille stylus and board, etc.).
- Help teens expand the view of who a person is beyond the limits of their own culture, race, or sexual orientation. Values clarification helps to reframe what the student holds as important in their own friends and family and hopefully allows them to see it is much more than physical traits.
- Focus on common adolescent concerns when working with groups composed of students from various backgrounds and cultures.
- For some students, it is a matter of anger management. Cognitive-behavioral intervention or group counseling can help.
- Engage students in helping to decorate the school for various holidays and theme days. Having students identify posters and pictures of peoples and events that celebrate another culture, race, or heritage is helpful.
- Encourage students to join larger clubs and activities (chorus, band, track, etc.) that will bring them into contact with a diverse group of students.
- Have a group of students walk blindfolded together and take turns leading one another. Discuss the experience of being without sight and relying on another.
- Develop an antidefamation or, more positively, a pro-uniqueness club and have the students discuss ways to change the school's atmosphere and culture.

Working with Teachers

- Help teachers develop cooperative learning groups in which the makeup of the group is heterogeneous across ethnic, socioeconomic, gender, and racial categories.
- Assign book reports or research reports on individuals or events depicting the experiences of one who is disabled, gay or lesbian, or of a marginalized population.
- If possible, have speakers (or students within the class) share their personal stories (e.g., what it is like to be blind).
- In social studies classes, have students share their rituals, food, and customs around major holidays.
- Have students provide peer tutoring to another student of a diverse background.
- Structure a class where students take notes only in an opposite seat desk (e.g., right-handed students should sit in a left-handed seat and vice versa) to emphasize difficulty with limited access.
- Teach part of the class with the lights off or provide a lecture in a very low volume and process the difficulties encountered by different students.
- Incorporate antibias lessons into coursework. Use illustrations and activities that reflect diversity.
- As a project, analyze television or print media for stereotyping messages.

REFERENCES

Bloom, J. (1995). The struggle with hate speech. Teaching strategy. *Update on Law-Related Education, 19*, 33–37.

Bureau of Justice Assistance (1999). *A policymaker's guide to hate crimes*. Washington, DC: U.S. Department of Justice.

D'Andrea, M., & Daniels, J. (1995). Helping students learn to get along: Assessing the effectiveness of a multicultural developmental guidance project. *Elementary School Guidance & Counseling, 30*(2), 143–155.

Katz, P. A., & Zalk, S. R. (1978). Modification of children's racial attitudes. *Developmental Psychology, 14*(5), 447–461.

Kowalski, K. (2003). The emergence of ethnic and racial attitudes in preschool-aged children. *Journal of Social Psychology, 143*(65), 677–690.

Leyser, Y., & Price, S. (1985). Improving attitudes of gifted children toward the handicapped. *Education, 105*(4), 432–437.

Louis Harris & Associates. (1990). *High school students' attitudes on human rights: Community activity and steps that might be taken to ease racial, ethnic and religious prejudice*. Study No. 902054, prepared for the Reebok Foundation and the Center for the Study of Sport in Society, Boston, MA.

National Education Association. (2002). *Report of the NEA task force on sexual orientation*. Available at www.nea.org/nr/02taskforce.html.

Sherman, L. (1999). Sticks and stones. *Northeast Education, 4*, 2–11.

Soriano, M., Soriano, F., & Jimenez, E. (1994). School violence among culturally diverse populations: Sociocultural and institutional considerations. *School Psychology Review, 23*, 216–235.

Van de Ven, P. (1995). Effects on high school students of a teaching module for reducing homophobia. *Basic & Applied Psychology, 17*(1/2), 153–173.

Yuker, H. E., Block, R. J., & Young, J. H. (1970). *The measurement of attitudes toward disabled persons.* Albertson, NY: Human Resource Center.

Zirkel, P. A. (1999). The "N" word. *Phi Delta Kappan, 80,* 713–715.

ADDITIONAL RESOURCES

INTERNET

www.edequity.org/. EEC is a not-for-profit organization that promotes bias-free learning through innovative programs and materials for administrators, teachers, and parents. EEC conducts training, workshops, and research and provides written and hands-on material for use in and out of the classroom.

www.kodak.com/global/en/consumer/education/lessonPlans/lessonPlan136.shtml. This Web site offers a lesson plan entitled "Erasing Handicapism: A Slide Show for Developing Positive Attitudes Toward Disabled Pupils."

www.projectappleseed.org/aaceptance.html. The Web site for the national campaign for public school improvement. Offers strategies for fostering able-bodied children's acceptance of disabled peers.

www.edchange.org/multicultural/index.html. Resources for educators, students, and activists to explore and discuss multicultural education, facilitate opportunities for educators to work toward self-awareness and development, and provide forums for educators to interact and collaborate toward a critical, transformative approach to multicultural education.

PRINTED MATERIALS

Hawley, W. D., & Jackson, A. W. (1995). *Improving race and ethnic relations in America.* San Francisco, CA: Jossey-Bass.

Lloyd, J., Kameenui, E. J., & Chard, D. (Eds). (1997). *Issues in educating students with disabilities.* Mahwah, NJ: Lawrence Erlbaum.

Sears, J., & Williams, W. (1997). *Overcoming heterosexism and homophobia: Strategies that work.* New York: Columbia University Press.

Walter, S. (1999). *Reducing prejudice and stereotyping in schools.* New York: Teachers College Press.

SECTION 3

HELPING STUDENTS WITH EMOTIONAL DIFFICULTIES

As noted in the preface, studies have demonstrated that over 20 percent of U.S. children and adolescents have a significant emotional impairment that requires treatment.

The interventions presented in Section III target the acute counseling needs of students who present with anxiety, stress, obsessive-compulsive disorder, poor self-esteem, depression, cutting, suicide ideation, grief, eating disorders, and substance abuse.

School counselors, with their primary roles centering on the facilitation of students' social, personal, and academic development, need to be aware that when presented with a child with severe behavioral and/or emotional concerns that referral is the first form of intervention. These children need to be thoroughly assessed and treated by those with specialized training. As such, the interventions presented in this section are offered as supportive or collateral interventions. As with all such treatments, they should not be undertaken without the appropriate training and supervision.

CHAPTER 12

ANXIETY: SEPARATION, SOCIAL, AND TEST

Anxiety is conceptualized as a complex pattern of behavioral responses (e.g., running away), physiological responses (e.g., increased heart rate, muscle tension), and subjective responses (e.g., unique images or thoughts). Responses (especially physiological) associated with anxiety have been connected to the "fight or flight" phenomenon, which is the psychological and physiological state of arousal that helps us respond to demands and threats.

Anxiety can be quite adaptive. Anxiety acts as an important signal that danger is imminent. It cues us to attend to important stimuli. Anxiety helps us to activate protective responses—actions that help us survive when confronted with danger and trouble. However, when the anxiety persists or is encountered in the absence of objective danger or threat, it can result in ineffective and self-defeating behaviors.

Although anxiety can be experienced in a variety of situations and presents in many forms, three specific forms of anxiety encountered by students—separation, social, and test—are the focus of the interventions presented within this chapter.

SEPARATION ANXIETY

It is not unusual as part of normal development for infants to experience distress when separated from their primary caretakers; however, this distress becomes problematic when it interferes with the child's ability to perform developmental appropriate tasks, such as attending school. Separation anxiety has been identified as the most common cause of school refusal in the preadolescent. Three-quarters of children who experience separation anxiety will eventually exhibit school reluctance or refusal (Last, Francis, Hersen, Kazdin, & Strauss, 1987). For this reason, school counselors need to be able to identify these children early on and address their needs in a systematic and supportive manner.

The DSM-IV-TR (APA, 2000) criteria for Separation Anxiety Disorder include any three of the following: recurrent excessive distress when separated from home or a major attachment figure (i.e., parent); worry about losing a parent or harm coming to a parent; an uncontrollable event leading to separation from a parent; reluctance to sleep alone or away from home; nightmares with separation themes; and/or physical complaints (e.g., stomachaches, headaches, nausea).

SOCIAL ANXIETY (SOCIAL PHOBIA)

Social anxiety involves an anxiety response related to the fear of being scrutinized by others, resulting in personal embarrassment or humiliation and ultimate avoidance of the feared social situation (APA, 2000). A student exhibiting social anxiety may experience distress when confronted with situations requiring social engagement and performance. These include activities such as speaking in public, reading aloud, engaging in conversation, or interacting in informal settings. It is not unusual for a child with social anxiety to refuse to attend classmates' birthday parties or join activities such as school clubs, scouts, or dances. The social withdrawal that is often employed as a coping mechanism isolates the child from normal and needed peer interaction and often leads to self-depreciation.

TEST ANXIETY

Test anxiety is an uneasiness or apprehension experienced before, during, or after an examination because of concern, worry, or fear. Test anxiety can be viewed as a general feeling of uneasiness, tension, or foreboding experienced by an individual prior to or during a testing situation. Although some anxiety has been demonstrated to be a motivator and a performance aid, too much anxiety has a detrimental effect on student performance (Rubenzer, 1988). In addition to negatively affecting academic performance, test anxiety can also result in withdrawal, outbursts, overactive behaviors, fatigue, avoidance of school, and other depressive symptoms (Rubenzer, 1988).

As demands and pressures are placed on students to achieve higher test scores, the need for school counselors to implement interventions to help reduce anxiety increases (Cheek, Bradley, Reynolds, & Coy, 2002).

OVERVIEW

Anxiety involves a cognitive element of concern or worry and a physio-emotional element that is best characterized as a heightened state of arousal and fight-flight preparation. Cognitive-behavioral interventions are most often the treatment of choice and are supported by randomized clinical trials with children and adolescents [see Silverman and Berman (2001) for review]. The interventions presented (Table 12.1) demonstrate the effectiveness of exposure, contingency management, and cognitive reframing in the treatment of anxiety disorders in children. The interventions presented not only reduced anxiety in students, but also helped to facilitate improved social interaction and academic performance.

TABLE 12.1 Overview of Studies Presented

TARGET PROBLEM	REFERENCE	K–6	6–9	9–12	OTHER SPECIFICATIONS
Reducing separation, social, and general anxiety	Bernstein, Layne, Egan, & Tennison (2005)	Y	Y	N	A randomized control group design using group treatment
Social anxiety	Spence, Donovan, & Brechman-Toussaint (2000)	Y	Y	Y	Randomized control group design
Separation anxiety	Dia (2001)	Y	N	N	Case study involving use of CBT with a 6-year-old boy
Test anxiety	Cheek, Bradley, Reynolds, & Coy (2002)	Y	N	N	Group intervention case study

SAMPLE INTERVENTIONS

FRIENDS Program

Authors: Gail Bernstein, Ann Layne, Elizabeth Egan, and Dana Tennison

Précis: A randomized control group study assessing the effectiveness of school-based group CBT as an intervention for anxious children.

Introduction

The study expanded on previous work by Barrett, Lowry-Webster, and Turner (2000a; 2000b; 2000c) assessing the effectiveness of FRIENDS, a manual-based CBT program. The FRIENDS program retains the essential elements of a cognitive-behavioral treatment for childhood anxiety, including exposure, relaxation, contingency management, and cognitive strategies. However, the program is unique in that it tailors the program to an individual's developmental needs and incorporates a family skills component. The current study was designed to test the differential effect of adding parent training to the child CBT intervention.

Multiple measures of child anxiety (i.e., clinician-report, child-report, and parent-report) demonstrated significant benefits of CBT treatments over the no-treatment control group, plus several instruments showed significantly greater improvement in child anxiety for group CBT plus parent training over group CBT alone.

Intervention

Students between the ages of 7 and 11 in 3 elementary schools ($n = 61$) who had been identified as exhibiting features or DSM-IV diagnoses of separation anxiety, social anxiety, or group anxiety were assigned at random by school to one of three conditions: group CBT, group CBT with parent training, or no treatment.

The FRIENDS program (Barrett, Lowry-Webster, & Turner, 2000a, 2000b, 2000c) is a manual-based family and peer group CBT intervention. Randomized clinical trials have demonstrated the effectiveness of the program (Shortt et al., 2001); the current study expanded the application of the intervention to a school setting and student population. The present study adapted the FRIENDS manual to include a broader, more intensive parental training component.

The FRIENDS acronym stands for:

F = Feeling worried?
R = Relax and feel good
I = Inner thoughts
E = Explore plans of action
N = Nice work, reward yourself
D = Don't forget to practice
S = Stay cool

The program consisted of 9 weekly 60-minute sessions and 2 booster sessions conducted 1 month and 3 months following completion of the treatment. The program followed the FRIENDS manual with one major modification: It combined sessions 9 and 10 because of time constraints. The FRIENDS program, although being a manual-based intervention, allows for flexibility in strategy implementation.

Reflection

Results indicated a significant reduction in anxiety for those in CBT as compared to the no-treatment condition. The addition of parent training combined with child group CBT, although more effective than no treatment, was not significantly more effective than the child group CBT alone.

Increasing amounts of data suggest the value of CBT as an effective treatment for anxiety disorders in children. The current study expands the utility of CBT by demonstrating an effective group-based cognitive-behavioral treatment for anxious children for use within a school setting. The group format, along with the structured, yet flexible, nature of this intervention program lends itself to use by school counselors.

Source: Bernstein, G. A., Layne, A. E., Egan, E. A., & Tennison, D. M. (2005). School-based interventions for anxious children. *Journal of the American Academy of Child and Adolescent Psychiatry, 44*(11), 1118–1126.

SAMPLE INTERVENTIONS

Social Anxiety: CBT and Social-Skills Training

Authors: Susan H. Spence, Caroline Donovan, and Margaret Brechman-Toussaint

Précis: A randomized control group study of the effectiveness of CBT involving social-skills training for childhood social phobia.

Introduction

Social phobia in children typically consists of fear and withdrawal from unfamiliar people as well as fear of negative evaluation by others. In children, the anxiety is typically encountered in performance situations, such as taking a test, presenting in front of the class, attending social events, or initiating social interaction. The current study was an attempt to employ a randomized controlled group design to test the applicability and effectiveness of a cognitive-behavioral intervention for the treatment of childhood social phobia.

Intervention

Fifty children between the ages of 7 and 14 who had a principal diagnosis of social phobia were randomly assigned to child-focused CBT, CBT plus parent involvement, or a wait-list control. The integrated cognitive-behavioral intervention involved intensive social-skills training combined with graded exposure and cognitive challenging.

The program included 12 weekly sessions followed by 2 booster sessions (at 3 and 6 months after treatment). Treatment was conducted in small groups (6 to 8 children) for 60 minutes followed by a 20-minute session for "games" during which the children practiced their social skills in a real, yet safe, encounter.

Social-skills training focused on developing microskills (e.g., eye contact, posture, tone, volume), asking questions, listening, engaging in prosocial behaviors (e.g., sharing, inviting, complimenting), and problem solving. Homework involving graded practice was assigned after each session. A detailed outline of the program is available in Spence (1995).

Reflection

Ratings of social anxiety and social-skills performance showed significant improvement for the treated group when compared to the wait-listed children, an improvement that was retained at a 12-month follow-up.

CBT has extensive support for its utility with adults exhibiting social anxiety. The current study extended its application to school-aged children. Although the group format, including the social-practice sessions, appears to be compatible with the role and function of the school counselor, the allocation of 90 minutes total to each session in the 12-week program may be somewhat prohibitive for many school counselors. Further, the expansive focus of treatment to include social-skills training, graded exposure, relaxation training, and cognitive challenging—all within the context of a problem-solving and self-instructional approach—may be too much to accomplish for all children within the 12-session limit. Perhaps, counselors would do well to test the possible effects of using an extended number of sessions, with a reduced length of time per session.

Source: Spence, S. H., Donovan, C., & Brechman-Toussaint, M. (2000). The treatment of childhood social phobia: The effectiveness of a social skills training-based, cognitive-behavioral intervention, with and without parental involvement. *Journal of Child Psychology and Psychiatry, 41*(6), 713–726.

SAMPLE INTERVENTIONS

Separation Anxiety: A Case Study using CBT

Author: David Dia

Précis: Case study of a 6-year-old boy investigating the use of CBT in the treatment of separation anxiety disorder (SAD).

Introduction

Separation anxiety can be seen in a child's difficulty in separating from his or her parents. Often, parents unwittingly reinforce this anxious, clinging behavior. Children experiencing separation anxiety perceive themselves to be incapable of managing the separation (low self-efficacy), thus increasing their anxiety. Children experiencing separation anxiety avoid separation situations, thus decreasing their anxiety. Therefore, the avoidance response is reinforced by the immediate relief that the child experiences.

The problem is that avoidance of separation does not allow the child to assess the danger in the separation situation more realistically, nor does it allow the child to develop coping abilities or increase perceptions of self-efficacy regarding his or her ability to handle the separation situation. Clearly, under these conditions extinction will not occur and intervention is required.

The current study examined the use of cognitive-behavioral therapy in the treatment of separation anxiety disorder. Prior to the actual treatment, both the client and his parent were informed about the nature of anxiety and the cognitive behavioral method to be employed.

Intervention

This case study focused on a 6-year-old male who would go into a panic attack if separated from parents. The student expressed concerns over the possibility of being kidnapped. The student met the criteria for separation anxiety (APA, 2000).

The treatment effort involved four phases:

1. **Psycho-education for the parents and child about the nature of anxiety and the cognitive-behavioral model**. The student was helped to understand the CBT model and learned how to label his thoughts, feelings, and behaviors by using stories of other little boys. For example, to help him understand the purpose of exposures, he was told a story of a little boy who was able to conquer his fear of the basement by going into the basement for progressively longer periods.
2. **Development of cognitive-behavioral coping strategies**. A variety of strategies were used to help the child cope with his anxiety during graded

exposures, such as contingency management, distraction techniques, and coping self-statements.

3. **Graded exposures and family work**. After forming a hierarchy of fear stimuli/situations, the child was exposed to the stimuli and was helped to employ a variety of distraction strategies, such as counting backward from 10, starting "blast off," and taking a deep breath (the counting game).
4. **Booster session**. The final session was used to review strategies and attribute the child's success to his use of the coping strategies.

Reflection

Although the use of CBT for the reduction of separation anxiety (or conversely, the increase in separation behaviors) is far from novel, what this case study highlights is the benefit of first establishing rational mind-sets prior to employing a behavioral intervention. It appears that helping the parents and child develop more functional, adaptive beliefs about anxiety increased their "ownership" of the program, thus ensuring their participation in the intervention. The article outlines creative strategies that are developmentally appropriate when employing CBT with young children (e.g., use of stories, games, etc.).

Although the case study provides an interesting way to look at exposure and cognitive restructuring as a means of reducing separation anxiety, the fact that the study employed a single subject means that caution is required when interpreting the validity and applicability of these findings to other age groups and settings.

Source: Dia, D. A. (2001). Cognitive behavioral therapy with a six-year-old boy with separation anxiety: A case study. *Health & Social Work, 26*(2), 125–129.

DETAILED INTERVENTION

Stop, Drop, and Roll to Reduce Test Anxiety

Introduction

Test anxiety may be viewed as an "invisible disability." Test anxiety not only causes children unpleasant feelings, but it can result in poor test performance and blocked recall and problem solving. The current study used a pretest-posttest format for 16 students who were identified by the school counselor as having failed to achieve 70 percent (the passing rate) on a statewide achievement test and who had exhibited or reported extreme feelings of anxiety and stress. The sample consisted of six third graders, five fourth graders, and five fifth graders. In interviews, the students reported feeling frustrated and anxious with regard to the testing and even noted feeling physically ill and vomiting.

All students reported less anxiety and being more relaxed during the administration of the statewide test as a result of participation in the group-based intervention. Of the 16 group members, only 2 failed both the reading and math sections, whereas in the pretest condition all students failed to reach the passing grade of 70 percent.

Method

The study included 16 students in grades three through five. The counselor developed a six-session group and classroom guidance intervention that taught the students stress management techniques.

- **Group Session 1**: The students were administered a test-anxiety exposure hierarchy consisting of 13 items. Using a scale of 0 (no anxiety) to 10 (debilitating anxiety), the students rated their individual reaction to each item on the hierarchy. These reactions served as a focal point for group relaxation techniques in subsequent sessions.
- **Group Session 2**: The students were taught to "Stop, Drop, and Roll." Students were instructed that when they felt the "fire" of anxiety and stress that they should:

  Stop . . . and put their pencils down, placing their hands on the table and focusing on the coolness of the surface.
  Drop . . . drop their heads forward, and
  Roll . . . roll their heads around gently while taking three deep breaths.

  The group members practiced this relaxation technique while the counselor played classical music.

- **Session 3**: The counselor presented items from the hierarchy and had the students practice relaxation during the imagined exposure. As the counselor read an item, a group member called "fire" when they started to experience anxiety. The group would then practice the Stop, Drop, and Roll technique.

- **Sessions 4–6**: The procedure was introduced as part of a classroom guidance unit on test-taking skills. The students from the group taught their classmates the Stop, Drop, and Roll technique and prior to the test administration a schoolwide assembly was held to motivate the students to practice this technique.

Reflection

The study provides an interesting use of desensitization and relaxation techniques, along with systemwide intervention to create a supportive culture for the application of the relaxation technique in vivo.

The use of this relaxation process has extensive support within the literature when applied to adolescents and adults. These authors have provided a creative and developmentally appropriate application of relaxation training to elementary-aged students in the form of the "Stop, Drop, and Roll" model. Beyond highlighting the value of this creative approach, the authors demonstrate both the importance and the value of utilizing a multisystemic format. Teachers, parents, in fact, the entire school community, were taught and encouraged to employ the relaxation technique, thus reducing the chance that the group members would be stigmatized for using it. Instead, a climate of acceptability and encouragement was developed for use of the strategy when experiencing test anxiety. This normalization of the intervention should help in making it a useful and usable strategy.

Although the results are encouraging and the intervention is intuitively appealing, additional controlled studies are called for in order to more fully demonstrate the specific treatment effect of "Stop, Drop, and Roll."

Source: Cheek, J. R., Bradley, L. J., Reynolds, J., & Coy, D. (2002). An intervention for helping elementary students reduce test anxiety. *Professional School Counseling, 6*(2), 162–164.

FROM THE FIELD

As with previous chapters, the following interventions, although touted by counselors working in schools, have not been tested for effectiveness using experimental design, and thus should be applied with caution.

Social Anxiety

- Have students "rehearse" self-disclosures.
- Ask the student to bring in items that may be of interest to other students. This may stimulate engagement and allow the student to share about something he or she feels competent and comfortable discussing.
- Pair the student with a more popular student while doing school projects or coursework.
- Invite the student to participate in a group volunteer project such as decorating for a holiday, preparing for a dance, organizing a food drive, and so on.
- Have the student participate in a poster club for the counseling center, where posters reflect healthy self-talk (e.g., we might not all be tall, but we are all important).
- Invite the student to be part of a play (drama). The student may find safety talking from and with another's voice.
- Help the child learn to distinguish between evaluation of conditions (e.g., hair color, clothes worn) and behaviors (e.g., striking out, stuttering, etc.) and the value of the person.
- Teach the student how to use active listening skills (reflection) as a way of engaging others.
- Teach the child to use self-control skills when anxiety strikes. The mnemonic STOP can be used: **s**cared **t**houghts, **o**ther thoughts I can do to handle my fear, and **p**raise myself for successful handling of my fear and exposure (e.g., saying, "I am really proud of myself," or "I feel good about how I'm improving").
- Help the child identify "safer" peers with whom to interact with, where "safe" is defined as more likely to be positive and engaging.
- Have the student set up small social engagement goals and then offer reinforcements when they are achieved.

Separation Anxiety

- Allow the parent to bring the child to school and even come in and sit for a few minutes (in the counselor's office) before allowing the child to go off to class.
- Have a classmate meet and greet the student at the door and walk to class together.

- Allow the student to phone home. However, make phoning home contingent on the student staying and performing in class. Increase the amount of time in class necessary prior to allowing the child to phone home.
- Allow the student to bring a comfort toy or item from home, perhaps a coin or something that the child could place in his or her pocket and rub when anxious.
- Allow the child permission to leave class to go to the bathroom. The child may become nervous about having an "accident" if anxious.
- For older students, use desensitization and successive approximations.
- Support parents' efforts to separate without a scene. Encourage parents to be nonchalant about leaving the student.
- Engage student in highly stimulating/attractive and interactive activity following separation as a means of refocusing attention.
- Help the child identify and develop his or her own coping skills and develop a sense of self-efficacy.
- Work with parents to make sure that incentives for staying home (such as watching television) are less than the incentives for coming to school (perhaps earning rewards or being able to participate in a desired activity).
- Have teachers make moderate modifications to the classroom setting or procedures. Perhaps allow the student to sit near the door, avoid calling attention to the child (especially if showing signs of being upset), reinforce all efforts to join in, and so on.
- The teacher should not show much sympathy for the crying, complaining child, but should be kind and firm. If class is disrupted by the child's crying, a mild time-out period in a corner of the classroom is recommended. The child rejoins the group when the crying stops, and the teacher reinforces any behavior except crying with attention and praise.

Test Anxiety

- Help the child identify and challenge negative thoughts such as "I always fail tests" or "There's no way I can pass."
- Teach the student to use rhythmic belly breathing to relax.
- Have the student practice positive self-talk such as "Tests measure my performance only on a test on a given day and NOT my worth as a student or a person."
- Have the student practice relaxation techniques while imagining coming to, sitting, and taking a test.
- Make sure the student has all of the supplies needed for the test.
- Tell the student to get enough sleep the night before and eat a low-fat, high-protein meal before the test.
- Study, study, study. It is better to overprepare!
- Before the test, allow the student to take a walk, go to the bathroom, walk up and down the stairs, and so on.

- During the test, advise the student to read the directions and start with the easiest question first.
- Tell the student to schedule "breaks" during the test, such as stretching the hands and fingers, rolling the head, and taking a couple of deep breaths.

REFERENCES

American Psychiatric Association. (2000). *Diagnostic and statistical manual of mental disorders* (4th ed., text revision). Washington, DC: Author.

Barret, P. M., Lowry-Webster, H., & Turner, C. (2000a). *FRIENDS program for children: Parents' supplement.* Brisbane: Australian Academic Press.

Barret, P. M., Lowry-Webster, H., & Turner, C. (2000b). *FRIENDS program for children: Group leaders manual.* Brisbane: Australian Academic Press.

Barret, P. M., Lowry-Webster, H., & Turner, C. (2000c). *FRIENDS program for children: Participants workbook.* Brisbane: Australian Academic Press.

Bernstein, G. A., Layne, A. E., Egan, E. A., & Tennison, D. M. (2005). School-based interventions for anxious children. *Journal of the American Academy of Child and Adolescent Psychiatry, 44*(11), 1118–1126.

Cheek, J. R., Bradley, L. J., Reynolds, J., & Coy, D. (2002). An intervention for helping elementary students reduce test anxiety. *Professional School Counseling, 6*(2), 162–164.

Dia, D. A. (2001). Cognitive behavioral therapy with a six-year-old boy with separation anxiety: A case study. *Health & Social Work, 26*(2), 125–129.

Last, C. G., Francis, G., Hersen, M., Kazdin, A. C., & Strauss, C. C. (1987). Separation anxiety and school phobia: A comparison using DSM-III criteria. *American Journal of Psychiatry, 144*, 653–657.

Rubenzer, R. L. (1988). *Stress management for the learning disabled.* Reston, VA: ERIC Clearinghouse on Handicapped and Gifted Children.

Shortt, A. L., Barrett, P. M., & Fox, T. L. (2001). Evaluating the FRIENDS program: A cognitive-behavioral group treatment for anxious children and their parents. *Journal of Clinical Child Psychology, 30*(4), 525–535.

Silverman, W. K., & Berman, S. L. (2001). Psychosocial interventions for anxiety disorders in children: Status and Future directions. In W. K. Silverman & P. D. A. Treffers (Eds.), *Anxiety disorder in children and adolescents: Research, assessment, and intervention* (pp. 313–334). Cambridge, UK: Cambridge University Press.

Spence, S. H. (1995). *Social skills training: Enhancing social competence with children and adolescents.* Windsor, UK: NFER-Nelson.

Spence, S. H., Donovan, C., & Brechman-Toussaint, M. (2000). The treatment of childhood social phobia: The effectiveness of a social skills training-based, cognitive-behavioral intervention, with and without parental involvement. *Journal of Child Psychology and Psychiatry, 41*(6), 713–726.

ADDITIONAL RESOURCES

INTERNET

www.counsel.ufl.edu/brochure.asp?include=brochures/test_anxiety.brochure.. Helpful information on reducing test anxiety prepared by Barbara Probert and the University of Florida Counseling Center.

www.socialanxietysupport.com. Online support group that provides information and special programs designed to assist those with social anxiety.

www.healthsystem.virginia.edu/ uvahealth/peds_mentalhealth/sepanxty.cfm. Provides general information on separation anxiety—presentation—causes and treatment as well as links to helpful information.

PRINTED MATERIALS

Bourne, E. J. (2000). *The anxiety and phobia workbook* (3rd ed). Oakland, CA: New Harbinger Publications, Inc.

Dacey, J. S., & Fiore, L. B. (2000). *Your anxious child: How parents and teachers can relieve anxiety in children.* San Francisco: Jossey-Bass.

Silverman, W. K., & Treffers, P. D. A. (Eds.). *Anxiety disorders in children and adolescents: Research, assessment, and intervention.* Cambridge, UK: Cambridge University Press. Schwarzer, R. (Ed.). (1986). *Self-related cognitions in anxiety and motivation.* Hillsdale, NJ: Lawrence Erlbaum.

CHAPTER 13

STRESS

Life in the twenty-first century is characterized by change, the need for multiple and rapid adaptation, and stress. Whether from in-school tests, a college entrance exam, or concerns about a school recital, making the team, or finding a prom date, children are not immune to stress, nor are they insulated from its negative psychological, social, and physiological effects.

It is clear that there is a relationship between major life stresses (e.g., divorce, illness, death, etc.) and psychological adjustment. It is also clear that everyday stressors, especially when experienced daily and in combination, can negatively impact children's health and well-being.

Children's ability to cope with everyday stress has been found to be significantly related to their psychological adjustment (Rutter, 1996). Evidence indicates that distress among young people is increasing. One study of a nationally representative sample in the United States involving over 1,200 adolescents suggested that 19.4 percent of ninth through twelfth graders experienced significant emotional distress (Resnick et al., 1997). Others (e.g., Roeser, 1998; Cunningham & Walker, 1999) have suggested that at any given time one-third of our youth may be experiencing difficulties in psychological functioning and coping with concerns and stresses of everyday life to the extent that it interferes with academic performance.

Research suggests that students who successfully employ cognitive and behavioral strategies to increase adaptive skills and reduce sources of stress and the negative arousal associated with it experience fewer of the negative impacts of stress (Connor-Smith & Compas, 2004; Compas, Malcarne, & Fondacaro, 1988). It appears, therefore, that school counselors should target their intervention and prevention efforts at assisting students to develop effective stress reduction and stress management strategies.

OVERVIEW

Because stress is so pervasive and all children can benefit from developing effective coping strategies, the techniques selected for inclusion in this chapter are felt to be useful for all students and lend themselves to delivery in group, whole-class, and general developmental guidance formats (Table 13.1).

TABLE 13.1 Overview of Studies Presented

TARGET PROBLEM	REFERENCE	K–6	6–9	9–12	OTHER SPECIFICATIONS
Skill-based stress reduction	DeWolfe & Saunders (1995)	Y	Y	N	Modified institutional cycles, quasi-experimental design, 157 sixth-grade students
Teaching optimistic thinking	Cunningham, Brandon, & Frydenberg, (2002)	Y	Y	N	Randomized pretest, posttest, control group design with treatment manual
Deep-muscle relaxation	deAnda (1998)	Y	Y	N	Pretest, posttest, control group design
CBT for stress reduction	Hains (1994)	N	N	Y	Randomized control group design

SAMPLE INTERVENTIONS

Stress—A Skills-Oriented Program

Authors: Alan S. DeWolfe and Antoinette M. Saunders

Précis: Demonstrates the utility of a skills-oriented stress prevention and management program in regular sixth-grade classrooms.

Introduction

Unlike many stress management programs that employ muscle relaxation, biofeedback, and meditation directed at relieving stress symptoms, such as autonomic reactions, this program focused on teaching skills that enable children to take an active role in confronting the causes of stress in their lives. The intervention employed (i.e., the "Capable Kid Program") focuses on teaching children skills such as identifying sources of stress in their lives, talking about their feelings, being positive, and solving problems. The authors reported significant improvement ratings of self-esteem and overall stress management following the intervention.

Intervention

A total of 157 sixth-grade students in two schools served as participants. The authors employed a recurrent institutional cycle quasi-experimental design, which provides a valid approach to research without employing random assignment or nontreatment control groups.

The stress management treatment program consisted of one-hour sessions over an eight-week period. The program was presented to classroom units consisting of all students in a class whose parents had signed a permission slip. The lessons include the presentation of information and practice exercises. The content of the sessions (the Capable Kid Program) was as follows:

- **Lesson 1**: "What Is Stress?" and "Learning to Relax" presented the effects of too much, too little, and just enough stress and instructed children in a relaxation technique (i.e., "breathing feet").
- **Lesson 2**: "Stress and My Body" helped the children to identify bodily indicators of stress.
- **Lesson 3**: "Switching Negatives to Positives" focused on self-talk, assisting the children to listen to what they tell themselves and then change the message by looking for the positive possibilities in situations.
- **Lesson 4**: "Why Listening Is Important" helped the students learn how to engage others in listening to them.
- **Lesson 5**: "Discovering My Feelings" discussed good and bad feelings and showed ways to gain control of love, joy, frustration, fear, and anger.

- **Lesson 6**: "Stress Solving" provided an approach for solving problems by stating the problem, finding options, rating the outcomes of the options, choosing the best option(s), putting it (them) into action, and, finally, taking responsibility for one's actions.
- **Lesson 7**: "Rules of Good Health" presented information about nutrition, exercise, and the effects of alcohol and drugs.
- **Lesson 8**: "Putting It All Together" helped each child select three stresses/problems to continue to work on and helped them select and employ skills that they had learned. The children then shared their thoughts and feelings with their classmates.

Reflection

The current study has a number of unique and valuable considerations for school counselors. First, the stress management program described differed from the more traditional therapy approach in that it focused on equipping the students with skills needed to prevent rather than manage stress. This developmental model would appear to lend itself for application within the school setting. Second, the study is of value in that it was used with normal grade-school children in regular classes rather than those identified for special service. Finally, the study reflected a unique design (i.e., a modified institutional-cycles, quasi-experimental research design, Campbell & Stanley, 1966), which provided control for internal threats to validity without the need to employ randomized assignment to treatment or the use of nontreated control groups, both elements that typically are not possible to employ within a school setting.

Source: DeWolfe, A. S., & Saunders, A. M. (1995). Stress reduction in sixth-grade students. *Journal of Experimental Education, 63*(4), 315–329.

SAMPLE INTERVENTIONS

Increasing Coping Skills with a School-based Program in Optimistic Thinking

Authors: Everarda G. Cunningham, C. M. Brandon, and Erica Frydenberg

Précis: Tested the effectiveness of an eight-week, manual-based program that taught students optimistic thinking skills using a randomly assigned pretest, posttest control group design.

Introduction

This intervention is based on research that suggests that a key factor that differentiates people who cope effectively from those who may not is their attributional style (Gladstone & Kaslow, 1995). For those with a pessimistic attributional style, negative events are perceived as permanent in time and global in effect and typically the result of their own limitations or fault. Those with an optimistic attributional style see bad events as temporary and limited to specific events for which there may be many causes beyond the self. Because the pessimistic attributional style has been associated with emotional distress, the authors hypothesized that changing a person's attributional style should effect changes in coping.

The eight-week program was implemented as part of the regular school curricula. Those students who participated in the training program reported significant improvement in coping efficacy when compared to controls.

Intervention

School psychologists and classroom teachers implemented an eight-week program in eight fifth and sixth grade classrooms as part of the regular school curricula. The treatment group (those receiving training) included 160 students; 135 students were in the control group. Pre- and posttest self-report questionnaires assessing children's attributional style, coping strategies, and perceived degree of control over internal states were used as dependent measures.

The program was the manual-based skills-training program "Bright Ideas: Skills for Positive Thinking" (Brandon & Cunningham, 1999). The program consists of eight weekly 60- to 90-minute sessions. The program covers basic optimistic thinking skills, including:

- Listening to self-talk
- Evaluating the accuracy of self-talk
- Generating alternative attributions
- Challenging catastrophic thinking

Throughout the program, students were taught to dispute negative self-talk in response to real and hypothetical events. The program, which is detailed elsewhere (Brandon, Cunningham, & Frydenberg, 1999), employed stories, cartoons, hypothetical examples, role-play, and practice to facilitate skill development.

Reflection

As hypothesized, children who received training reported a significant increase in coping efficacy, reflecting a greater sense of control over their internal states and changes in the perceived nature of stressors encountered. Beyond the positive outcome, what is noteworthy about the intervention is that it provides an example of an effective universal program that has application within a normal school setting. Future research may want to consider outcome measures other than student self-report and assess the durability of the intervention over time.

Source: Cunningham, E. G., Brandon, C. M., & Frydenberg, E. (2002). Enhancing coping resources in early adolescence through a school-based program teaching optimistic thinking skills. *Anxiety, Stress and Coping, 15*(4), 369–381.

SAMPLE INTERVENTIONS

Muscle Relaxation and Cognitive Coping Strategies

Author: Diane deAnda

Précis: Tested the effectiveness of a 10-week stress management program emphasizing cognitive-control coping strategies and relaxation methods.

Introduction

Citing supportive research, the author notes that the amount of stress experienced by adolescents and their *concomitant lack of coping skills* are linked to their experience of psychological and emotional disturbance. The development and employment of coping skills served as the focus for this study. It was hypothesized that providing adolescents with instruction in employing coping strategies would prove effective in reducing the degree of stress experienced. The program developed was therefore designed to teach the adolescent specific cognitive coping strategies (e.g., accurate self-talk and problem solving) and behavioral coping techniques (e.g., muscle relaxation). The author reported that the adolescents in the intervention program not only employed cognitive control coping strategies more frequently than the control group, but also reported significantly less stress than those in the control group.

Intervention

The author employed a pretest, posttest control group design to test the effectiveness of a 10-week stress management program for 36 middle school students. The program was conducted on a weekly basis over a 10-week period. The program employed didactic and group methods to instruct the participants in cognitive and behavioral coping skills.

The participants were taught to distinguish between stress and stressors, to identify healthy (eustress) and unhealthy (distress) stress; and to understand the physiology of stress. Following this introduction, participants were taught to observe and analyze self-talk in order to evaluate the meaning of the stress that they experienced. Next, participants were instructed in the "Calm Body, Clear Mind" method of coping with stress (see deAnda, Darroch, Davidson, Gilly, & Morejon, 1990), which emphasizes muscle relaxation and accurate self-talk.

Reflection

Lazarus and Folkman (1986) proposed that the relationship between the individual and the environmental stressor is mediated by a person's appraisal of both the threat value of the stressor and the effectiveness of the coping strategies. The current study addressed both of these factors by teaching participants rational problem solving, cognitive reframing, and relaxation techniques. The program demonstrated the effectiveness of systematic instruction in cognitive behavioral strategies for coping with stress, with participants reporting significant increases in their ability to cope with the stress they experienced in their daily lives.

The intervention's relatively brief treatment period and the use of structured instruction lends itself to use by school counselors, even as a developmental guidance unit. However, as with all such studies, a major concern is the degree to which the technique and findings can be generalized to other populations given the small sample size employed in the study and the self-selection of participants.

Source: deAnda, D. (1998). The evaluation of stress management program for middle school adolescents. *Child and Adolescent Social Work Journal, 15*(1), 73–85.

DETAILED INTERVENTION

A School-based Stress Management Program

Introduction

Adolescence has often been referred to as a period of "sturm und drang" (storm and stress). Whether attempting to cope with parent–teen conflict, academic and social pressures, dating anxiety, or education or career decisions, adolescents encounter stress daily as part of their normal developmental transition. The impact of this stress on the psychological and physical well-being of the adolescent and its potential contribution to increased anxiety, depression, and chronic illness highlights the importance of counselors developing strategies to help adolescents more successfully cope with stress.

The current study describes a school-based cognitive stress management intervention program that resulted in improvement on self-report measures of trait anxiety, self-esteem, depression, and trait anger.

Method

The study employed a randomized, pretest, posttest design with volunteer juniors in a parochial high school. A total of 19 students participated: 10 in the treatment group, 9 in the wait-list control group. The participants were assessed pre- and post-treatment using the State-Trait Anxiety Scale; the State-Trait Expression of Anger Scale, the Coopersmith Self-Esteem Inventory, and the Reynolds Adolescent Depression Scale.

The cognitive behavioral training paralleled the three-phase, stress inoculation training model developed by Meichenbaum (1985). The three phases of this model are as follows:

1. **Conceptualization phase**. Each student in the treatment group participated in a 50-minute group session followed by two 30-minute individual sessions. Participants were trained to identify stress events; to reconceptualize stress in terms of physiological reactions, behaviors, emotions, and cognitions; and to identify negative, self-defeating cognitions.

   The 50-minute group meeting involved the following activities:

- Students provided examples of experienced stress and were prompted to define them in terms of behavioral, physiological, and cognitive components.
- Students were provided a definition for the term *cognitive*, and the role of cognition in emotional arousal (negative) was explained.
- Students were introduced to the purpose and process of self-monitoring and were given examples of cognitive distortions. They were provided self-monitoring sheets and practiced filling them out.

In the individual sessions, participants reviewed homework (self-monitoring sheets), identified cognitive distortions (e.g., all or nothing, catastrophizing, etc.), and practiced additional self-monitoring.

2. **Skill-acquisition phase**: Again, using a format of a 50-minute group session and two 30-minute individual sessions, students were taught cognitive restructuring strategies. They were trained to question their self-defeating thoughts by examining evidence for and against their thoughts and by looking for alternative explanations for stress events.

   During the group session, participants discussed challenging negative thoughts and replacing them with realistic thoughts. They were introduced to questions for challenging self-defeating thoughts (e.g., "What is the evidence for or against this belief?").

   In the 30-minute individual sessions, participants reviewed self-monitoring and restructuring efforts (homework). They also recalled (using imagery) a stress situation and identified self-defeating thoughts that they then challenged by re-imaging the scene using adaptive rational cognitions.

3. **Application phase**. Using two, 30-minute sessions, students were given additional practice with cognitive restructuring. Participants identified a possible upcoming stressful event and applied cognitive restructuring while in imagery.

The first of the application-phase sessions included the following activities:

- Participants reviewed the self-monitoring sheets.
- Participants described a likely stressor and narrated the self-defeating cognitions as they imagined the situation.
- Participants practiced re-imagining with an adaptive, rational response.
- Participants completed a self-monitoring sheet following the incident.

The second of the application-phase sessions included the following activities:

- Participants reviewed the previous meeting and its effect on their preparation for the anticipated stressor.
- They repeated the preparation process for another anticipated stress event.
- They discussed generalization and continued use of the strategies learned.

Reflection

Research supports the use of cognitive behavioral procedures within stress management programs. What is somewhat unique to this study was its application not only with an adolescent population, but with its use of a school-based group and individual session format. It would appear that given this population, the school is the logical setting for prevention and intervention efforts, and counselors are the professionals best situated to implement these programs. The approach outlined here appears to have utility not just for those teens exhibiting extreme stress reactions, but for those experiencing the stress typically associated with developmental transitions and adolescent life. The one caution noted by the author and emphasized here is that the absence of follow-up makes it difficult to assume that the treatment continued to prove effective beyond the post-assessment phase.

Source: Hains, A. A. (1994). The effectiveness of a school-based, cognitive-behavioral stress management program with adolescents reporting high and low levels of emotional arousal. *School Counselor, 42*(3), 114–125.

FROM THE FIELD

The following suggestions emphasize the need to educ
stress, its impact, and the attitudes and behaviors that can
successfully cope with stress. As with the other "From the Field"
following have not been tested using experimental control.

Working with Students—Attitudes and Beliefs

- Educate students about the physiology of stress so that they can normalize their feelings. Help students develop an understanding of their symptoms and the source of these reactions.
- Have students conduct a "reality check." Help students to distinguish between real-life demands and their consequences and self-imposed demands with cognitively distorted consequences and importance. It's important that students understand that how one sees the situation is key to how one experiences it.
- Decatastrophize! Have students identify a reality-based worse-case scenario as opposed to exaggerated concerns.
- Tell students that if the source of their concern and stress is worry over other people's opinions, they should act as if they don't care. Sometimes faking it helps to make it.
- Reframe. Rather than feeling burned out or loaded down by stress, students should try to see it as a push, a motivator, to get moving.
- Help students learn to prioritize. When trying to have and do it all, sometimes students simply need to identify that which is most important and let the rest wait until another day.

Working with Students—Behavior

- Help students learn time management and organizational skills as a way of reducing demands.
- It's okay to take time out. Help students remember that sometimes it's okay to simply walk away for awhile, to stop for a moment, to refocus and relax.
- Eat, sleep, exercise, and be healthy. Help students understand that a healthy body is better able to deal with life's demands.
- Take a walk, listen to music, or take a five-minute break when stressed with homework or study.
- When stressed, relax with a nice warm bath.
- Breathe, breathe, breathe. Help students learn to belly breathe with slow, rhythmic, smooth breaths. Use the image of a swing as a guide to breathing, with a pattern of a slow in breath, a slight hesitation, and then reversing to a smooth exhale.

- Teach the student progressive muscle relaxation.
- Nurture imagery of safe, relaxing places. Take time to mentally envision a scene of comfort and relaxation. It's important to distinguish this from a fun place with lots of activity (and stress).
- Talk it out. Invite students to simply vent—with a parent, a friend, or the counselor—as a way of gaining distance, perspective, and support.
- Practice saying "no" to things that really are not that important and that the student really doesn't want to do.
- Laugh! A sense of humor is very good for stress management. Help students identify movies, television shows, or special friends that make them laugh!

Working with Teachers

- As much as possible, spread out tests and assignments across classes.
- Help students anticipate, plan, and begin major assignments or study for tests.
- Prior to test taking, help the class focus by doing a cleansing breath. After a test have the class stretch and move to shake out the stress.
- Model a rational, stress-reduced approach to the day by employing cleansing breaths before the start of a class, being organized, and verbalizing a plan of the day.
- When students are clearly frustrated with a task, name it for them and teach them to stop, take a time-out, center and relax, take care of the self, and then return to task.

REFERENCES

Brandon, C. M., & Cunningham, E. G. (1999). *Bright ideas manual.* Australia, Melbourne: Oz Child.

Brandon, C. M., Cunningham, E. G., & Frydenberg, E. (1999). Bright Ideas: A school based program teaching optimistic thinking skills in pre-adolescence. *Australian Journal of Guidance and Counseling, 9,* 153–163.

Cunningham, E. G., Brandon, C. M., & Frydenberg, E. (2002). Enhancing coping resources in early adolescence through a school-based program teaching optimistic thinking skills. *Anxiety, Stress and Coping, 15*(4), 369–381.

Campbell, D. T., & Stanley, J. C. (1966). *Experimental and quasi-experimental designs for research.* Boston: Houghton Mifflin.

Compas, B. E., Malcarne, V. L., & Fondacaro, K. M. (1988). Coping with stressful events in older children and young adolescents. *Journal of Consulting and Clinical Psychology, 56,* 405–411.

Connor-Smith, J. K., & Compas, B. E. (2004). Coping as a moderator of relations between reactivity to interpersonal stress, health status, and internalizing problems. *Therapy & Research, 28*(3), 347–368.

Cunningham, E. G., & Walker, G. A. (1999). Screening for at-risk youth: Predicting adolescent depression from coping styles. *Australian Journal of Guidance and Counseling, 8*, 37–47.

Cunningham, E. G., Brandon, C. M., & Frydenberg, E. (2002). Enhancing coping resources in early adolescence through a school-based program teaching optimistic thinking skills. *Anxiety, Stress and Coping, 15*(4), 369–381.

deAnda, D. (1998). The evaluation of stress management program for middle school adolescents. *Child and Adolescent Social Work Journal, 15*(1), 73–85.

deAnda, D., Darroch, P., Davidson, M., Gilly, J., & Morejon, A. (1990). Stress management for pregnant adolescents and adolescent mothers: A pilot study. *Child and Adolescent Social Work Journal, 7*(1), 53–67.

DeWolfe, A. S., & Saunders, A. M. (1995). Stress reduction in sixth-grade students. *Journal of Experimental Education, 63*(4), 315–329.

Hains, A. A. (1994). The effectiveness of a school-based, cognitive-behavioral stress management program with adolescents reporting high and low levels of emotional arousal. *School Counselor, 42*(3), 114–125.

Gladstone, T. R. G., & Kaslow, N. J. (1995). Depression and attributions in children and adolescents: A meta-analytic review. *Journal of Abnormal Child Psychology, 23*, 597–606.

Lazarus, R. S., & K. Folkman, S. (1986). Cognitive theories of stress and the issue of circularity. In M. H. Appley & R. Trumbull (Eds.), *Dynamics of stress: Physiological, psychological, and social perspectives* (pp. 63–80). New York: Plenum Press.

Meichenbaum, D. (1985). *Stress inoculation training*. New York: Pergamon Press.

Resnick, M. D., Bearman, P. S., Blum, R. W., Bauman, K. E., Harris, K. M. Jones, J., Tabor, J., Beuhring, T., Sieving, R. E., Shew, M., Ireland, M., Bearinger, L. H., & Udry, R. (1997). Protecting adolescents from harm: Findings from the national longitudinal study on adolescent health. *The Journal of the American Medical Association, 278*, 823–832.

Rocscr, R. W. (1998). On schooling and mental health: Introduction to special issues. *Educational Psychologist, 33*, 129–135.

Rutter, M. (1996). Stress research: Accomplishments and the tasks ahead. In R. J. Haggerty, L. Sherrod, & N. Garmezy (Eds.), *Stress, risk, and resilience in children and adolescents: Processes, mechanisms, and interventions* (pp. 354–386). New York: Cambridge University Press.

ADDITIONAL RESOURCES

INTERNET

www.mindtools.com/smpage.html. The Mind Tools Web site is a good source for articles and self-help information for stress management, project planning, and organizational and time management skills.

www.imt.net/~randolfi/StressLinks.html. This Web site features stress management and emotional wellness links organized by subcategories and intervention strategies.

http://heartmath.org. The Institute of HeartMath is a research and education organization. Its primary mission is to help people achieve balance between the mind and heart when making decisions.

PRINTED MATERIALS

Adamson, E. (2002). *The everything stress management book: Practical ways to relax, be healthy and maintain your sanity*. Avon, MA: Adams Media.

Humphrey, J. H. (1998). *Helping children manage stress: A guide for adults*. Washington, DC: Child Welfare League, Inc.

Pincus, D. B., & Friedman, A. G. (2004). Improving children's coping with everyday stress: Transporting treatment interventions to the school setting. *Clinical Child and Family Psychology Review, 7*(4), 223–240.

Sluke, S. J., & Torres, V. (2002). *The complete idiot's guide to dealing with stress for teens.* Indianapolis, IN: Alpha Books.

Warren, M. P. (2002). *Behavioral management guide: Essential treatment strategies for the psychotherapy of children, their parents and families.* Nortvale, NJ: Jason Aronson, Inc.

CHAPTER 14

OBSESSIVE-COMPULSIVE DISORDER

Childhood Obsessive-Compulsive Disorder (OCD) is a complex psychological condition. It can be debilitating to the child experiencing it and disruptive to his or her family or classroom. OCD is not simply trying to get something right or having a case of the worries. According to the DSM-IV (APA, 2000), the essential features of OCD are recurrent obsession or compulsions. *Obsessions* are inappropriate, intrusive, and persistent ideas, thoughts, impulses, or images that cause marked anxiety or distress. *Compulsions* are repetitive behaviors that are used to prevent or reduce anxiety or distress and do not in themselves provide pleasure. These obsessions and compulsions are severe enough to be time consuming or cause marked distress or significant impairment of functioning.

Although the average age of onset is in the early 20s, OCD has been observed in children with a surprising rate of incidence. It has been estimated that one-third to one-half of those diagnosed with OCD are under the age of 15 (Zohar, 1999). In childhood, OCD is often associated with deterioration in school performance (Toro, Osejo, & Salamero, 1992) and poor peer relationships (Allsopp & Verduyn, 1988). In addition, childhood OCD is often associated with disruptions to family life, with significant distress experienced by parents and siblings (Calvocoressi, Lewis, Trufan, et al., 1995; Cooper, 1996).

In children, the symptoms of OCD often appear insidiously and may be misidentified or mistaken for behavioral difficulties. For example, the student who tends to take too long with homework or who resists turning in assignments may be reflecting perfectionist tendencies, rather than simply a lack of interest in school. Similarly, the child who frustrates both teachers and parents by refusing to perform science lab work may be thought to be oppositional and defiant, when in fact such refusal is based on an intense fear of contamination.

It is important, therefore, that counselors recognize the various signs and forms of OCD and be prepared to serve both as a referral source when needed and as an agent of therapeutic change when permitted. The studies presented are but a few examples of interventions demonstrated to be effective with children and adolescents exhibiting OCD. A review of the literature, however, suggests that the approach of choice is cognitive-behavioral therapy (CBT), with or without medication (see Franklin & Foa, 2002). As such, the studies that follow employ a variety of behavioral, cognitive, and psychopharmacological strategies for the treatment of OCD in children and adolescents.

OVERVIEW

As noted in Table 14.1, the studies reported targeted clinically diagnosed individuals (children and adolescents). Although the populations for which the techniques have been employed (i.e., those who have been clinically diagnosed with OCD) may not reflect those with whom a school counselor will work, it is this author's opinion that the interventions may prove effective for students who struggle with ruminations and behavioral rituals even when they fail to meet the criteria for DSM-IV diagnosis. In addition, the interventions described may be useful adjunctive to and in collaboration with clinical services provided to those students who have been diagnosed.

TABLE 14.1 Overview of Studies Presented

TARGET PROBLEM	REFERENCE	K–6	6–9	9–12	OTHER SPECIFICATIONS
OCD	Kearney & Silverman (1990)	N	N	y	Single case study of 14-year-old male
OCD	The Pediatric OCD Treatment Study Team (2004)	Y	Y	Y	Study of a clinical population ages 7 to 17
OCD	Himle, Fischer, VanEtten, Janeck, & Hanna (2003)	N	Y	Y	Structured two-year group intervention
OCD	Piacentini & Langley (2004)	N	Y	N	Case study, 12-year-old, Asian American male

SAMPLE INTERVENTIONS

Response Prevention with an Adolescent

Authors: Christopher A. Kearney and Wendy K. Silverman

Précis: A case study using both response prevention and cognitive therapy to treat a 14-year-old boy with severe OCD.

Introduction

Only in recent years has research begun to examine treatment issues related to childhood OCD. As with adult OCD, CBT has been the treatment of choice (Waters, Barrett, & March, 2001; Wever & Rey, 1997). The current case study represents one of the few early applications of cognitive therapy to the treatment of adolescent OCD. The study compared cognitive therapy and response prevention as treatments of the checking behaviors and worries over contracting rabies for a 14-year-old, depressed OCD adolescent.

Intervention

The case study employed multiple observations and comparison of treatment to baseline data depicting the frequency of checking behavior, self-reported anxiety, and depression. Treatment employed an alternating design of response prevention and cognitive therapy. The client was instructed to use only the method being tested at any one phase of the treatment.

- **Response prevention**. The student was asked to predetermine a percentage goal for reducing checking behavior. He then had two sessions with the therapist to develop alternative responses to employ when he felt the need to check.
- **Cognitive therapy**. The student met with the therapist to examine obsessions, identify the irrationality of the obsessions, and use various reality-checking methods to test the validity of the belief. For example, providing the client with information on how rabies is contracted and treated served as data from which to confront and debate irrational concerns of contracting rabies by way of contact with bat saliva on a window sill.

Treatment procedures over 24 sessions eliminated the compulsive behaviors and reduced self-reported anxiety. The authors reported that each treatment mode appeared to have successful, yet differential, outcomes. The response prevention resulted in a significant decrease (by over 90 percent from baseline) of window checking. The cognitive intervention appeared to lend to a total disappearance of saliva checking by the end of treatment. Further, the authors reported that a six-month follow-up confirmed that the student's checking behaviors were gone and his anxiety and depression were greatly reduced.

Reflection

The case study, although reporting on a clinically diagnosed adolescent treated within a clinical setting, can still prove instructive for the school counselor. The case is not only an early illustration of the use of CBT strategies for children with OCD, but the creative alternating design employed may also have special value in treating OCD in children.

The OCD Expert Consensus guidelines (March, Francis, Carpenter, & Kahn, 1997) recommend exposure-based CBT as the first line of treatment of choice for all prepubertal children who present with primary OCD and for adolescents with mild or moderate OCD. The alternating of the two intervention strategies may also help to reduce the tendency of some clients who fail to comply with the demanding and potentially anxiety-provoking homework typically employed in an exposure-plus-response-prevention approach.

Since this study, others have found cognitive-behavioral interventions (such as differential reinforcement, thought stopping, cognitive restructuring, relaxation training) to be therapeutically productive (Boyarsky, Petrone, Lee, & Goodman, 1991; Clarizio, 1991).

Although primary treatment responsibility falls outside of the role and function of the school counselor, the school counselor can serve in an adjunctive capacity. Counselors can provide support to students in their application of cognitive-debating and restructuring strategies and continuing the psycho-educational process by informing the student about the nature of the disorder.

Source: Kearney, C. A., & Silverman, W. K. (1990). Treatment of an adolescent with obsessive-compulsive disorder by alternating response prevention and cognitive therapy: An empirical analysis. *Journal of Behavioral Therapy and Experimental Psychiatry, 21*, 39–47.

SAMPLE INTERVENTIONS

Cognitive-Behavioral Treatment and Medication Alone or in Combination

Authors: The Pediatric OCD Treatment Study (POTS) Team

Précis: A randomized controlled group design to test the efficacy of CBT alone, medical management with the selective serotonin reuptake inhibitor sertraline alone, or CBT and sertraline combined as initial treatment for children and adolescents with OCD.

Introduction

Although research supports the efficacy of CBT in the treatment of OCD in children and adolescents, questions remained regarding the relative combined efficacy of CBT with medical management with selective serotonin reuptake inhibitors (SSRIs). The current study was designed to test the relative and combined efficacy of CBT and an SSRI.

Intervention

The Pediatric OCD Treatment Study employed a balanced, masked randomized controlled trial using a volunteer outpatient sample of 112 patients aged 7 through 17 years with a primary diagnosis of OCD. The dependent measure employed was the Children's Yale-Brown Obsessive-Compulsive Scale (CY-BOCS). Participants were randomly assigned to receive CBT alone, sertraline alone, combined CBT and sertraline, or a pill placebo for 12 weeks. The authors reported significant improvement on CY-BOCS scores for each of three treatment conditions (i.e., CBT alone, SSRI alone, and the combined treatment). The authors concluded that children and adolescents with OCD should begin treatment with a combination of CBT plus a selective serotonin reuptake inhibitor or CBT alone.

Reflection

At a time when many within our society are seeking a "quick fix" to life's challenges through use of modern medicine, this study demonstrates the effectiveness of an alternative to medicine—CBT (with or without medication)—for the treatment of childhood and adolescent OCD.

Although prescribing, or even recommending, medication is clearly outside the competencies and ethical boundaries of the school counselor, the current study is provided as a means of increasing counselor awareness of the two approaches (i.e., CBT and psychopharmacology) most often cited as treatments for OCD. It is also helpful for counselors to be aware that cognitive methods appear especially useful for children who have what are sometimes called overvalued ideas—

obsessions that carry so much conviction that they are close to being delusions. Although a counselor or therapist may attempt to use an exposure–response–prevention approach with OCD children, they may not respond well to this behavior therapy if they firmly believe that their parents will die unless they constantly wash their hands. Under such conditions, cognitive therapy will help challenge such children's exaggerated sense of responsibility and fear of catastrophe.

Source: The Pediatric OCD Treatment Study Team. (2004). Cognitive-behavior therapy, sertraline, and their combination for children and adolescents with obsessive-compulsive disorder. *JAMA, 292,* 1969–1976.

SAMPLE INTERVENTIONS

Group Behavioral Treatment

Authors: Josepha A. Himle, Daniel J. Fischer, Michelle L. Van Etten, Amy S. Janeck, and Gregory L. Hanna

Précis: A noncontrolled clinical investigation on the use of group CBT for OCD with 19 adolescents aged 12 to 17 years showing both tic-related and non–tic-related symptoms.

Introduction

OCD has been found to co-occur with tic disorders, so much so that some authors (e.g., Leckman et al., 2000) believe that the presence of a tic is a meaningful distinction or subtype of OCD. When used as a distinguishing criterion, tics have been implicated in the differential effects of specific treatment approaches. For example, McDougle and colleagues (1994) found that individuals with tic-related OCD showed significant improvement with haloperidol added to fluvoxamine. However, similar studies have not been conducted to test the possible differential effect of psychotherapeutic models of treatment for tic related and non–tic-related OCD. The current study presents a noncontrolled clinical trial of group CBT for adolescents with either tic-related or non-tic-related OCD.

Intervention

The treatment consisted of 7 weekly, 90-minute group CBT sessions conducted over a 2-year period. For specific details of the group therapy format, the reader should see Fischer, Himle, and Hanna (1998). The groups were closed ended and included four to six patients. Treatment provided general education about the nature of OCD and CBT principles. The six educational topics presented were on the nature of OCD, the principles of behavioral therapy, the causes of OCD, family life and OCD, specialized techniques for making CBT more effective, and lifestyles and OCD. In addition to the educational component, group sessions focused on OCD symptoms, and not tics, using exposure and response prevention conducted in-session, as well as training in a cognitive framework for externalizing OCD as an enemy to battle.

The authors reported significant improvements for all subjects on the Yale-Brown Obsessive Compulsive Scale ratings of obsessions, compulsions, and total OCD symptoms.

Reflection

Although the school counselor may not be concerned with the differential diagnosis of OCD as tic-related and non-tic-related presentations or the differential treatment effect given these subtypes, what may be of use is the group approach to supporting and treating teens with OCD.

Some school counselors may find that running therapeutic groups for teens diagnosed with OCD is outside their job definition and professional training, and thus they should not attempt such an intervention. However, all counselors may offer assistance by providing psycho-education. This study demonstrates the effectiveness of providing adolescents with educational information as well as a supportive environment in which to experience exposure and response prevention and the use of cognitive reframing skills.

Two concerns about the empirical support provided by the study need to be highlighted. First, the lack of the use of a control group requires that the interpretation of an actual treatment effect needs to be done with caution. Second, and more practically, the study extended over a two-year period, which is not feasible for most school counselors. Counselors may want to consider using the same group approach but having more sessions (i.e., more than once a week) over a shorter time period (perhaps over one semester). If such modification is employed, it is important for counselors to monitor changes (good or bad) in student experience of obsessions and compulsions. As with all such interventions, counselors should not attempt to implement them unless they are sanctioned, trained, and supervised.

Source: Himle, J. A., Fischer, D. J., VanEtten, M. L., Janeck, A. S., & Hanna, G. L. (2003). Group behavioral therapy for adolescents with tic-related and non-tic-related obsessive-compulsive disorder. *Depression and Anxiety, 17,* 73–77.

DETAILED INTERVENTION

The Use of Exposure and CBT

Introduction

The study describes the use of exposure-based CBT for the treatment of childhood OCD. As noted by the authors, insight-oriented play therapy and family therapies have not been shown to be effective in treating OCD. Although there is strong support for the efficacy of exposure-based CBT, much of that research has been with adults.

The value of the current case study is that it highlights the need for adjusting traditional adult CBT approaches in order to address the developmental differences that exist. Specifically, the use of exposure can be made more difficult by the fact that children may have difficulty in describing specific obsessions or even recognizing the connection between the obsession and the rituals. Some approaches using CBT with children have incorporated rewards for compliance, increased family involvement, and age-appropriate metaphors to facilitate cognitive restructuring (e.g., Piacentini, 1999).

Results indicated that following 12 sessions the client showed a significant decrease in OCD symptoms as indicated by a score of 9 (subclinical) on the Children's Yale-Brown Obsessive Compulsive Scale (CY-BOCS). Further, the client was reported to be better able to concentrate in school and was completing homework within a normative time frame.

Method

The case study involved a 12-year-old, Asian American male who exhibited the following OCD symptoms: obsessions about germ-related contamination; fear of spreading such contaminants; ritualized hand wiping and washing; excessive seeking of reassurance from parents; disturbing sexual and violent images; and excessive checking of schoolwork and homework for errors and rereading until it felt "just right."

The client received a pretreatment score of 25 (moderate/severe) on the CY-BOCS. Academically, although a straight-A honors student, he was exhibiting difficulty concentrating in class and was spending excessive hours completing homework. His behaviors were occurring at such a level that they interfered with his extracurricular activities and his sleep.

Interventions

Based on his clinical presentation, exposure-based CBT was selected as the treatment of choice. Because of family involvement and concern, additional family intervention components were included in the treatment protocol.

The course of treatment was as follows:

- **Psycho-education**. The client and his family were provided with psycho-education regarding OCD. OCD was presented as a neurobehavioral disorder in order to reduce feelings of blame and conflict among family members and to help reduce the stigma and anger often associated with OCD. Specifically, OCD was presented as an attempt to adjust to anxiety, and anxiety was presented as a universal and adaptive phenomenon. The final part of the educational component presented the rationale for CBT treatment of OCD. Analogies were employed to convey key concepts to the client and his family. For example, habituation was explained by using the analogy of one's body adjusting to a cold swimming pool.
- **Ranking**. A complete symptom list was developed, and the symptoms were rank ordered using a scale of 1 (least distressing) to 10 (most distressing). The therapist created an OCD fear thermometer as a way of graphically displaying levels of distress. The therapist and client then selected an initial symptom with which to begin exposure therapy. The symptom selected (touching a trashcan without washing afterward) was chosen because it was relatively low on the distress scale (3) and was easy to re-create in session.
- **Cognitive restructuring**. The client was taught to distance himself by recognizing and relabeling his obsessive thoughts and feelings in a more realistic fashion. He used challenges such as "What are the chances that if I touch this door handle I will get sick?" and coping statements such as "My friends touch this door handle every day and they aren't sick."
- **Exposure-plus-response prevention**. The therapist typically modeled or shaped the trial for the client. Once the exposure started, the client was instructed to resist urges to ritualize in response to the stimulus in both treatment and nontreatment settings. During the presentation of the stimulus, the client would employ the fear thermometer to rate the experience. Exposure would continue until the fear thermometer rating returned to baseline or decreased to at least 50 percent of baseline.
- **Addressing obsessions**. The therapist asked the client to use a journal to describe his thoughts and images. As the therapist would read the journal entries, they would turn them into silly songs, reading them backwards, and change the images into something innocuous or humorous. In one example, the therapist had the client recite a frightening obsessional image to the tune of his favorite hip-hop song, thus removing the anxiety-provoking valence.

Reflection

Although the use of exposure-and-response prevention strategies to treat OCD is far from new or novel, what is significant about the current study is the modification of typical CBT procedures to make them more developmentally sensitive. Further, the treatment included a cognitive-restructuring component that provided the client with tools for continuing to address obsessive images and thoughts directly following the conclusion of the therapy. When including this element (i.e., cognitive restructuring), one must consider the developmental level of the client. Such restructuring may prove difficult to employ with very young or cognitively impaired youth.

The apparent utility of CBT, when employed with insight and sensitivity to the developmental needs of the client, along with the relatively brief length of treatment (i.e., 12 sessions), suggests that this approach provides the school counselor with an effective strategy for assisting those children exhibiting debilitating anxiety and ritualized behavior.

Source: Piacentini, J., & Langley, A. K. (2004). Cognitive-behavioral therapy for children who have obsessive-compulsive disorder. *Journal of Clinical Psychology, 60*(11), 1181–1194.

FROM THE FIELD

A quick search of the popular and professional literature will produce a large quantity of position statements, narratives, and general recommendations for parents, teachers, and counselors working with children with OCD. The recommendations listed in this section reflect suggestions from those who are working as counselors with children with OCD. They reflect only the singular, personal experience of the recommending counselor and thus need to be embraced and applied with caution.

Working with Teachers

- Avoid punishing the student for OCD-related behaviors.
- Be sensitive to child's experience of anxiety, but set limits and establish consequences for behaviors such as incomplete work, tardiness, etc.
- Highlight the child's areas of competency to boost self-esteem.
- When possible, use small group/cooperative instruction to foster peer relationships.
- Monitor all student teasing and establish a zero-tolerance policy for classroom teasing.
- Communicate with counselors, especially if behaviors seem to change or other behaviors begin to emerge.
- Reinforce the student for all small gains in controlling behaviors.
- Establish a signal that would allow the student to leave the room when feeling overwhelmed by the OCD.

Working with Students

- Use a classroom guidance unit to educate students about conditions such as OCD, AD/HD, asthma, epilepsy, etc.
- Encourage the student with OCD to develop short, easily understood responses to questions about his or her OCD that may be posed by peers.
- Be attentive to changes in a student's behavior that may result from taking medication.
- Become familiar with OCD medications and their side effects.
- Establish a process through which the student can seek "safety" in the counselor's office when overwhelmed by OCD symptoms.
- Help teachers appreciate the intensity of the OCD symptoms so that they can be more sensitive to the student's experience.
- Help the student develop strategies for dealing with negative social situations or confrontations.
- Encourage the student to participate in outside social activities (e.g., Boy Scouts, Girl Scouts, or other clubs) to promote the development of social skills and build self-esteem.

- Keep lines of communication open; be sure to discuss progress with families as frequently as possible. What may appear to be an inconsequential gain may actually be monumental for the child.
- Make notes and collect data that may demonstrate changes in behavior that may be occurring and use reinforcement for student's resistance to engage in compulsive behaviors.

REFERENCES

Allsopp, M., & Verduyn, C. (1988). A follow up of adolescents with obsessive compulsive disorder. *British Journal of Psychiatry, 154*, 829–834.

American Psychiatric Association. (2000). *Diagnostic and Statistical Manual* (4th ed., text revision). Washington, DC: Author.

Boyarsky, B. K., Petrone, L. A., Lee, N. C., & Goodman, W. K. (1991). Current treatment approaches to Obsessive Compulsive Disorder. *Archives of Psychiatric Nursing, 5*, 299–306.

Calvocoressi, L., Lewis, B., Harris, M., Trufan, S. J., et al. (1995). Family accommodation in obsessive-compulsive disorder. *American Journal of Psychiatry, 152*, 441–443.

Clarizio, H. E. (1991). Obsessive-compulsive disorder: The secretive syndrome. *Psychology in the Schools, 28*, 106–115.

Cooper, M. (1996). Obsessive-compulsive disorder: Effects on family members. *American Journal of Orthopsychiatry, 66*, 296–304.

Fischer, D. J., Himle, J. A., & Hanna, G. L. (1998). Group behavioral therapy for adolescents with obsessive-compulsive disorder: Preliminary outcomes. *Research on Social Work Practice, 8*, 629–636.

Franklin, M. E., & Foa, E. B. (2002). Cognitive behavioral treatments for obsessive compulsive disorder. In P. E. Nathan & J. M. Gorman (Eds.), *A guide to treatments that work* (2nd ed.) (pp. 367–410). New York: Oxford University Press.

Himle, J. A., Fischer, D. J., VanEtten, M. L., Janeck, A. S., & Hanna, G. L. (2003). Group behavioral therapy for adolescents with tic-related and non-tic-related obsessive-compulsive disorder. *Depression and Anxiety, 17*, 73–77.

Kearney, C. A., & Silverman, W. K. (1990). Treatment of an adolescent with obsessive-compulsive disorder by alternating response prevention and cognitive therapy: An empirical analysis. *Journal of Behavioral Therapy and Experimental Psychiatry, 21*, 39–47.

Leckman, J. F., McDougle, C. J., Pauls, D. L., Peterson, B. S., Grice, D. E., King, R. A., Scahill, L., Price, L. H., & Rasmussen, S. A. (2000). Tic-related versus non-tic-related obsessive-compulsive disorder. In W. K. Goodman, M. V. Rudorfer, & J. D. Maser (Eds.), *Obsessive–compulsive disorder: Contemporary issues in treatment* (pp. 23–42). Mahwah, NJ: Lawrence Erlbaum Associates, Inc., Publishers.

March, J., Frances, A., Carpenter, D., & Kahn, D. (1997). Expert consensus guidelines: Treatment of obsessional-compulsive disorder. *Journal of Clinical Psychology, 58*, 1.

McDougle, C. J., Goodman, W. K., Leckman, J. F., Lee, N. C., Heninger, G. R., Price, L. H. (1994). Haloperidol addition in fluvoxamine in obsessive-compulsive disorder: A double blind placebo-controlled study in patients with and without tics. *Journal of Clinical Psychopharmacology, 51*, 302–308.

Pediatric OCD Treatment Study Team. (2004). Cognitive-behavior therapy, sertraline, and their combination for children and adolescents with obsessive-compulsive disorder. *JAMA, 292*, 1969–1976.

Piacentini, J. (1999). Cognitive behavior therapy for child and adolescent OCD. *Child and Adolescent Clinics of North American, 8*, 599–618.

Piacentini, J., & Langley, A. K. (2004). Cognitive-behavioral therapy for children who have obsessive-compulsive disorder. *Journal of Clinical Psychology, 60*(11), 1181–1194.

Toro, J., Cervera, M., Osejo, E., & Salamero, M. (1992). Obsessive compulsive disorder in childhood and adolescence: A clinical study. *Journal of Child Psychology and Psychiatry and Allied Disciplines, 33*, 1025–1037.

Waters, T., Barrett, P., & March, J. (2001). Cognitive-behavioral family treatment of childhood obsessive-compulsive disorder: An open clinical trial. *American Journal of Psychotherapy, 55*, 372–387.

Wever, C., & Rey, J. (1997). Juvenile obsessive-compulsive disorder in children and adolescents. *Child Psychiatric Clinics of North America, 8*, 445–460.

Zohar, A. H. (1999). The epidemiology of obsessive-compulsive disorder in children and adolescents. *Child and Adolescent Psychiatric Clinics of North America, 8*, 445–460.

ADDITIONAL RESOURCES

INTERNET

www.ocfoundation.org/. The Obsessive Compulsive Foundation Web site includes links for the definition of OCD, related disorders, and how OCD is treated. It also provides information and advice on medications for children and adults suffering from OCD. A mental health referral list and support group is also available on this site.

http://www.ocdaction.org.uk/youngpeople.htm. The OCD Action Web site includes information on OCD, its causes, how to help someone with OCD, treatment, advice for parents, and self-help and support groups.

www.livingwithocd.co.uk/index1.htm. This site provides information on the types of OCD, the symptoms and feelings involved in the disorder, who gets OCD, and how to beat it. It also offers an opportunity to share and read about others suffering from the disorder.

PRINTED MATERIALS

Baer, L. (2000). *Getting control: Overcoming your obsessions and compulsions (rev. ed.).* New York: Plume/Penguin Books.

March, J. S., & Mulle, K. (1998). *OCD in children and adolescents: A cognitive-behavioral treatment manual.* New York: Guilford.

Reinecke, M. A., Dattilio, F. M., & Freeman, A. (2003). *Cognitive therapy with children and adolescents: A casebook for clinical practice* (2nd ed.). New York: Guilford.

CHAPTER 15

IMPROVING AND MAINTAINING SELF-ESTEEM

For most school counselors, it is painfully obvious that a student's self-esteem is correlated with academic performance, peer relationships, and general emotional well-being. Fostering and maintaining self-esteem in students is often the target for counselor intervention and prevention programs, particularly those counselors working with at-risk populations.

Self-esteem is a global evaluation or judgment of one's self-worth. A high self-esteem indicates a personal sense of self-respect and self-worth, whereas a low self-esteem implies self-dissatisfaction, self-rejection, and even self-contempt (Rosenberg, 1979). Self-esteem has been described as a judgment based on the discrepancy that one perceives between who they are and who they would like to be (Harter, 1990). Because self-esteem involves a comparison of what one is to what one perceives to be the standards of what he or she "should be," any change in standards without a concomitant change in the child's ability to meet that standard can result in a drop in self-esteem. Place this within the context of the rapid changes and expectations that occur around puberty, and one can understand the reason for the drop noted in adolescent self-esteem (e.g., Eccles, Lord, & Midgley, 1991).

Although the topic of self-esteem has become a media favorite, and often the overdone concern of those in education, research does suggest that self-esteem is an important correlate to academic achievement (see Bankston & Zhou, 2002; Lockett & Harrell, 2003; Schmidt & Padilla, 2003). Self-esteem has been systematically linked to many at-risk behaviors (Rosenberg, Schooler, & Schoenback, 1989); emotional problems, including anxiety and depression (Hammond & Romney, 1995; Weiten & Lloyd, 1994); and suicide attempts (Overholser, Adams, Lehnert, & Brinkman, 1995). As such, measures that can be taken to enhance positive self-esteem in students and provide them with the skills and competencies needed to maintain their own feelings of self-worth are important parts of a school counselors' armament.

OVERVIEW

The interventions presented (Table 15.1) focus on the promotion of trusting social relationships, the development of personal competencies, and the utilization of positive cognitive processes. They attempt to affect positive changes in student self-esteem by targeting two major contributors to self-esteem: (1) the student's cognitive processes and (2) the expectations and behaviors of parents, teachers, and peers who stand as "standard setters."

TABLE 15.1 Overview of Studies Presented

TARGET PROBLEM	REFERENCE	K–6	6–9	9–12	OTHER SPECIFICATIONS
Cognitive and self-esteem training	Barrett, Hayley, & Wallis (1999)	N	N	Y	Random pretest, posttest design
Low self-esteem, feelings of inferiority	Wells, Miller, Tobacyk, & Clanton (2002)	N	N	Y	Pretest, posttest, single group design
Guided emotive imagery for self-esteem	Omizo, Omizo, & Kitaoka (1998)	Y	Y	N	Randomized control group design
Adlerian adventure-based counseling for self-esteem	Wick, Wick, & Peterson (1997)	Y	N	N	Pretest, posttest, single group design

SAMPLE INTERVENTIONS

Psychosocial Prevention Program

Authors: Paula M. Barrett, Hayley M. Webster, and Jeffrey R. Wallis

Précis: Assessed the effect of a school-based psychosocial prevention program for adolescents focusing on self-esteem, negative cognitive processes, and peer isolation.

Introduction

Previous research (Christopher, Nangle, & Hansen, 1993; Oglivy, 1994) has pointed to the importance of social interactions for current and future psychological well-being and functioning. Further, research has demonstrated that the willingness to engage socially requires more than social skills. Teens need to believe in their social competence and acceptability; that is, they need to have a positive self-esteem in terms of social relationships if they are to engage in positive social interactions.

The current study investigated the effect of social cognitive training as a means of improving adolescent self-esteem, self-related perceptions and cognitions, and peer relationships. The authors noted significant improvement in the self-esteem and self-statements of those participants in the social cognition training group when compared to the control groups.

Intervention

A pretest, posttest control group design using multiple outcome measures was used to test the impact of a school-based psychosocial prevention program for adolescents. The study included 51 tenth-grade students who were randomly assigned to one of three groups: the Social Cognitive Training (SCT) group, the Attention Placebo Comparison (APC) group, or the Wait-list (WL) control group.

All of the students completed pretest and posttest measures assessing self-esteem, self-related cognitions, perceptions, and perceived peer relationships. Those receiving training were engaged in a four-session social cognitive training experience. The training program focused on developing the students' knowledge and skills relevant to the issues of self-esteem, self-talk, and modification of negative thinking and the use of positive thinking, communication, problem solving, and perception. The group employed direct instruction, coaching, modeling, rehearsal, peer feedback, and reinforcement. In addition, participants completed weekly homework assignments relevant to the topic.

Reflection

The study provides support for the value of group social cognitive training in improving adolescent self-esteem. Additionally, post-session questioning of the participants revealed that the students rated the social cognitive program as useful and relevant to their lives. The perception of program relevance should help to reduce dropout rates, which is often a problem for any school counselor attempting to run a voluntary counseling group program. Further, the relatively brief duration of treatment (four sessions) and the possibility of delivering the intervention in a group format make this intervention attractive to the school counselor faced with a tight schedule and a large caseload.

Source: Barrett, P. M., Hayley, W. M., & Wallis, J. R. (1999). Adolescent self-esteem and cognitive skills training: A school-based intervention. *Journal of Child and Family Studies, 8*(2), 217–227.

SAMPLE INTERVENTIONS

Psycho-educational Approach

Authors: Don Wells, Mark Miller, Jerome Toabcyk, and Robert Clinton

Précis: An eight-week psycho-educational program designed to change self-concepts, self-esteem, and dropout rates of 80 high-risk adolescents was investigated.

Introduction

Research on high school dropouts indicates that multiple factors contribute to a teen's decision to drop out. For some, the decision is facilitated by the fact that they have lost all confidence in their ability to succeed in school (Nunn & Parish, 1992) and have developed feelings of inferiority (Cairns, Cairns, & Neckerman, 1989). This study describes a program targeting issues of feelings of inferiority and low self-esteem in at-risk adolescents in an attempt to reduce dropout rates. Results indicated significant reductions in dropout rates and increased self-esteem among participants.

Intervention

In an intensive eight-week summer program, 80 students who had been identified by their school counselors as being at high risk for dropping out were enrolled in a total-immersion curriculum at a local college. The program included four hours of academic instruction and four hours of vocational instruction. Each evening the students received one to four hours of individual and group counseling, performed by counseling psychology graduate students. Analysis of pretest and posttest results on the Coopersmith Self-Esteem Inventory School Form (1986) revealed a statistically significant difference in pretest and posttest self-esteem scores. A follow-up study of participants' school-retention rates revealed that the first year after intervention the dropout rate was zero, and the second year the dropout rate of participants was 6 percent. For a control group of similar individuals not receiving intervention, the dropout rate was 21.2 percent for the same time period.

Reflection

Previous research has supported the theory that there is a correlation between self-concept, self-esteem, and achievement in school. Successful students have a greater sense of personal worth and feel somewhat better about themselves (Garzarelli, Everhart, & Lester, 1993; Liu, Kaplan, & Risser, 1992). Additional research (e.g., Chiu, 1990; Munson, 1992) has noted that adolescents who have identified career goals for themselves have higher self-esteem than those lacking career goals. It appears that the current intervention supports these notions by demonstrating that academic and career counseling contribute to the increased self-esteem of this particular sample.

The results need to be viewed with caution given the failure to control for such possible influences of increased peer acceptance (at least among the 80 participants), changed expectations of family and teachers, and so on. Further, the "intensity" of the treatment would most likely make it difficult for most school counselors to employ. However, the importance of vocational direction, academic support, and peer-group acceptance cannot be underestimated in helping at-risk students increase their self-esteem and positive self-concepts.

Source: Wells, D., Miller, M., Tobacyk, J., & Clanton, R. (2002). Using a Psycho-educational approach to increase the self-esteem of adolescents at high risk for dropping out. *Adolescence, 37*(146), 431–434.

SAMPLE INTERVENTIONS

Guided Imagery

Authors: Michael M. Omizo, Sharon A. Omizo, and Sean K. Kitaoka

Précis: Investigates the efficacy of guided affective and cognitive imagery in enhancing self-esteem.

Introduction

The current study focused on the self-esteem of Hawaiian children. The authors noted that Hawaiians, like other minority cultures, often experience an array of social, economic, educational, and political disadvantages. Further, they experience conflicts with the dominant cultural values system, and as a result often feel inadequate and helpless within that culture.

According to these authors, such problems may be exacerbated by the fact that the U.S. system of education gives an inherent advantage, although unintentionally, to mainstream American children. As a result, Hawaiian children are often unsuccessful in the mainstream educational system. These factors contribute to the development of low self-esteem and adjustment problems among these children. The authors attempted to use guided affective and cognitive imagery to assist and improve Hawaiian children's self-esteem.

Intervention

Sixty children from the fourth, fifth, and sixth grades of one elementary school were randomly selected and assigned to treatment or control groups. Pretest and posttest measurements of self-esteem were employed as the dependent measure. Results indicated significant improvement in the general self-esteem and academic/school-related self-esteem scores for the treatment group.

The intervention consisted of 10 weekly guided affective and cognitive imagery sessions. Each session lasted approximately 45 minutes. The goals of the sessions were to (1) use a script or provide directions that would invoke images to reinforce for the children; (2) provide opportunities to increase students' awareness of self and others; (3) develop life skills, such as problem solving, coping, and stress management; and (4) enhance self-esteem. Guided affective imagery was used to help each child develop an awareness and acceptance of his or her own strengths and areas for improvement. Guided cognitive imagery was used to develop skills and accelerate mastery of cognitive material. The activities involved as many senses as possible (touch, smell, taste, hearing) as well as the children's feelings. The following is a brief description of the 10 sessions:

- **Session 1: Introduction and Rules of the Group**. In addition to establishing group rules, the first exercise involved creating an image of students' positive characteristics and writing these three traits around their names. They were then asked to close their eyes and imagine (a) someone special who loves them, (b) something that they have accomplished that they are proud of, (c) something that they like to do when they have free time, and (d) a place that they like to visit. These were all shared with the group.

- **Session 2: Trip to the Beach**. The children imagined going to their favorite beach—the feelings, sights, sounds, etc. The children shared their images.
- **Session 3: Floating on a Cloud**. The children imagined floating on a safe, comfortable cloud.
- **Session 4: I Am Special**. The children imagined a person who loves them and shared the reasons.
- **Session 5: Relaxation Training**. The children were taught progressive muscle relaxation.
- **Session 6: My Family**. Children were asked to imagine their roles in their family and describe why that is an important role.
- **Session 7: Sculpture and Self-Affirmation**. Using modeling clay, the children were asked to make a sculpture while imagining past experiences that made them feel good or strong. After sharing their creations, they closed their eyes and imagined self-affirmations such as "I am a capable person," "I am smart and can do well in school," and so on.
- **Session 8: Self-Defeating Behaviors**. After discussing the nature of self-defeating behaviors, the children identified one of their own behaviors that they wanted to discontinue. They then imagined doing the self-defeating behavior, paying the price for the behavior, and choosing not to do the behavior.
- **Session 9: Problem Solving**. The children were taught problem solving and then imaged using each step.
- **Session 10: Summary, Sharing, and Closure**.

Reflection

Guided imagery is a strategy of focused concentration where visual images of sights, sounds, music, and words are used to create feelings of empowerment and relaxation. The ability to engage in healing imagery has been shown to support both physiologic and psychologic wellness (Dreher, 1998). Teachers have also used guided imagery to increase artistic expression, personal awareness, and concentration in students (Witmer & Young, 1987). Guided imagery has been used to help students to stay on task and manage their classroom behaviors (Matthews, 1986).

Given the history and use of guided imagery, it is not unusual to see it as a tool within a school counselor's repertoire of intervention strategies. The current study expands the possible use of this technique by school counselors. However, a number of caveats need to be considered before wholeheartedly employing this technique. The results may not be generalizable to other children, specifically non-Hawaiian children. Further, the very nature of the group interaction and sharing, along with the attention and support received from the counselor, may have contributed to the positive outcome beyond the effect of imagery. Thus, caution and careful monitoring need to guide the school counselor's use of this technique as a strategy for addressing the issue of low self-esteem.

Source: Omizo, M. M., Omizo, S. A., & Kitaoka, S. K. (1998). Guided affective and cognitive imagery to enhance self-esteem among Hawaiian children. *Journal of Multicultural Counseling and Development, 26*(1), 52–60.

DETAILED INTERVENTION

Adlerian Adventure-based Counseling

Introduction

A person's self-esteem is clearly affected by both self-evaluation of competence and feedback from those who are personally significant. One approach to increasing adolescents' self-esteem targets competence and group support and acceptance. Adventure-based counseling, a nontraditional approach to counseling, takes the teen away from the familiar and adds the challenge of taking risk and testing limits. The goal of adventure-based counseling is to develop positive self-esteem through trust building, goal setting, and problem solving.

The current study investigated the efficacy of an Adlerian-based adventure therapy to improve self-esteem and increase social competence. The results of this pretesting and posttesting using the Piers-Harris Children's Self-Concept Scale revealed significant improvement in self-esteem scores following the six intervention sessions. In addition to their statistical significance, reports from teachers suggested the students were mediating their own problems and reporting that they had more friends than before the intervention.

Method

The study involved 42 fifth grade students from an urban elementary school. The students were primarily of lower socioeconomic status. The students participated in 6 weeks of adventure-based sessions lasting 30 minutes each. The students participated in the tasks in small groups of approximately 10. New groups were created at random each week to avoid the formation of cliques. The posttest on the Piers-Harris Children's Self-Concept test occurred following the final treatment session.

Interventions

The intervention involved two phases. The participants engaged in an adventure activity and then processed the experience. The specific tasks were selected to blend an unfamiliar environment with a difficult, noncompetitive task that required cooperative group effort. The goals for the task became increasingly difficult, yet remained achievable. This required the counselor to adapt the goals to the skills of each group.

The activities included:

1. **Brick and boards across the Lava**. The counselor randomly places boards and bricks. Students are asked to build a bridge that they can walk across without touching the ground from the start to stop points. Increasing the distance or eliminating boards increases the difficulty of the task.

2. **Brick and Board Walk Carrying Basketball**. With boards, blocks, and bricks randomly placed on the ground, students are asked to build a bridge using all components. Students are then asked to pick up and carry basketballs without using their hands. They are to then carry the basketballs and walk on the boards that have been laid across the blocks.
3. **Basketball Carrying with Plastic Pipe**. Basketballs and PVC pipe pieces are placed on the floor, and students are asked to work in a group and carry a basketball from start to stop using only the end of the pipe. Different numbers of individuals are asked to carry the balls, and the group decides the optimum number per ball.
4. **Basketball Passing with Towels**. Students are asked to stand in two lines facing each other. Each pair holds on to one end of a towel. The counselor indicates a stop point that is beyond the end of the line of students. The first pair tosses the basketball to the pair next to them. The first pair then runs to the end of the line. The second pair repeats this process. The basketball is passed from one pair to another as the line moves toward the stop point. Once the ball reaches the stop point, the distance and the number of basketballs is increased.
5. **Trust Fall**. Students are asked to fall back and "trust" that the group will catch them. Doing this one student at a time, the group catches each student.
6. **Tent Construction**. The group is provided the components of a tent. They are asked to work together to assemble it. When completed, the group enters the tent. The group also deconstructs the tent and places it in its carrying bag.

Following each task, the counselor would use the task as a metaphor for real-life experiences, such as trust or inappropriate gender biases. This discussion was followed up later in that day or the next day in a second 15-to 30-minute discussion about the experience of the task.

Reflection

Adventure-based counseling has become popular over the course of the past 30 years. Although many adventure-based programs take place outdoors, that need not be a requirement. What is needed, however, is a break from the familiar and an element of risk and challenge (Priest, 1990).

Because the dynamics of an adventure-based group parallels those of traditional counseling groups, they can be incorporated within the repertoire of a school counselor's activities. The focus on challenge, risk, group support, noncompetiveness, and success-oriented activities allows for the counselor to be creative in designing the program. For example, although physical activities such as those employed in this study can be used, other activities, such as creating group murals, community projects, or even dances, can also be used. Further, the processing of the experience allows the counselor to not only focus on the here and now of the event, but also to lead the students to discuss their feelings and how they are the same or different from those experienced in the recess yard or at home.

The major limitations to the current study was the lack of a control group and any measure of long-term impact. However, other outcome- and process-oriented research (e.g., Cason & Gillis, 1994; Welch & Steffan, 1993; Hastie, 1992; Davis-Berman, & Berman, 1994) has demonstrated the effectiveness of adventure programming.

Source: Wick, D. T., Wick, J. K., & Peterson, N. (1997). Improving self-esteem with Adlerian adventure therapy. *Professional School Counseling, 1*(1), 53–56.

FROM THE FIELD

The following are interventions employed by counselors in the field. As noted, some are to be employed by the counselor, whereas others can be implemented by the teacher within a classroom. These later suggestions may be useful for the school counselor operating from a consultation mode. Each of these suggestions have been reported, anecdotally, by a counselor in the field but have not been empirically tested for effectiveness; as such, they should be used with caution and their impact closely monitored.

Working with Students

- Teach students to develop positive self-talk.
- Help students develop confidence and competence in school work.
- Connect the student with supportive peer(s) by enrolling the student in a school activity, club, or project.
- Have students keep a list of things they did well each day in an affirmation journal and have them review the journal affirming their own contribution and value.
- Assist students in preparing to participate in class. Review materials, role-play questions and answers, and identify one specific question a student can ask or answer in an upcoming class.
- Use group counseling formats to help students recognize that they are not the only ones with feelings of insecurity and experiences of failure. Group cohesion provides evidence of acceptability and increases esteem.
- Assist students in developing the skills and attitudes necessary to express their own needs while respecting the rights of others.
- Help students develop appropriate social skills, including eye contact, voice volume, posture, and so on.
- Practice "faking it until you make it." Have the student identify a role model and act as if he or she were that model.
- Have students read *My Best Friend Is Me* (available from Childswork/Childsplay, LLC) and have them share a list of their good qualities.
- Help students identify personal self-evaluations and check evidence and correct negative beliefs.
- Help students to articulate realistic academic, vocational, and social goals. Develop a monitoring plan so that students can see evidence of progress toward their goals.
- Develop a list of 5 to 10 positive affirmations about the student and have him or her read them daily.

Working with Teachers

- Help students focus on doing their personal best rather than competing with one another. Focusing on growth and improvement will facilitate positive self-statements and esteem.

- When providing negative feedback be sure to separate the person from their behavior and provide specific instruction on steps to take to improve.
- Reinforce both improvement in performance and any signs of positive self-statements.
- ILAC: I am loveable and capable. Have the students practice this self-affirmation.
- Help students identify tasks and skills (one each) that they have and that are valuable in class (e.g., listening, responding, remembering, taking turns, etc.). Praise the children, noting their use of these specific skills.
- Have students in the class practice positive affirmation of other students in the class (e.g., "I think Laura did really well at the board today," "I like the way John takes turns with the microscope," etc.).
- Provide the student with a classroom duty (e.g., hand out or collect papers, record milk orders, feed the classroom pet, etc.) and verbally praise the student for competence.

REFERENCES

Bankston, C. L. III., & Zhou, M. (2002). Being well vs. doing well: Self-esteem and school performance among immigrant and nonimmigrant racial and ethnic groups. *International Migration Review, 36*(2), 389–415.

Barrett, P. M., Hayley, W. M., & Wallis, J. R. (1999). Adolescent self-esteem and cognitive skills training: A school-based intervention. *Journal of Child and Family Studies, 8*(2), 217–227.

Cairns, R. B., Cairns, B. D., & Neckerman, H. J. (1989). Early school dropout: Configuration and determinants. *Child Development, 60*, 1436–1452.

Cason, D., & Gillis, H. L. (1994). A meta-analysis of outdoor adventure programming with adolescents. *Journal of Experiential Education, 17*, 40–47.

Chiu, I. (1990). The relationship of career goals and self-esteem among adolescents. *Adolescence, 25*, 593–597.

Christopher, J. S., Nangle, D. W., & Hansen, J. (1993). Social skills interventions with adolescents—current issues and procedures. *Behaviour Modification, 17*, 314–338.

Coopersmith, S. (1986). *Self-esteem inventory*. Palo Alto, CA: Consulting Psychologist Press.

Davis-Berman, J., & Berman, D. S. (1994). Research update: Two-year follow-up report for the Wilderness Therapy Program. *Journal of Experiential Education, 17*, 48–50.

Dreher, H. (1998). Mind-body interventions for surgery: Evidence and exigency. *The Journal of the Institute for the Advancement of Health, 14*(3), 207–222.

Eccles, J. S., Lord, S., & Midgley, C. (1991). What are we doing to early adolescents? The impact of educational contexts on early adolescents. *American Journal of Education, 99*, 521–539.

Garzelli, P., Everhart, B., & Lester, D. (1993). Self-concept and academic performance in gifted and academically weak students. *Adolescence, 28*, 235–237.

Hammond, W. A., & Romney, D. M. (1995). Cognitive factors contributing to adolescent depression. *Journal of Youth and Adolescence, 24*, 667–683.

Harter, S. (1990). Processes underlying adolescent self-concept formation. In R. Monte-Mayor, G. R. Adams, & T. P. Gullota (Eds.), *From childhood to adolescence: A Transitional period?* (pp. 205–239). Newbury Park, CA: Sage.

Hastie, P. A. (1992). Secondary school students' enjoyment of outdoor adventure experience. *Journal of Experiential Education, 15,* 43–47.

Liu, X., Kaplan, H. B., & Risser, W. (1992). Decomposing the reciprocal relationships between academic achievement and general self-esteem. *Youth and Society, 24,* 123–148.

Matthews, D. B. (1986). Discipline: Can it be improved with relaxation training? *Elementary School Guidance & Counseling, 20,* 194–200.

Munson, W. W. (1992). Self-esteem, vocational identity and career salience in high school students. *The Career Development Quarterly, 40,* 361–368.

Nunn, G. D., & Parish, T. S. (1992). The psychosocial characteristics of at-risk high school students. *Adolescence, 27,* 435–440.

Oglivy, C. M. (1994). Social skills training with children and adolescents: A review of the evidence on effectiveness. *Educational Psychology, 14,* 73–83.

Omizo, M. M., Omizo, S. A., & Kitaoka, S. K. (1998). Guided affective and cognitive imagery to enhance self-esteem among Hawaiian children. *Journal of Multicultural Counseling and Development, 26*(1), 52–60.

Overholser, J. C., Adams, D. M., Lehnert, K. L., & Brinkman, D. C. (1995). Self-esteem deficits and suicidal tendencies among adolescents. *Journal of the American Academy of Child and Adolescent Psychiatry, 34,* 919–928.

Priest, S. (1990). The semantics of adventure education. In J. C. Miles & S. Priest (Eds.), *Adventure education* (pp. 113–117). State College, PA: Venture.

Rosenberg, M. (1979). *Conceive the self.* New York: Basic.

Rosenberg, M., Schooler, C., & Schoenbach, C. (1989). Self-esteem and adolescent problems: Modeling reciprocal effects. *American Sociological Review, 54,* 1004–1018.

Schmidt, J. A., & Padilla, B. (2003). Self-esteem and family challenge: An investigation of their effects on achievement. *Journal of Youth & Adolescence, 32*(1), 37–47.

Weiten, W., & Lloyd, M. A. (1994). *Psychology applied to modern life: Adjustment in the 90's* (4th ed.). Pacific Grove, CA: Brooks/Cole.

Welch, J. D., & Steffan, J. P. (1993). Stages of adjustment to an adventure-based program. *Journal of Humanistic Education and Development, 31,* 116–123.

Wells, D., Miller, M., Tobacyk, J., & Clanton, R. (2002). Using a psycho-educational approach to increase the self-esteem of adolescents at high risk for dropping out. *Adolescence, 37*(146), 431–434.

Wick, D. T., Wick, J. K., & Peterson, N. (1997). Improving self-esteem with Adlerian adventure therapy. *Professional School Counseling, 1*(1), 53–56.

Witmer, J. M., & Young, M. E. (1987). Imagery in counseling. *Elementary School Guidance & Counseling, 22,* 5–15.

ADDITIONAL RESOURCES

INTERNET

www.childdevelopmentinfo.com/parenting/self_esteem.shtml. A Web site for helping your child develop self-esteem. Includes "words of encouragement" for parents and audiotapes and videotapes for children's self-image and successful teens.

www.kidsource.com/kidsource/content2/strengthen_children_self.html. The Kidsource Online Web site includes information on self-esteem and how we can help children develop a healthy sense of self-esteem.

www.more-selfesteem.com/low_self_esteem.htm. Low self-esteem can be cured! Defines self-esteem and discusses children and self-esteem, body image, self-image, and exercise and esteem. The site also features a self-esteem test and a self-help section on self-talk, self-discipline, and other self-help resources.

PRINTED MATERIALS

Herod, L. (1999). *Discovering me: A guide to teaching health and building adolescents' self-esteem.* Boston: Allyn and Bacon.

Page, R. M., & Page, T. S. (2003). *Fostering emotional well-being in the classroom.* Sudbury, MA: Jones and Bartlett Publishers.

Mruk, C. J. (1999). *Self-esteem: Research, theory, and practice.* New York: Springer.

CHAPTER 16

DEPRESSION

It may be too easy to dismiss a child or adolescent's sadness, irritability, and moodiness as simply a characteristic of his or her development. It is also true that for some, the experience of sadness or dysphoria, social withdrawal, decreased academic performance, increased anxiety, and somatic complaints may signal child or adolescent depression. Differentiating the developmental "downs" from clinical depression is not always easy, and understanding the nature and presentation of childhood and adolescent depression is challenging. At present, separate diagnostic categories for mood disorders in children or adolescents are not found in the DSM-IV. The symptoms required to be diagnosed with a major depressive episode are the same for children, adolescents, and adults—with one variation. Table 16.1 lists the diagnostic symptoms listed in the DSM-IV for a major depressive episode. For a person to be diagnosed, he or she must exhibit: (1) five or more of the symptoms listed, (2) one of the symptoms must be either depressed (or irritable) mood or loss of pleasure, and (3) the symptoms must be present for at least two weeks.

TABLE 16.1 Symptoms of Major Depressive Disorder Common to Adults, Children, and Adolescents

- Persistent sad or irritable mood
- Loss of interest in activities once enjoyed
- Significant change in appetite or body weight
- Difficulty sleeping or oversleeping
- Psychomotor agitation or retardation
- Loss of energy
- Feelings of worthlessness or inappropriate guilt
- Difficulty concentrating
- Recurrent thoughts of death or suicide

Five or more of these symptoms must persist for two or more weeks before a diagnosis of major depression is indicated.

With children and adolescents, the exception is that an irritable mood can be substituted for a depressed mood. Table 16.2 provides a list of signs that may be associated with depression in children and adolescents.

Because of the various ways depression has been defined, estimates as to its prevalence vary widely. According to Lewinsohn, Rohde, and Seeley (1998), major depressive disorder is the most prevalent affective disorder among children and adolescents. The onset of major depressive disorders (MDD) is most often between the ages of 13 and 19 (Birmaher, Ryan, & Williamson, 1996). Recent reports (see Kessler, Avenevoli, & Merikangas, 2001) suggest that major depression among our youth is on the rise. Current epidemiological studies indicate that up to 2.5 percent of children and up to 8.3 percent of adolescents in the United States suffer from depression (Birmaher et al., 1996). These findings take on additional significance in light of research indicating that depression may have more extreme consequences for adolescents than for adults (Schraedley, Gotlib, & Hayward, 1999).

Research into the causes or factors influencing the development of depression has targeted biological factors as well as social-psychological factors. Although research on the involvement of biological factors (i.e., genetics and biochemistry) has focused primarily on adults, recently researchers have begun to target children and adolescents in their investigations (e.g., Rutter, Silberg, O'Connor, & Simonoff, 1999). Genetic influences are generally thought to contribute to depression in children and adolescents, although the supportive re-

TABLE 16.2 Signs That May Be Associated with Depression in Children and Adolescents

- Frequent vague, nonspecific physical complaints such as headaches, muscle aches, stomachaches, or tiredness
- Frequent absences from school or poor performance in school
- Talk of or efforts to run away from home
- Outbursts of shouting, complaining, unexplained irritability, or crying
- Being bored
- Lack of interest in playing with friends
- Alcohol or substance abuse
- Social isolation, poor communication
- Fear of death
- Extreme sensitivity to rejection or failure
- Increased irritability, anger, or hostility
- Reckless behavior
- Difficulty with relationships

search is less clear than that typically found with adults (Rice, Harold, & Thapar, 2002). One of the major difficulties when examining the biological correlates of depression in children and adolescents is the paucity of normative data on these functions. Similarly, when reviewing the information on psychological influences on child and adolescent depression it becomes clear that most of the theories are derived from research on depressed adults. Thus, theories explaining depression as a response to separation or loss, inadequate interpersonal skills, or faulty cognition are generally taken from work with adults and generalized to children and adolescents.

The specific application of these theories to the treatment of children and adolescents with depression has begun to receive some attention (Asarnow, Jaycox, & Tompson, 2001). However, many of the reported treatment approaches still reflect the generalization of findings from treatment efficacy with adult populations, and therefore need to be viewed with caution when applied to children and adolescents.

The literature on the treatment of childhood and adolescent depression is far less extensive than that concerning adults. Some evidence is now beginning to appear to support short-term counseling and psychotherapy, especially cognitive-behavioral therapy (e.g., Birmaher, Brent, & Benson, 1998; Reinecke, Ryan, & DuBois, 1998); the use of medication; and a combination of the two. Additionally, interpersonal therapy (IPT), which focuses on helping the person with disturbed personal relationships, has been found to lead to greater improvement in adolescents with depression than clinical contact alone (Mufson et al., 1999).

OVERVIEW

Students experiencing clinical depression need to be referred for assessment and treatment. As such *the primary role of the school counselor working with clinically depressed students will be that of referring the student to a support professional.* However, in some situations the counselor is in the unique position to serve both as an interventionist and as a preventionist. The child or adolescent presenting with subthreshold depression may seek out the help of the school counselor as the first line of assistance. The counselor confronted by these situations should find the treatment modalities presented within this chapter (Table 16.3) helpful. Further, as suggested by Rice and Meyer (1994), the school counselor may also be able to assist adolescents learn skills that will decrease their susceptibility to depression, and thus play an important prevention role.

TABLE 16.3 Overview of Studies Presented

TARGET PROBLEM	REFERENCE	K–6	6–9	9–12	OTHER SPECIFICATIONS
CBT for moderate depression	DeCuyper, Timbremont, Braet, DeBacker, & Wullaert (2004)	Y	Y	N	Randomized control group design, manual-based treatment
Psycho-educational prevention model	Rice & Meyer (1994)	N	Y	Y	Randomized control group design
Ecological model for treating depression	Abrams, Theberge, & Karan (2004)	Y	Y	Y	Case study format
CBT	Kahn & Kehle (1990)	Y	Y	N	Pretest and posttest control group design

SAMPLE INTERVENTIONS

Cognitive-Behavioral Treatment Program for Schoolchildren

Authors: Sandy DeCuyper, Benedikte Tibremont, Caroline Braet, Vicky De-Backer, and Tina Wullaert

Précis: This article demonstrates the effectiveness of an 18-session cognitive-behavioral treatment program for schoolchildren exhibiting moderate depressive symptoms.

Introduction

Research suggests the importance of attending to children exhibiting subthreshold levels of depressive symptomatology. The current study was designed to evaluate the efficacy of a cognitive behavioral program for children, ages 10 to 12, with subthreshold profiles. The participants were engaged in a program employing affective education, problem solving, cognitive restructuring, and engagement in enjoyable activities. Child self-reports and parent reports were used as outcome measures. At a four-month follow-up, significant improvement was noted from baseline when compared to a wait-list control group.

Intervention

The study employed a randomly assigned pretest, posttest group design in which 11 students were assigned to a treatment group and 11 to a wait-list control group. The participants were selected after being assessed as having subthreshold depressive profiles.

The cognitive-behavioral program "Taking Action" was used in this study. The manual was designed for use with children between the ages of 9 and 13 diagnosed with unipolar depressive disorder, dysthmia, or depressed mood. The treatment consisted of 16 weekly, 1-hour sessions.

In the first session, the children were helped to gain a better understanding of their emotional experiences and the connection between thoughts and feelings and behaviors. The remaining sessions focused on teaching the children problem-solving procedures. The participants were also taught self-monitoring strategies and techniques for altering negative thoughts.

The authors reported statistically significant improvement in symptoms (pre-post test) for the treatment group, as compared to the control, wait-listed subjects.

Reflection

The use of a manual-based treatment protocol over the course of 16 one-hour weekly sessions suggests that such an approach may be viable for use by a school counselor. It is important to note that the target for the intervention were students who presented as "at risk" and not students manifesting full-blown clinical depression. Again, this is an important consideration for school counselors, because with the latter group the role of the counselor should shift to that of referral agent.

Source: DeCuyper, S., Timbremont, B., Braet, C., DeBacker, V. & Wullaert, T. (2004). Treating depressive symptoms in schoolchildren. *European Child and Adolescent Psychiatry, 13*, 105–114.

SAMPLE INTERVENTIONS

Preventing Depression

Authors: Kenneth G. Rice and Aleta Meyer

Précis: A psycho-educational group intervention designed to facilitate transition to and through adolescence.

Introduction

The study examined a program designed to help adolescents learn skills that will decrease their susceptibility to depression during adolescence. The program was implemented in 3 schools and involved over 145 students. Although the work is a preliminary investigation, which focused on the process variables of the number of sessions attended, group cohesion, and the degree to which the program was implemented as intended, ratings from leader self-reports were relatively high for each school when assessing the effectiveness of the activity portion of each session.

Intervention

A total of 145 adolescents participated in this study. Slightly less than one-third of the students were categorized using a self-report measure of emotional well-being as being high risk for developing depression. Students were randomly assigned to program and control groups. The control group members participated in school group activities such as art classes, hunter safety classes, and so on.

The intervention employed a psycho-educational approach to teaching adaptive emotional, cognitive, and behavioral responses to stressors or challenges. Emphasis was placed on adaptive coping to chronic strains, stressful life events, developmental transitions, and hassles. The 16 small group sessions (lasting 40 minutes each) each targeted specific activities designed to actualize a session's topic through role-play, group problem solving, and cooperative and competitive games. As noted by the authors, ratings were relatively high across all sessions when assessing the effectiveness of the activity portion of each session.

Reflection

The utilization of a brief, small group, psycho-educational model of intervention makes this approach "culturally compatible" with most school settings. A major limitation to this pilot study is the absence of short- and long-term results indicating the effectiveness of the program, beyond the immediacy of each session, in enhancing coping skills and subsequently reducing the appearance of depressive symptomatology. As such, employment of this program should be done with caution and with an eye to collecting outcome data.

Assuming additional data supports the carryover effect of these sessions, one could see how the inclusion of a program such as this within the guidance curriculum could assist counselors in their efforts to impact large portions of the school population and in so doing serve as an agent of prevention.

Source: Rice, K. G., & Meyer, A. L. (1994). Preventing depression among young adolescents: Preliminary process results of a psycho-educational intervention program. *Journal of Counseling and Development, 73*, 145–152.

SAMPLE INTERVENTIONS

An Ecological Approach

Authors: Karen Abrams, Susan K. Theberge, and Orv C. Karan

Précis: A case study depicting ways a counselor can use an ecological framework for identifying sources of depression as well as areas for intervention.

Introduction

The authors report on an ecological model originally developed by Urie Bronfenbrener (Brofenbrener & Morris, 1998) that provides a systematic approach to identifying factors contributing to a student's depression. By incorporating factors inherent both within the student as well as within the school, family, and community in which that student operates, the model provides a contextual map for understanding the many different factors contributing to the student's depression as well as finding focus points for intervention strategies.

Intervention

The authors present a variety of case samples that illustrate how the ecological model directs interventions at an individual level or at a broader systemic level.

Focusing on the Individual

The focus here is on the student's physical, cognitive, and/or social-emotional functioning. For example:

- A high school junior presenting with limited energy and headaches found that his patterns of caffeine and sugar consumption contributed to the problem. (Physical focus)
- A fourth-grade student found that group relaxation exercises helped with anger and depression. (Physical focus)
- Middle school student provided assistance in developing learning strategies that helped reduce frustration and increase achievement, thus decreasing irritability and social withdrawal. (Focus on cognitive processing)
- High school senior employed cognitive/behavioral strategies to reframe a breakup with boyfriend. (Focus on cognitive processing)

Focus on Microsystems: Family, Peers, School, and Community

- Third-grade student employed solution-focused strategies to reduce the quizzing she received from her mother, following her visit to her divorced father's girlfriend's house. (Family)

- Elementary student participated in friendship group to develop effective social skills and increase peer interaction. (Peer)
- Linking students to community-based support services (e.g., Big Brother/Sister, Al-Anon, etc.). (Community)

Reflection

The case nature of the presentation fails to provide the empirical data needed to support the efficacy of this approach. However, with this as a major caveat, the description, rationale, and case illustration help to make the approach intuitively appealing, especially for use by the school counselor.

One value of the ecological approach is that it provides a framework for school counselors to begin to conceptualize both the nature of a student's problem (e.g., depression) as well as identify multiple targets for intervention. Although the school counselor cannot be a master of all, the ecological model widens the horizon of intervention and invites collaboration. One final potential value of such a framework is that it provides opportunities for the counselor to serve both as interventionist and preventionist. New-found opportunities are found by expanding the focus from simply working with the student to servicing the microsystem of family, peers, and community and impacting the macrosystem of cultural values, social conditions, and education.

Source: Abrams, K., Theberge, S. K., & Karan, O. C. (2004). Children and adolescents who are depressed: An ecological approach. *Professional School Counseling, 8*(3), 284–291.

DETAILED INTERVENTION

Cognitive-Behavioral Therapy, Relaxation, and Self-Monitoring

Author: James S. Kahn and Thomas J. Kehle

Précis: The efficacy of short-term cognitive-behavioral therapy, relaxation training, and self-modeling interventions for the treatment of depression among middle school students was investigated.

Introduction

Confronting early signs of depression for at-risk students is clearly preferable than waiting until the syndrome is clearly developed with full-blown symptomatology. The study presented here was one of the first to address the effectiveness of school-based interventions with depressed middle school students.

The authors attempted to replicate and extend the depression treatment literature to a group of early adolescent middle school students by using an adolescent version of the "Coping with Depression" (CWD) course (Clarke & Lewinsohn, 1984; Lewinsohn & Clarke, 1984), relaxation training, and a self-modeling approach as active interventions.

Results indicated that all treatment conditions, relative to the wait-list control, evidenced a significant decrease in depression and an increase in self-esteem. Parent-report data, as well as data from treated control subjects, provided further support for the potential effectiveness of the short-term structured school-based intervention.

Method

A pretest, posttest control group design with therapy group and/or therapist nested within the active treatment condition was employed. Sixty-eight moderate to severely "experimentally diagnosed" latency age and depressed early adolescent subjects (ages 10 to 14) were assigned randomly to one of three active treatments or the wait-list control. Experimental subjects participated in one of three short-term, intensive intervention programs for depression that served as the independent variable. Wait-list control subjects received no unique interventions for depression until follow-up posttesting was completed. Posttesting occurred at two different data points: immediately upon completion of the active intervention programs and again at one-month follow-up.

Intervention

All treatments were structured short-term, group, psycho-educational intervention programs employing structured therapist manuals as well as workbook materials and/or relevant handouts for subjects.

Cognitive-Behavioral Intervention

The current study employed a slightly modified cognitive-behavioral treatment program previously employed with adolescents [i.e., The CWD course (adolescent version), Clarke & Lewinsohn, 1984]. Students were instructed in specific skills and strategies (i.e., constructive thinking, self-reinforcement, pleasant events scheduling, and social skills) to cope with problems demonstrated to be related to depression. The program consisted of 15 two-hour sessions held twice weekly, with 1- and 6-month follow-up booster sessions.

Group sessions began with an introduction to the group and presentation of the rationale underlying the cognitive-behavioral treatment of depression. Materials (treatment folders and workbooks) were distributed, and instruction was presented in self-observation and monitoring of mood. Session 2 addressed such self-change skills as pinpointing problems, discovering antecedents and consequences, goal setting, and self-reinforcement. Sessions 3 and 4 addressed pleasant activities and depression and the formulation of a pleasant activities plan. Sessions 5 and 6 explored thinking and depression, positive and negative thoughts, and constructive thinking. Session 7 focused on communication skills. Sessions 8 and 9 promoted negotiation and problem-solving skills. Session 10 highlighted social skills and depression. Session 11 focused on the utilization of social skills. Session 12 explored maintaining and generalizing gains.

Relaxation Treatment

Students received information on progressive relaxation and generalization procedures. Assessment and home practice activities were provided. Activities were conducted identifying stress-related situations and symptoms. Sessions 6 through 11 focused on variations of basic relaxation training, including relaxation procedures for fewer muscle groups, relaxation through recall, relaxation by counting, the use of mental imagery in relaxation, breathing exercises, and generalization of relaxation skills across situations noted to produce tension.

Self-Modeling

Subjects participating in this treatment program received an explanation of intervention procedures and rationale. Target behaviors included appropriate eye contact, body posture, positive affect–related expression (smiling, gesturing, pleasant voice tone), and verbalizations of positive prosocial self-attributions regarding personal, family, school and social functioning, and pleasant events. Subsequent to videotaping the subjects' behaviors during the baseline phase, subjects were provided a rationale for the self-modeling procedure and were verbally instructed to behave in a manner that was incompatible with their typically depressed behavior (e.g., verbalizations and body posture). Subjects were then given opportunities for behavioral rehearsal of the "nondepressed" behaviors prior to final videotaping. The instruction and rehearsal were intended to reduce the amount of editing needed; however, it was still necessary to edit out instances of "depressed" behavior to produce a three-minute treatment videotape that portrayed each subject in a nondepressed manner. Treatment entailed 10- to 12-minute sessions with each subject, which were conducted twice weekly for 6 to 8 weeks. During treatment, subjects were instructed by the therapists to observe the three-minute tape of themselves behaving in a nondepressed manner. No therapist reinforcement of these behaviors was provided, as subjects were merely instructed to "watch the tape."

Reflection

This investigation demonstrated support for the efficacy of all three active interventions (cognitive-behavioral therapy, relaxation, and self-modeling) in the treatment of moderately and severely depressed early adolescents. Self-report and interview data reflected fairly substantial and significant gains for each of the treatments versus the wait-list control. The authors noted that analysis of one-month follow-up data suggested that subjects maintained these treatment gains.

It is important to note that the study supported the utility of a cognitive-behavioral treatment package for middle school students. The "group" and structured course format of this cognitive-behavioral treatment program may extend the viability of this intervention for use within a school setting.

Source: Kahn, J. S., & Kehle, T. J. (1990). Comparison of cognitive-behavioral, relaxation, and self-modeling interventions for depression among middle school students. *School Psychology Review, 19*(29), 196–211.

FROM THE FIELD

Although the primary role of the school counselor working with students experiencing depression is to refer and support, sometimes students present with less than clinical depression. Under these conditions, some counselors have suggested the following strategies that may prove helpful for the student. Again, these suggestions reflect the experience and anecdotal reporting of counselors engaged in school counseling and have not been tested using experimental design. As personal suggestions, they need to be employed with caution and their impact monitored.

Working with Students

- Set goals that are doable and achievable.
- Fake it until you make it . . . ! Tell students that they may not want to go out and be with friends, but that they should force themselves to do so.
- Engage in at least one pleasurable activity each day.
- Try some mild exercise or engage in a ball game.
- One should not make major life decisions, such as picking a school or deciding whether to go to college or not, when depressed. Tell students to just keep notes about the things they want to work on when they regain their energy.
- Try to force yourself to do the things you know are good for you (even if they don't immediately feel real good). Be sure to eat, rest (not too much or too little), and attack small pieces of your chores or your work.
- Try to hear your negative thinking and argue with it. Write your thoughts down and check for the evidence of their truth.
- When working with adolescents who are depressed, a critical therapeutic issue is the extent to which they experience a sense of belonging with peers.
- Helping young girls identify feelings they have about themselves in relation to current friendships, friendships they would like to have, and conflicts with peers should help clarify the extent to which connectedness to peers is affecting current problems and the sense of self.
- Journal writing that facilitates dialogue with the adolescents about their thought processes may be useful in helping them uncover connections between their thoughts and current depressive symptomatology.
- Teaching relaxation and coping skills and other cognitive-behavioral approaches may also be key in helping to ease anxieties and raise self-esteem.
- Teaching the adolescent how to interact assertively with peers may also help them become less vulnerable to being socially isolated.
- Modeling, teaching, and practicing social skills may be successful interpersonal techniques for counselors working with socially isolated youth who are depressed.
- Role-plays and homework assignments that help the adolescents transfer new social approaches to other environments should support the development of the skills and self-confidence they need to begin to form new connections with peers.

- Counselors can help adolescents identify and explore their fears and the possibilities of what will happen should those fears become reality.
- Counselors working with young girls who are depressed should remain cognizant of the strong hormonal fluctuations that occur at this age. Helping female adolescents compare their depressive symptomatology with biological changes may highlight the role of their hormones in intensifying symptoms of depression.

Working with Teachers and Parents

- Help them to accept that this is not just a case of being "moody" or having the "blahs." Teachers and parents should not accuse adolescents of faking depression.
- Be aware of the signs that a student is becoming depressed and seek referral for treatment:
  - A decline in the quality of schoolwork and grades
  - Persistent looks of boredom
  - Inability to engage with peers or to have fun
  - Talks about or writes about being sad
  - Withdraws from social interaction with peers
  - Changes in behavior and style (i.e., a previously outgoing student becomes withdrawn or a quiet, passive child becomes aggressive)
  - Lethargy
  - Difficulty concentrating (when previously that was not a problem)
  - Expressions of worthlessness or guilt
  - Morbid preoccupation with death and dying
  - Dramatic weight gain or loss
  - General change in demeanor (e.g., slower speech and movement; decreased personal care, such as with hair, clothing, etc.)
- Provide emotional support, be a listener. Reach out and engage the student in conversation.
- Invite the student to become actively engaged in nongraded class activities as a way of providing both social interaction and diversion.
- Assist the student in breaking tasks down into small components and attacking them one at a time.
- Invite the student to assist another student in an area in which they have a special talent or competence.

REFERENCES

Abrams, K., Theberge, S. K., & Karan, O. C. (2004). Children and adolescents who are depressed: An ecological approach. *Professional School Counseling, 8*(3), 284–291.

Asarnow, J. R., Jaycox, L. H., & Tompson, M. C. (2001). Depression in youth: Psychosocial interventions. *Journal of Clinical Child Psychology, 30*, 33–47.

Birmaher, B., Brent, D. A., Benson, R. S. (1998). Summary of the practice parameters for the assessment and treatment of children and adolescents with depressive disorders. American Academy of Child and Adolescent Psychiatry. *Journal of the American Academy of Child and Adolescent Psychiatry, 37*(11), 1234–1238.

Birmaher, B., Ryan, N. D., Williamson, D. E., et al. (1996). Childhood and adolescent depression: A review of the past 10 years. Part I. *Journal of the American Academy of Child and Adolescent Psychiatry, 35*(11), 1427–1439.

Bronfenbrener, U., & Morris, P. (1998). The ecology of developmental process. *The handbook of child psychology, 1*, 992–1029.

Clarke, G. N., & Lewinsohn, P. M. (1984). *The Coping with Depression course, adolescent version: A psycho-educational intervention for unipolar depression in high school students.* Eugene, OR: Peter M. Lewinsohn.

DeCuyper, S., Timbremont, B., Braet, C., DeBacker, V., & Wullaert, T. (2004). Treating depressive symptoms in schoolchildren. *European Child and Adolescent Psychiatry, 13*, 105–114.

Kahn, J. S., & Kehle, T. J. (1990). Comparison of cognitive-behavioral, relaxation, and self-modeling interventions for depression among middle school students. *School Psychology Review, 19*(29), 196–211.

Kessler, R. C., Avenevoli, S., & Merikangas, K. R. (2001). Mood disorders in children and adolescents: An epidemiological perspective. *Biological Psychiatry, 49*, 1002–1014.

Lewinsohn, P. M., & Clarke, G. N. (1984). *The Coping with Depression course, adolescent version: Instructor's manual for parent course.* Eugene, OR: Castalia Publishing Company.

Lewinsohn, P. M., Rohde, P., & Seeley, J. R. (1998). Major depressive disorder in older adolescents: Prevalence, risk factors, and clinical implications. *Clinical Psychology Review, 18*, 765–794.

Mufson, L., Weissman, M. M., Moreau, D., & Garfinkel, R. (1999). Efficacy of interpersonal psychotherapy for depressed adolescents. *Archives of General Psychiatry, 56*(6), 573–579.

Reinecke, M. A., Ryan, N. E., & DuBois, D. L. (1998). Cognitive behavioral therapy of depression and depressive symptoms during adolescence: A review and meta-analysis. *Journal of the American Academy of Child and Adolescent Psychiatry, 37*(1), 26–34.

Rice, K. G., & Meyer, A. L. (1994). Preventing depression among young adolescents: Preliminary process results of a psycho-educational intervention program. *Journal of Counseling and Development, 73*, 145–152.

Rice, F., Harold, G., & Thapar, A. (2002). The genetic aetiology of childhood depression: A review. *Journal of Child Psychology and Psychiatry, 43*, 65–79.

Rutter, M., Silberg, J., O'Connor, T., & Simonoff, E. (1999). Genetics and child psychiatry: II Empirical research findings. *Journal of Child Psychology and Psychiatry, 40*, 19–55.

Schraedley, P. K., Gotlib, I. H., & Hayward, C. (1999). Gender differences in correlates of depressive symptoms in adolescents. *Journal of Adolescent Health, 25*, 98–108.

ADDITIONAL RESOURCES

INTERNET

www.nimh.nih.gov/publicat/depression.cfm. National Institute of Mental Health (NIMH) Web site on depression.

www.about-teen-depression.com. Excellent site for information on symptoms and treatment options for teens who are depressed.

www.nmha.org/infoctr/factsheets/24.cfm. Depression facts and resource guide on the National Mental Health Association Web site.

PRINTED MATERIALS

Dudley, C. D. (1997). *Treating depressed children: A therapeutic manual of cognitive behavioral interventions.* Oakland, CA: New Harbinger Publications, Inc.

Koplewicz, H. S. (2002). *More than moody: Recognizing and treating adolescent depression.* New York: Putnam.

Merrell, K. W. (2001). *Helping students overcome depression and anxiety: A practical guide.* New York: Guilford Press.

Mondimore, F. M. (2002). *Adolescent depression: A guide for parents.* Baltimore: Johns Hopkins.

Weissman, M. (1999). Treatment of depression in the twenty-first century. Washington, DC: American Psychiatric Association Press.

CHAPTER 17

SUICIDAL IDEATION AND BEHAVIOR

Suicidal behavior includes not only completed suicide, but also suicide attempts and suicide ideation. Although suicide is relatively rare among youths under age 15 (300 suicide deaths for 10- to 14-year-olds in 2000), the rate has increased by 70 percent since 1981 (CDC, 2002). When the age group studied is expanded to 10- to 19-year-olds, suicide becomes the third-leading cause of death (CDC, 2000). According to the Centers for Disease Control, 1 out of every 5 high school students has reported seriously considering attempting suicide, and 1 in 13 have actually attempted suicide (CDC, 1998). More teenagers die from suicide than from cancer, heart disease, AIDS, birth defects, stroke, pneumonia and influenza, and chronic lung disease combined (U.S. Public Health Service, 1999). However, these statistics alone fail to show the full picture.

Suicide is a singular act with plural effects (Parsons, 1996). In addition to the potential for "copycat" suicides, family, loved ones, peers, teachers, and school personnel experience years of pain, anger, guilt, and self-doubt. Student suicide is a devastating problem, one requiring the attention and involvement of all school personnel, especially school counselors.

The school counselor is in an important position from which to serve a role as a preventionist. School counselors are able to identify at-risk students as well as consult with and educate faculty and school professionals on the facts of teen suicide. Counselors can provide teachers and other school professionals with essential information about early warning signs, effective interventions, and referral steps to undertake when confronted with a suicidal student (Popenhagen & Qualley, 1998). Further, as will be demonstrated in the studies to be reported, counselors can provide programs that assist students in recognizing the early signs of suicide and developing the skills to help their peers find available support services when necessary (McCarthy, Brack, & Lambert, 1996). Finally, the school counselor can provide school-based prevention programming targeted at reducing at-risk behaviors and attitudes and increasing protective factors.

It is important to note that research in the area of suicide intervention and prevention is limited in two general aspects. First, the studies typically lack controls and "experimental" rigor. Most of the work published is of a clinical/descriptive nature. Thus, questions of treatment effects and generalizability must be kept in the forefront. A second limitation to be considered when reviewing the interventions is that the programs cited are designed and used with adolescent populations. This author was unable to find specific interventions targeted at suicidal children. Therefore, although each of the programs provides models, directions, and some support for treatment, they all must be viewed as limited with the aforementioned caveats in mind.

OVERVIEW

As noted in Table 17.1, the studies to be reported targeted adolescent populations. As such, the findings should not be automatically generalized to middle school or elementary school populations.

TABLE 17.1 Overview of Studies Presented

TARGET PROBLEM	REFERENCE	K–6	6–9	9–12	OTHER SPECIFICATIONS
Suicide ideation and suicidal behavior, school-based prevention program	Eggert, Thompson, Herting, & Nicholas (1995)	N	N	Y	Prevention program administered by counselors, teachers, or school nurse
Suicide ideation and behavior, brief prevention protocols	Randell, Eggert, & Pike (2001)	N	N	Y	Single-session intervention process
Suicide ideation and behavior, "Successful Negotiation Acting Positively" (SNAP)	Rotheram-Borus, Piacentini, Cantwell, Belin, & Song (2000)	N	N	Y	Focused on adolescent females
Suicide ideation and behavior, the "Signs of Suicide" (SOS) program	Aseltine & DeMartino (2004)	N	N	T	Large sample involving five high schools

SAMPLE INTERVENTIONS

Reducing Suicide Potential—A School-based Prevention Program

Authors: Leona L. Eggert, Elaine A. Thompson, Jerald R. Herting, and Liela J. Nicholas

Précis: Tested the efficacy of a school-based prevention program for reducing suicide potential among high-risk youth.

Introduction

Although much has been known about factors increasing suicide risk among teens, the application of this knowledge to the development of prevention programming has been lacking. Schoolwide prevention programs tested throughout the 1980s and 1990s (e.g., Eggert, Thompson, & Herting, 1994; Overholser, Hemstreet, Spirito, & Vyse, 1989; Shaffer et al., 1990) found that although some students had positive responses, some exposed to the programs were more likely to endorse suicide as a "reasonable solution" (Shaffer et al., 1991). The recommendations that followed this early research was for school-based prevention programs to (1) include social support enhancement and skills training, (2) focus on common and multiple risk and protective factors related to suicidal behavior and other problem behaviors, (3) target distinct suicide-risk groups, and (4) be intensive and comprehensive.

The current study attempted to test the effectiveness of a program that attended to these recommendations. The authors employed a three-group, repeated measures design with a sample of 105 youth at risk for suicide. The study provides support for the efficacy of a comprehensive school-based prevention program featuring targeted, brief, supportive interventions. The authors noted that the experimental "personal growth class" prevention program was effective in reducing suicide-risk behaviors, depression, hopelessness, stress, and anger; and in increasing the protective factors of personal control, self-esteem, and support resources. These effects were present post-intervention and maintained in follow-up five months later.

Intervention

The experimental procedure involved a comprehensive assessment protocol along with participation in a personal growth class (PGC). The class was conducted in small groups of 12 students and taught either by a teacher, counselor, or school nurse. The PGC groups met daily for 55-minute periods in regular classrooms, with students receiving elective credit.

The fundamentals of the program components were (1) a small group work component featuring social support and the exchange of help; (2) weekly monitoring of activities targeting changes in mood management, school performance and attendance, and drug involvement; and (3) life-skills training in decision making, personal control (including anger, depression, and stress management skills), and self-esteem enhancement. Pro-suicidal attitudes (i.e., as viable solution) and behaviors (e.g., attempts) were negated in the decision-making skills unit (e.g., in personal problem-solving activities) and counteracted in the personal control skills unit (e.g., by teaching depression and management skills) and in the interpersonal communication unit by engaging a support network.

Reflection

The study appears to provide support for a comprehensive school-based prevention program. One factor to be highlighted is the suggested potential value of targeted, but brief, supportive interventions targeting the development of skills and attitudes needed to effectively manage depression, stress, and anger and navigate conflicting relationships.

The use of health promotion and prevention programs, although clearly less expensive (in time and resources) than one-on-one counseling efforts, are often deemed as "nice" but not "needed," because they are typically targeted to entire school populations. The current study illustrated the importance of targeting a high-risk population for prevention efforts. Such targeting not only reduces the resources needed but also allows for population-specific needs to be addressed, thus increasing effectiveness.

Source: Eggert, L. L., Thompson, E. A., Hertin, J. R., & Nicholas, L. J. (1995). Reducing suicide potential among high-risk youth: Tests of a school-based prevention program. *Suicide and life-threatening behavior, 25*(2), 276–296.

SAMPLE INTERVENTIONS

Counselor Interview as Prevention Intervention

Authors: Brooke P. Randell, Leona L. Eggert, and Kenneth C. Pike

Précis: This study evaluated the immediate effects of two brief suicide prevention protocols: a brief interview—Counselors CARE (C-CARE)—and C-CARE plus a 12-session Coping and Support Training (CAST) peer-group intervention.

Introduction

The authors previously found that a brief assessment protocol worked to decrease suicidal behaviors and related indicators of emotional stress (Eggert et al., 1995; Thompson, Horn, Herting, & Eggert, 1997). These findings suggested that a single counseling session could be an efficient and cost-effective means of reducing suicide-risk behavior.

The current study attempted to test the value of a targeted single counseling session. The study employed a randomly assigned control group design. The authors concluded that the brief prevention program was effective in reducing suicide risk behaviors, increasing anger control, and reducing family distress.

Intervention

The study targeted 341 adolescents in grades 9 through 12 who had been identified as at-risk for both school dropout and suicide. Students were assigned randomly to C-CARE plus CAST, C-CARE only, or "intervention as usual."

- **C-Care**. Students in the C-Care group participated in an individual, computer-assisted interview that provided a comprehensive assessment of direct suicide risk factors, related risk factors, and protective factors. The program also provided the students with a brief motivational counseling intervention designed to provide empathy and support, reinforce positive coping skills and help-seeking behaviors, and increase access to help and social support.
- **CAST**. The students in the CAST treatment group received the standardized C-Care intervention and then began a 6-week CAST small group skills training program that entailed 12 one-hour sessions. The focus of the training was on group support, goal setting, self-esteem, decision making, anger/depression management, drug use, relapse prevention, and recognizing progress/staying on track.

The impact of these programs was assessed using trend analyses on data available from three repeated measures. C-CARE and CAST led to increases in personal control, problem-solving, coping, and perceived family support. Both C-CARE plus CAST and C-CARE only led to decreases in depression and to enhanced self-esteem and the meeting of family goals.

Reflection

A significant feature of this study is the apparent validation of a short-term, counselor-directed intervention that resulted in a reduction of suicide risk factors for at-risk adolescents. The use of a brief standardized form of intervention designed for administration within a school setting makes this a viable option for the school counselor. The one major caveat in embracing the results is that the authors only tested the immediate effects of the programs. A follow-up study of relative permanence of treatment effect is needed.

Source: Randell, B. P., Eggert, L. L., & Pike, K. C. (2001). Immediate post-intervention effects of two brief youth suicide prevention interventions. *Suicide and Life-Threatening Behavior, 31*(1), 41–61.

SAMPLE INTERVENTIONS

Cognitive-Behavioral Structured Intervention—SNAP

Authors: Mary Jane Rotheram-Borus, John Piacentini, Coleen Cantwell, Thomas R. Belin, and Juwon Song

Précis: A specialized emergency room (ER) care intervention was evaluated over an 18-month period.

Introduction

Adolescent suicide attempters (SAs) are at increased risk for repeat attempts, long-term psychiatric symptoms, and academic, social, and behavioral problems (Shaffer & Piacentini, 1994). Sadly, research (e.g., Piacentini et al., 1995; Rotheram-Borus, Piacentini, Miller, Graae, & Castro-Blanco, 1994) demonstrates that very few adolescent suicide attempters either engage in, or continue with, follow-up psychotherapy once out of crisis.

The school counselor's role and level of engagement with a student who is suicidal will most often be in the context of a crisis, with the primary goal being crisis intervention followed by referral. Given this research pointing to the tendency of the adolescent not to follow through or continue in counseling, counselors must employ strategies that not only help in the moment of crisis but also increase the likelihood of such engagement in therapy following a crisis. The current study tested the effectiveness of a brief, cost-effective technique for increasing an adolescent's motivation and commitment to engage in therapy following an initial experience of suicidal behavior.

Intervention

Using a quasi-experimental design, this study assigned 140 female adolescent SAs, ages 12 to 18 years, and their mothers (88% Hispanic) to receive either specialized ER care or standard ER care during their ER visit. The baseline assessment was conducted shortly after the ER care, and then the SNAP therapy (Rotheram-Borus, Piacentini, & Miller, 1994) was delivered.

The specialized ER care included a videotaped orientation to the family regarding the dangers of ignoring suicide attempts and the potential benefits of treatment and delivery of a structured family therapy session while the adolescent and her mother were in the ER.

The specialized ER care was designed to frame or define the suicide attempt as:

- An ineffective problem-solving strategy
- A critical event requiring immediate therapeutic intervention to prevent its likely reoccurrence

- A roadblock to the positive, loving feelings shared by the SAs and their parents
- A problem that could be addressed in six sessions of therapeutic intervention

Parents were asked to endorse attendance for themselves and their child at Successful Negotiation Acting Positively (SNAP), a six-session outpatient program that was designed to be interesting and rewarding.

The study reported that the adolescents in the specialized ER care condition were significantly less depressed and reported less suicidal ideation after receipt of this intervention than those receiving standard ER care.

Reflection

The strength of the study is in its use of a consecutive cohort as a control and the use of a standardized treatment (SNAP). The use of the video to increase interest and compliance in continued counseling and the brief counseling format (six sessions) makes this approach feasible for school counselors who operate under time constraints.

The primary concern with the study was the unique nature of the sample employed. Not only were the adolescents seen in an emergency room—at the height of their crises—but the sample was limited to urban, Hispanic females. Questions of the generalizability of these findings outside of an emergency room setting or with males or females from other regional and cultural backgrounds need to be addressed.

Source: Rotheram-Borus, M. J., Piacentini, J., Cantwell, C., Belin, T. R., & Song, J. (2000). The 18-month impact of an emergency room intervention for adolescent female suicide attempters. *Journal of Consulting and Clinical Psychology, 68*(6), 1081–1093.

DETAILED INTERVENTION

Suicide Prevention Program—SOS

Introduction

Numerous approaches to suicide prevention have been employed in school settings. However, few of these programs have been tested for efficacy using rigorous evaluation methods. One exception is the following study, reporting on the effect of the "Signs of Suicide Program" (SOS).

The SOS program is designed to reduce the incidence of suicide among adolescents. SOS is a school-based prevention program that combines curricula designed to raise awareness of suicide and its related issues along with a screening test of depression and risk factors associated with suicidal behavior. The current study demonstrates a significant treatment effect for those experiencing the SOS program.

Method

The study employed a randomized, control group posttest only experimental design; 2,100 students in 5 high schools were randomly assigned to intervention or control groups. A self-administered questionnaire (Columbia Depression Scale) was used as the dependent measure. Results indicated a significantly lower rate of suicide attempts, greater knowledge. and more adaptive attitudes about depression and suicide for the students in the treatment groups compared to those in the control groups.

Interventions

SOS, a school-based prevention program, incorporates two suicide prevention strategies: self-screening and education:

- **Self-screening component**. The Columbia Depression Scale (CDS) was administered to the participants. The questionnaire included items assessing suicide attempts and ideation; knowledge and attitudes about depression and suicide; and help-seeking behaviors. Using self-report methods, students were asked to evaluate their own depressive symptoms and suicidal thoughts.
- **Education component**. Students were taught to understand that suicide is not a typical or normal response to stress or upset. They were taught to recognize the signs of suicide and depression and the specific action steps necessary to respond to these signs.

Teaching materials included a video (*Friends for Life: Preventing Teen Suicide*) and a manual. The video featured dramatizations that depicted signs of suicidal thoughts and depression and recommended ways to react to someone who is depressed and suicidal. Following the presentation of the video, students were taught specific action steps to put their knowledge into motion. The steps were taught using the acronym ACT:

- A—*Acknowledge* the signs of suicide that others display and take them seriously.
- C—Let the person know that you *care* and that you want to help.
- T—*Tell* a responsible adult.

In addition to the specific training, flyers and posters were hung around the school to promote general awareness and cohesiveness within the school.

Reflection

The SOS program is unique in that it is one of a very few school-based programs for which a reduction in self-reported suicide attempts has been demonstrated using a randomized experimental design. The treatment components (i.e., self-assessment and education) are clearly compatible with the culture of the school and the role and function of the school counselor. Further, the treatment allows for group implementation (e.g., in a health class) and thus provides a prevention strategy that is both effective and relatively easy to employ. One additional benefit of the program is that the focus on peer intervention (i.e., teaching teens to recognize signs of depression and empowering them to respond) expands the intervention/prevention base within the school.

As with any such study, additional research is needed to demonstrate that the program will be as effective for students from different schools and backgrounds. Also, data are reported only at one point, a three-month follow-up. It is important to assess the longer-term impact of this program. As is true for the application of any clinical program, counselors are advised to carefully monitor the impact and outcome (short and long term) of this program as applied to their specific students.

Source: Aseltine, R. H., & DeMartino, R. (2004). An outcome evaluation of the SOS suicide prevention program. *American Journal of Public Health, 94*(3), 446–451.

FROM THE FIELD

As with all of the previous "From the Field" recommendations, these recommendations, although reflecting suggestions from counselors and specialists currently working in the field, need to be viewed as just that—personal recommendations.

Symptoms and Early Indicators

The American Psychiatric Association recommends seeking help if a child or teen:

- Withdraws from friends and family
- Shows an inability to concentrate
- Sleeps too much or too little
- Talks of suicide
- Has dramatic changes in personal appearance
- Loses interest in favorite activities
- Expresses hopelessness, helplessness, or excessive guilt
- Exhibits self-destructive behavior (such as reckless driving, drug abuse, or promiscuity)
- Seems preoccupied with death
- Bequeaths favorite possessions

It is particularly important to pay attention to all statements that indicate a student is thinking about suicide. Contrary to popular belief, people who talk about suicide *are* likely to follow through.

Working with Students

- Assess the imminent risk of suicide, negotiate a no-harm contract, limit the availability of lethal means, and provide support and 24-hour contact information.
- Don't leave the student alone; remove dangerous objects and stabilize the student.
- Inform parents, the building principal, and the crisis team (if one is formed). It helps to have at least two school personnel present when informing parents.
- Be direct when interviewing the student as to whether he or she is thinking about killing him- or herself. Be careful not to rush into a solution or dismiss the student's perspective. Be nonevaluative but affirm that you value the student's life.
- Communicate caring, support, and trust. Provide encouragement that the student can cope and that together you can develop ways to make the coping easier and more effective.

- Be hopeful, but don't offer simple answers to serious questions, ready-made solutions, or platitudes.
- Listen!!!
- Ask the student to assess the degree to which he or she is at risk. You can employ a "subjective distress scale" where 10 is "I can't take it, and can't control myself" and 1 is "I'm okay and in control of my feelings."
- Initially target feelings of hopelessness, then as the crisis subsides focus on remediation of skill deficits in the short term and improving self-image and interpersonal functioning in the long term.
- Try to move toward identifying the problem and the goal. Shape both so that they are realistic and doable.
- Have the student identify alternative ways to respond to the perceived problems. Identify strategies that have been employed (successfully) in the past.
- Try to engage the student in some future-oriented goal.
- When feasible, connect the student to clubs and activities.
- Help the student understand the need and value for referral.

Working with Teachers and Parents

- Address the seriousness of the situation and dispel myths, such as the student is only seeking attention or that the student is only talking about it.
- Provide in-service for teachers on identifying signs of risk for suicide.
- Help teachers increase sensitivity to the experienced crisis the student is going through so that there is no mocking, criticism, or dismissal of the student's behavior.
- Develop a fact sheet and referral information for parents and teachers.
- Work with teachers to develop a curricula that highlights the signs of risk and the steps to take if a friend (or self) is at risk.
- If one doesn't already exist, create a crisis intervention process and policy and inform teachers and parents of the plan.
- Be available to support the teacher after initial identification, often the experience can be emotionally distressing.
- Include suicide prevention education in the teaching curriculum.
- Debrief all involved to allow an opportunity to process feelings, concerns, and suggestions.

REFERENCES

Aseltine, R. H., & DeMartino, R. (2004). An outcome evaluation of the SOS suicide prevention program. *American Journal of Public Health, 94*(3), 446–451.

Centers for Disease Control and Prevention. (1998). Youth risk behavior surveillance—United States, 1997. *Morbidity and Mortality Weekly Report, 47*(SS-3), 1–89.

Centers for Disease Control and Prevention. (2000). *Data Source: NCHS National Vital Statistics System for numbers of deaths, U.S. Bureau of Census for population estimates. Statistics compiled using WISQARS™ produced by the Office of Statistics and Programming, NCIPC, CDC.* Atlanta: Author.

Centers for Disease Control and Prevention. (2002). Youth risk behavior surveillance—United States, 2001. *Morbidity and Mortality Weekly Report, 51*(SS-4), 6.

Eggert, L. L., Thompson, E. A., & Herting, J. R. (1994). Prevention research program: Reconnecting at-risk youth. *Issues in Mental Health Nursing, 15*(2), 107–135.

Eggert, L. L., Thompson, E. A., Herting, J. R., & Nicholas, L. J. (1995). Reducing suicide potential among high-risk youth: Tests of a school-based prevention program. *Suicide and Life-Threatening Behavior, 25*(2), 276–296.

Hoyert, D. L. (1999). Deaths: Final data for 1997. National Vital Statistics reports: From the Centers for Disease Control and Prevention, National Center for Health, *National Vital Statistics, 47*(19), 1–104.

Overholser, J. C., Hemstreet, A. H., Spirito, A., & Vyse, S. (1989). Suicide awareness programs in the schools: Effects of gender and personal experience. *Journal of the American Academy of Child and Adolescent Psychiatry, 28*(6), 925–930.

Parsons, R. D. (1996). Student suicide: The counselor's postvention role. *Elementary School Guidance & Counseling, 31*, 77–80.

Piacentini, J., Rotheram-Borus, M. J., Gillis, J. R., Graae, F., Trautman, P., Garcia-Leeds, C., Cantwell, C., & Shaffer, D. (1995). Demographic predictors of treatment attendance among adolescent suicide attempters. *Journal of Consulting and Clinical Psychology, 63*, 469–473.

Pophenhagen, M. P., & Qualley, R. M. (1998). Adolescent suicide: Detection, intervention and prevention. *Professional School Counseling, 1*(4), 30–35.

Randell, B. P., Eggert, L. L., & Pike, K. C. (2001). Immediate post-intervention effects of two brief youth suicide prevention interventions. *Suicide and Life-Threatening Behavior, 31*(1), 41–61.

Rotheram-Borus, M. J., Piacentini, J., & Miller, S. (1994). Brief cognitive-behavior treatment for adolescent suicide attempters and their families. *Journal of the American Academy of Child and Adolescent Psychiatry, 22*(4), 508–517.

Rotheram-Borus, M. J., Piacentini, J., Cantwell, C., Belin, T. R., & Song, J. (2000). The 18-month impact of an emergency room intervention for adolescent female suicide attempters. *Journal of Consulting and Clinical Psychology, 68*(6), 1081–1093.

Rotheram-Borus, M. J., Piacentini, J., Miller, S., Graae, F. & Castro-Blanco, D. (1994). Brief cognitive-behavioral treatment for adolescent suicide attempters and their families. *Psychiatry, 33*, 508–517.

Shaffer, D., & Piacentini, J. (1994). Suicide and suicide attempts. In M. Rutter, L. Hersov, & E. Taylor (Eds.), *Child and adolescent psychiatry* (3rd ed., pp. 407–424). London: Blackwell Scientific.

Shaffer, D., Garland, A., Vieland, V., Underwood, M., & Busner, C. (1991). The impact of curriculum-based suicide prevention programs for teenagers. *Journal of the American Academy of Child and Adolescent Psychiatry, 30*(4), 588–596.

Shaffer, D., Vieland, V., Garland, A., Rojas, M., Underwood, M., & Busner, C. (1990). Adolescent suicide attempters: Response to suicide prevention programs. *Journal of the American Medical Association, 264*(24), 3151–3155.

Thompson, E. A., Horn, M., Herting, J. R., & Eggert, L. L. (1997). Enhancing outcomes in an indicated drug prevention program for high-risk youth. *Journal of Drug Education, 27*, 19–41.

U.S. Public Health Service. (1999). *The Surgeon General's Call to Action to Prevent Suicide*. Washington, DC: Author.

ADDITIONAL RESOURCES

INTERNET

http://kidshealth.org/parent/emotions/behavior/suicide_p3.html. A good source of information for parents on the what, why, and what to do about teenage suicide.

www.save.org. SAVE stands for "Suicide Awareness Voices of Education." This Web site includes a suicide and depression glossary, facts, and a question and answer section. Provides warning signs of suicide and common misconceptions. Includes a link for those coping with a loss.

www.preventsuicidenow.com. Web site includes suicide warning signs, causes, FAQs, and articles. Also provides suicide statistics, e-mail support groups, and telephone hotlines. Links to suicide myths, survivor stories, and disorders related to suicide.

www.suicideinfo.ca/csp/go.aspx?tabid=1. Web site for the Center for Suicide Prevention. Provides information for you or someone you know who may be suicidal. Includes a FAQ section, resources, and a support link for counseling and crisis centers.

PRINTED MATERIALS

Berkan, W. A., & Deaton, R. L. (1995). *Planning and managing death issues in the schools.* Westport, CT: Greenwood Press.

Brock, S. E., Lazarus, P. J., & Jimerson, S. R. (Ed.). (2002). *Best practice in school crisis prevention and intervention.* Bethesda, MD: National Association of School Psychologists.

Jamison, K. R. (1999). *Night falls fast: Understanding suicide.* New York: Knopf.

Shea, S. C. (2002). *The Practical art of suicide assessment: A guide for mental health professionals and substance abuse counselors.* New York: Wiley.

CHAPTER 18

TRAUMA, LOSS, AND THE GRIEVING PROCESS

Recent data from the National Vital Statistics System suggest that approximately 40,000 families each year experience the death of a child under the age of 15 (Minino & Smith, 2001). These sobering statistics highlight the unfortunate salience of death in the lives of children and adolescents in our country.

Children, like adults, experience change, loss, and death in their lives. Although we may typically think of grieving as associated with the death of a loved one, such as a parent, sibling, grandparent, or friend, a child can experience grief as a result of parents divorcing, families relocating, and even the shattering of one's athletic dream as a result of an injured knee. These are all significant losses for a child, and they need to be grieved.

Although it is true that children are resilient, and some researchers have shown that they can develop strategies to cope with grief and loss, other evidence suggests that many children are unable to cope with grief, especially when the grief is the result of a traumatic event such as a violent crime, a horrible accident, or terrorism. These children and others having difficulty moving through the grieving process may find it difficult to concentrate, complete tasks, or even engage with peers (Webb, 1993). Those youth struggling with loss may be at risk for more serious behavioral problems, morbidity, and suicide (Valente, Saunders, & Street, 1988).

It is crucial for counselors to be sensitive to students who have experienced death and other significant losses in their lives. A caring counselor can help a child struggling with losses (Lane & Dickey, 1988).

OVERVIEW

Although the literature identifies programs, services, and activities aimed at assisting children and adolescents cope with trauma, loss, and grief, very few have been tested for effectiveness using the rigors of scientific research. Further, those that have attempted to test the effectiveness of such programs are often limited by methodological problems such as lack of control groups, variations in time lapse since loss, and unique samples. As such, counselors employing these strategies with their students need to do so with caution and employ measures to monitor their immediate, short-term, and long-term impacts. Table 18.1 presents the grief-related studies detailed in this chapter.

TABLE 18.1 Overview of Studies Presented

TARGET PROBLEM	REFERENCE	K–6	6–9	9–12	OTHER SPECIFICATIONS
Trauma and grief group work	Saltzman, Pynoos, Layne, Steinberg, & Aisenberg (2001)	Y	Y	Y	Pretest, posttest, non-control group design with manual-based treatment
School-based intervention for children suffering loss through divorce	Stolberg & Mahler (1994)	Y	N	N	Manual-based treatment with intact control group design
Puppet play with grief	Carter (1987)	Y	N	N	Case study, female
Childhood traumatic grief	Brown, Pearlman, & Goodman (2004)	Y	N	N	A single-subject, time series design, case study

SAMPLE INTERVENTIONS

School-based Group Treatment Protocol

Authors: William Saltzman, Robert Pynoos, Christopher Layne, Alan Steinberg, and Eugene Aisenberg

Précis: Study tested the effectiveness of group intervention for middle school students exposed to trauma.

Introduction

The authors noted the high incidence with which children are exposed to severe stress and trauma, citing a study by Kilpatrick, Saunders, Resnick, and Smith (1995) that found 23 percent of adolescents surveyed had been both a victim of assault and a witness to violence. What makes this statistic more concerning is research that has demonstrated the adverse affect of such exposure to violence on academic achievement, social relationships, and emotional adjustment (e.g., Kilpatrick, Aciermo, Saunders, Resnick, & Best, 2000; Saigh, Mroueh, & Bremmer, 1997).

The current study described the effectiveness of a school-based trauma and grief-focused group psychotherapy program for middle school students.

Intervention

Following a screening of 812 students, ages 11 to 14, 56 students were identified as meeting one of two criteria: (1) reporting one or more forms of significant exposure to trauma, violence, or loss and reporting at least moderate levels of Post-Traumatic Stress Disorder (PTSD) symptomatology or (2) reporting the death of a close friend or family member and reporting significant symptoms of depression or complicated grief.

Groups of five to seven members were formed; efforts were made to maximize group homogeneity in terms of whether the primary treatment issue centered on trauma versus traumatic death, as well as the severity of the trauma or loss and the developmental level of the student. Groups met once a week for one 50-minute period over the course of 20 consecutive weeks. A manual-based protocol was followed that employed four separate modules. Module I focused on building group cohesion, educating the members regarding loss and trauma, normalizing distress reactions, and developing coping skills. Module II targeted therapeutic processing of selected traumatic experiences, including trauma-narrative-exposure work and restructuring maladaptive cognitions associated with the negative emotions. Module III included psycho-education about grief symptoms, information on processing angry reactions to losses, and re-creating nontraumatic images of the deceased. The final module (Module IV) focused on problem solving current stress, challenging maladaptive core life beliefs, and initiating normal developmental progression.

Using a pretest, posttest, noncontrol group design, the authors reported that group participation was associated with a reduction in PTSD symptoms and complicated grief symptoms and improved academic performance.

Reflection

A survey of the current literature reveals numerous recommendations and suggestions for assisting students who are grieving; however, almost all of these are based on anecdotal reporting and/or clinical experience. The current study is one step in the direction of empirically testing the effectiveness of a treatment program for students who are grieving.

The time-limited (20 sessions), manual-based approach adds to the utility of this program for application within a school setting. Further, the evidence of improved academic functioning certainly makes this group approach one to be considered by school counselors.

Source: Saltzman, W. R., Pynoos, R. S., Layne, C. M., Steinberg, A. M., & Aisenberg, E. (2001). Trauma- and grief-focused intervention for adolescents exposed to community violence: Results of a school-based screening and group treatment protocol. *Group Dynamics: Theory, Research and Practice, 5*(4), 291–303.

SAMPLE INTERVENTIONS

School-based Intervention for Children Suffering Loss from Divorce

Authors: Arnold L. Stolberg and Jeffrey Mahler

Précis: Presents a 14-week program consisting of 3 major components: support or special topics, skill building, and skills transfer.

Introduction

The alarming divorce rate in the United States has placed a severe demand on children's educational and mental health facilities. One approach to ameliorating the harmful effects of divorce on students has been to provide child-centered support groups within the schools (Grych & Fincham, 1992). These touted programs have pointed to the successful use of peers as a therapeutic element in that they provide social support and shared perspectives and experiences.

Two of these early group programs (Pedro-Carroll & Cowen, 1985; Stolberg & Garrison, 1985) focused on assisting students with anger control, relaxation, and communication skills as a means of helping them with the stressors associated with divorce.

The current study expanded the previous model (Stolberg & Garrison, 1985; Pedro-Carroll & Cowen, 1985) by adding home workbooks for children and parents and increasing the use of game-like activities to engage participants.

Intervention

The study involved children in third through fifth grades in 11 suburban elementary schools. A total of 103 students were identified for treatment, and a group of students from intact families was recruited and served as a nonstressed, intact control group.

Treatment involved a comprehensive 14-week program consisting of 3 major components: support or special topics, skill building, and skills transfer. All program procedures were presented in the *LeadersGuide* (Stolberg, Zacharias, & Camplair, 1991).

Following two introductory group sessions, the next four sessions targeted support or special topics. During these sessions, the students were engaged in component discussion of specific themes. This was accomplished through the use of cartoon and pictorial stimulus material, newspaper articles, and games developed for the intervention. During the next five sessions, the focus was on skill building. During these sessions, students were assisted in learning how to label feelings, associate them with causal events, and combine the feelings and events into statements to others. Self-control and anger-control procedures were taught in all of the next three sessions. The final session was devoted to termination activities.

In addition to in-school group work, skills transfer was introduced through use of a combined *KidsBook* and *ParentsBook* (Stolberg et al., 1991) and a series of four parent workshops. The *KidsBook* is an activity and home workbook that helps children prepare for upcoming sessions, provides practice opportunities for skills learned in the group, and encourages parent–child communication. Through drawing and writing exercises, the *KidsBook* encouraged children to examine their thoughts, feelings, and behaviors related to divorce and to evaluate their progress. Material in the *KidsBook* corresponded to the sequencing and content of the in-school sessions.

The *ParentsBook* encouraged parents to be involved in their child's experience with the transfer, skills, and support condition. It directed parents to encourage the use of skills learned and to initiate the discussion of important divorce-related topics. It recommended procedures to address issues that may have affected the parent–child relationship and suggested ways in which parents could give support and understanding to their child. Material in the *ParentsBook* corresponded to the sequencing and content of the in-school sessions and *KidsBook* activities.

The authors noted that participation in the skill-building components yielded significant adjustive gains beyond those displayed by the divorce controls. The skills and support condition yielded the most immediate gains, specifically in reductions in internalizing and externalizing behavior and total pathology in the home.

Reflection

Although school counselors will encounter children impacted by traumatic grief, it is more likely, given current statistics, that they will engage with students experiencing significant loss as a result of parents going through a divorce or separation. These children are also grieving and trying to cope with the stress of significant loss.

The current study provides the school counselor with an effective, school-based group intervention. The time-limited (14 sessions), manual-based approach adds to the utility of this program for application within a school setting.

Source: Stolberg, A. L., & Mahler, J. (1994). Enhancing treatment gains in a school-based intervention for children of divorce through skill training, parental involvement and transfer procedures. *Journal of Consulting and Clinical Psychology, 62*(1), 147–156.

SAMPLE INTERVENTIONS

Use of Puppets to Treat Traumatic Grief

Author: Stephanie R. Carter

Précis: Puppet therapy as a "natural" form of play facilitating a child's expression of grief.

Introduction

The author noted that children often present as resistant to grief counseling. Further, even for those willing to share, many lack the appropriate skills to do so. The use of puppet therapy as a form of play has been used in many settings. Puppet therapy can be used in a directive, structured manner, in which the counselor designs the activities, the rules, and the medium to be employed, or in an unstructured manner, where the child is free to choose what to use and how to use it. The current study presents the use of nondirective (unstructured) play as a means of assisting a 10-year-old, fifth-grade student who, at the age of 8, saw his father murdered.

Since the time of the incident, the client had been extremely aggressive and destructive in his behavior, using profanity with peers and teachers. Further, his academic progress had essentially stopped in the third grade.

Intervention

The counselor employed nondirective play. The client selected his own medium (puppets) and was allowed to set his own rules in using the materials. An unstructured approach was used in order to provide the client with the free, unpressured environment necessary to explore his trauma and experience the stages of bereavement.

Sessions were weekly, lasting 50 to 60 minutes each. The first two sessions were employed as a means to help the client feel comfortable with the counselor. Beginning with the third session, toys were displayed, and the client elected to play with the puppets with no further instruction or prompting from the counselor. During this session, the client named the puppets as family members and acted out the murder he had witnessed. In subsequent sessions, puppets were engaged in continuous fighting; however, in the eighth session, the client—through the "little boy" puppet—grieved for his father. Following this session, the client began to talk more freely to the counselor about his father and the circumstances of the murder; and his teachers began to report positive changes. The client was also now able to separate and distinguish his emotions—expanding beyond only anger to allow for sadness, joy, and frustration as separate feelings.

The client continued in counseling for the next two years, during which time three other people close to him died. The client was able to grieve these deaths both as himself and as the "little boy" puppet.

Reflection

The case study provides a good illustration of the value of play therapy, especially as a tool for working with "resistant" clients. The nondirected nature of the puppet therapy provided this client with the needed freedom and control to progress at a comfortable pace and in a direction that assured the level of safety desired. What is of particular value is that this child, who had previously expressed strong resistance to "talking" with the counselor, began almost immediately talking through the puppets and by the eighth session was able to be more directly involved in the grief counseling.

The use of play materials and play therapy as a medium for working with children appears to be a very useful approach for school counselors to include in their repertoire of intervention strategies. It should be noted, however, that as with any specialized technique, the use of puppet therapy should not be engaged without appropriate training and supervision.

Source: Carter, S. R. (1987). Use of puppets to treat traumatic grief: A case study. *Elementary School Guidance & Counseling, 21*(3), 210–215.

DETAILED INTERVENTION

Childhood Traumatic Grief

Introduction

Occasionally, a child experiences the death of a loved one under conditions that could best be described as traumatic (e.g., car accident, violent death, environmental disaster, etc.). Some children are overwhelmed by the trauma experienced to the degree that they are unable to begin the normal grieving process. Under such conditions, the child is described as experiencing Childhood Traumatic Grief (CTG) (Cohen et al., 2002).

In addition to grieving the loss of a loved one, the child with CTG experiences the symptoms of one with Post-Traumatic Stress Disorder (PTSD). The child has episodes of re-experiencing the trauma; avoids situations, events, and other activities associated with the trauma; and has a heightened level of arousal. The reaction to the traumatic nature of the loss may interfere with the child moving through the grieving process. School counselors encountering students exhibiting such trauma-based grief need to act as support and referral agents. However, although providing appropriate referral for treatment, it is important that the school counselor understand strategies that can be extended into the school and serve as school-based support for children experiencing trauma-based grief. The current case study demonstrated the effective use of cognitive-behavioral therapy for a five-year-old boy whose father, a firefighter, died in the line of duty at the World Trade Center on September 11, 2001.

Method

Children were identified as a result of an outreach effort to assist those whose fathers worked in uniformed services (i.e., New York Fire and Police Departments, Port Authority and Emergency Medical Services) and were killed on September 11, 2001. The case under report was that of Brian, a 5-year-old boy who lived with his mother and younger sister.

The case was a single-subject, time-series design. Brian was assessed four times (pretreatment, midtreatment, posttreatment, and a six-month follow-up), using the Diagnostic Interview Schedule for Children: Predictive Sales, Global Assessment of Functioning, Behavioral Assessment System for Children, and the Student-Teacher Relationship Scale.

Intervention

The family was assigned to traumatic grief cognitive-behavioral therapy (TG-CPT), a manual-based program (Coehn & Mannarino, 2001). The program provides a progression of skill development, cognitive and affective processing of the traumatic event, and engagement in the bereavement process. Flexibility is built into the program to allow the therapist to adapt it to the unique developmental needs of the client.

The TG-CBT program has two modules: the Trauma-Focused Children's Module and the Grief-Focused Children's Module.

- **Trauma-Focused Children's Module**. During the first two sessions, the child was helped to identify feelings and label them as traumatic grief. The child was also taught to see the relationship between emotions, thoughts, and behaviors. In the third and fourth sessions, the child was provided with relaxation training and taught cognitive restructuring strategies as a way of reducing stress. In sessions 5 through 7, a trauma narrative was created to habituate the child to cues surrounding the trauma. The counselor assisted the child in processing cognitions and affect tied to the re-experience. In the eighth session, a joint parent–child session, the parent was taught to reinforce the child's new coping strategies.
- **Grief-Focused Children's Module**. During the ninth and tenth sessions, the child was encouraged to mourn the loss of the loved one discussing death, in general, and specifically as it applied to his relationship with the deceased. In the eleventh session, the child was taught to preserve positive memories (memory making). In the next two sessions the child was assisted with social skills and reconnecting. In sessions 14 and 15, the child was assisted in reframing and making meaning out of the trauma and loss. In the final session, a joint parent–child session, both strategized about how they will address future challenges (e.g., anniversaries).

The author reported that in a six-month follow-up evaluation, the client was symptom free and was below criteria for any mental disorder.

Reflection

Childhood Traumatic Grief is a newer term in the literature. The experiences of September 11, 2001, have helped to sharpen our awareness of the interplay between the post-traumatic reaction and the grieving process. The current case study provides a clear, replicable, and effective method (TG-CBT) for treating children with CTG. The major limitation to this study, and all case studies, is its limited potential for generalization. Although additional randomized and controlled studies need to be implemented, the school counselor seeking a structure—a paradigm—for approaching the counseling of a student experiencing the traumatic loss of a loved one would do well to review Cohen, Mannarino, & Rogal (2001) or Cohen, Greenberg, Padio, et al. (2001) on cognitive-behavioral therapy for traumatic bereavement.

Source: Brown, E. J., Pearlman, M. Y., & Goodman, R. F. (2004). Facing fears and sadness: Cognitive behavioral therapy for childhood traumatic grief. *Harvard Review of Psychiatry, 12*(4), 187–198.

FROM THE FIELD

Numerous reports from the field offer intuitively appealing recommendations for working with children struggling through trauma, loss, and grief (e.g., Costa & Holliday, 1994). The following recommendations have been gleaned from these clinical/anecdotal reports. As personal suggestions, they need to be employed with caution and their impact monitored.

Working with Students

- Acknowledge the pain and grief and assure the student that it is normal to grieve.
- Be supportive and empathetic; relate don't resolve.
- Books and stories pertaining to death can help the student label feelings and respond to the loss.
- Journal writing may be useful to help the student identify thoughts and feelings and serve as a way for reconstructing memories.
- Kandt (1994) suggests the use of a memory book and family tree as a means of helping the youth to evaluate the different roles that family members have played in his or her life. The memory book can include photos, poems, letters, and other memorabilia related to the deceased. This provides concrete objects to connect the adolescent to the deceased and encourages sharing.
- When working with the student, remember the 5 T's (tears, touch, talk, time, together). Help the student "normalize" what they are going through (i.e., grieving). There is no need to apologize for spontaneous tears or feelings of anger; these are part of the healing process.
- Help the student accept that each of us experiences and expresses grief differently. The student doesn't have to go through grief like his or her parents, siblings, or friends. Everyone grieves in their own way.
- Don't attack or take away the student's defenses, especially during the early stages of grief. The student will embrace as much of the truth as he or she can handle at any one moment.
- Be accessible—physically and emotionally—and be aware of your own unresolved grief.
- Assure the child (especially younger children) that he or she was not responsible or that more deaths are not imminent.
- Be comfortable and accepting of all the child's questions—accepting that you will not know all the answers.
- Provide the student with relaxation techniques.
- In the case where it is a student or teacher who has died, others in the school should be informed of the death by someone who is trusted and seen as an authority figure, with the most logical choice being the principal.
- School counselors should make sure that the affective concerns of the student body are attended to, and not just the information disseminated.
- If the class or school is grieving, showing a film (such as *But He Was Only Seventeen—The Death of a Friend*) can be an excellent conversation starter.

- Suggest ways that students might express their grief, both verbally and nonverbally. Expressing one's loss through drawing a picture, writing a poem, being by oneself, going for a walk in a park, or creating some type of memorial are ways that some students have been helped.
- Help students to be realistic with themselves in their grief work. Encourage them to be patient with themselves or with others who are grieving and to not expect too much too soon.
- Encourage children to take breaks from their grieving. Suggest that they spend time playing and talking with their friends. Assure them that it is okay to take such breaks from the grieving process.
- Even though it may be difficult for some students to grasp the idea, encourage them to eat properly, exercise, and to get sufficient sleep and rest. Help them to understand that they must take care of themselves physically.

Working with Teachers and Parents

- In the classroom, issues of death, loss, and transitions can be addressed with the goal to help students embrace the grieving process and begin to recognize if and when they need support.
- Conduct an in-service workshop for teachers about loss, death, and grief in the lives of their students and how they might respond to students facing these issues.
- Help teachers accept that the student's loss will also affect them.
- Help teachers to understand that children and young people grieve many losses, some of which may not seem very significant to the adult, but which are important to the child. Do not evaluate the child's grief by comparing it to the way you grieve as an adult, but take the child's importance of the loss and his or her developmental stage into account.
- If appropriate to class material or assignments, allow students to express their grief through drawings, writing a poem, and so on.
- Develop a means by which the child can indicate a need to leave the class, see the counselor, or simply stop working while he or she gathers him- or herself.
- Help teachers understand the need to be available but not "impose" help on the student.
- Refrain from setting timetables for children's recovery. Every loss is unique for the persons involved; each person must grieve in his or her own time and way. Some heal rather quickly; others take longer.
- Be encouraging and hopeful. Assure students that eventually they will remember the person or object they have lost without hurting so much.
- Encourage students to remember the good times and to cherish them. Assure them that those memories can never be taken away.
- Discipline and appropriate limits should continue to be set and enforced. Day-to-day routines help in the adjusting process, but students need to feel a sense of caring.

- Teachers can educate children about death and provide support to grieving children in ways both similar to and different from those of parents. With regard to this notion, Crase and Crase (1995) identified three functions of teachers: (1) to help children feel safe and acknowledge the reality of the death, (2) to promote an inviting environment where children can talk about their feelings, and (3) to provide appropriate learning opportunities and curricular materials about death.
- Teachers can educate their classes about death issues and help bereaved children create memorials honoring the deceased.
- In talking with students, use normal tone of voice and words such as *dead* and *dying* rather than euphemisms to soften the blow.
- Listen! Answer the child's questions, but let him or her talk.
- Accept the emotions expressed and try not to discount them with a platitude ("everything will be ok").
- If others in the class know about the death, allow them some time in class to process their feelings.
- If students share their experiences, ask them to talk about what they miss the most, the things they used to do, with the hope of rekindling positive memories.
- Be patient. The student may need time to get back completely on track.
- Be sensitive to mood and behavioral changes, especially around anniversaries or special occasions (holidays).
- Offer to accompany the student to the counselor's office if you feel that additional support is needed.

REFERENCES

Brown, E. J., Pearlman, M. Y., & Goodman, R. F. (2004). Facing fears and sadness: Cognitive behavioral therapy for childhood traumatic grief. *Harvard Review of Psychiatry, 12*(4), 187–198.

Carter, S. R. (1987). Use of puppets to treat traumatic grief: A case study. *Elementary School Guidance & Counseling, 21*(3), 210–215.

Cohen, J. A., Greenberg, T., Padlo, S., et al. (2001). *Cognitive behavioral therapy for traumatic bereavement in children treatment manual.* Rev. ed., Pittsburgh, PA: Center for Traumatic Stress in Children and Adolescents, Department of Psychiatry, Allegheny General Hospital.

Cohen, J. A., Mannarino, A. P., & Rogal, S. (2001). Treatment practices for childhood posttraumatic stress disorder. *Child Abuse & Neglect, 25*(1), 123–135.

Cohen, J. A., Mannarino, A. P., Greenberg, T., Padlo, S., & Shipley, C. (2002). Childhood traumatic grief: Concepts and controversies. *Trauma Violence Abuse, 3*, 307–327.

Costa, L., & Holliday, D. (1994). Helping children cope with the death of a parent. *Elementary School Guidance & Counseling, 28*(3), 206–213.

Crase, D. R., & Case, D. (1995). *Responding to a bereaved child in the school setting.* (Eric Document Reproduction Service No. 3946555).

Grych, J. H., & Fincham, F. D. (1992). Interventions for children of divorce: Toward greater integration of research and action. *Psychological Bulletin, 111*, 434–454.

Kandt, V. E. (1994). Adolescent bereavement: Turning a fragile time into acceptance and peace. *The School Counselor, 41*, 203–211.

Kilpatrick, D., Aciermo, R., Saunders, B., Resnick, H., & Best, C. (2000). Risk factors for adolescent substance abuse and dependence: Data from a national sample. *Journal of Consulting and Clinical Psychology 65*, 1–12.

Kilpatrick, D. G., Saunders, B. E., Resnick, H. S., & Smith, D. W. (1995). *The national survey of adolescents: Preliminary findings of lifetime prevalence of traumatic events and mental health correlates*. Charleston, SC: Medical University of South Carolina, National Crime Victims Research and Treatment Center.

Lane, K. E., & Dickey, T. (1988). New students and grief. *School Counselor, 35*(5), 359–362.

Minino, A. M., & Smith, B. L. (2001). *Deaths: Preliminary data for 2000* (Vol. 49, No. 12). National Vital Statistics System. Washington, DC: Department of Health and Human Services.

Pedro-Carroll, J. L., & Cowen, E. L. (1985). The Children of Divorce Intervention Program: An investigation of the efficacy of a school-based prevention program. *Journal of Consulting and Clinical Psychology, 53*, 603–611.

Saigh, P. A., Mroueh, M., & Bremmer, J. D. (1997). Scholastic impairments among traumatized adolescents. *Behavior Research and Therapy, 35*, 429–436.

Saltzman, W. R., Pynoos, R. S., Layne, C. M., Steinberg, A. M., & Aisenberg, E. (2001). Trauma- and grief-focused intervention for adolescents exposed to community violence: Results of a school-based screening and group treatment protocol. *Group Dynamics: Theory, Research, and Practice, 5*(4), 291–303.

Stolberg, A. L., & Garrison, K. M. (1985). Evaluating a primary prevention program for children of divorce. *American Journal of Community Psychology, 13*, 111–124.

Stolberg, A. L., & Mahler, J. (1994). Enhancing treatment gains in a school-based intervention for children of divorce through skill training, parental involvement and transfer procedures. *Journal of Consulting and Clinical Psychology, 62*(1), 147–156.

Stolberg, A. L., Zacharias, M. A., & Camplair, C. W. (1991). *Children of divorce: LeadersGuide, KidsBook, and ParentsBook*. Circle Pines, MN: American Guidance Service.

Valente, S. M., Saunders, J., & Street, R. (1988). Adolescent bereavement following suicide: An examination of the relevant literature. *Journal of Counseling and Development, 67*, 174–177.

Webb, N. B. (Ed.). (1993). *Helping bereaved children*. New York: Guilford Press.

Wolfert, A. D. (1997). Death and grief in the school setting. In T. N. Fairchild (Ed.), *Crisis intervention strategies for school-based helpers* (pp. 199–244). Springfield, IL: Charles C. Thomas.

ADDITIONAL RESOURCES

INTERNET

www.growthhouse.org/death.html. Web site includes links for getting help and finding grief support groups. Also provides resources for bereaved families.

www.nim.nih.gov/medlineplus/bereavement.html. Medline provides information on grief and bereavement as well as excellent links to information on the grieving process and self help.

www.healthatoz.com/healthatoz/Atoz/dc/caz/ment/grif/grif_gen_ovw.jsp. Offers information on grief and grieving. Provides links and responses to frequently asked questions.

PRINTED MATERIALS

Allen, J. (2002). *Using literature to help troubled teenagers cope with end-of-life issues*. Westport, CT: Greenwood.

Rowling, L. (2003). *Grief in school communities: Effective support strategies*. Philadelphia: Open University.

Webb, N. B. (2002). *Helping bereaved children: A handbook for practitioners*. New York: Guilford Press.

CHAPTER 19

EATING DISORDERS

Go to any newsstand and scan the article titles in popular preteen and teen magazines. You are sure to find titles such as "How to Drop 5 lbs Before Prom," "You Can Be a Size 4 by April," and "The New 10-Minute Routine to a New, Better You." Children and teens are bombarded with commercial messages that tout the benefits of being slim—if not skinny. Most of these messages imply or explicitly state that one's personal worth increases as his or her weight decreases. It is no wonder that the number of clinical and subclinical cases of anorexia and bulimia are on the rise (Lucas & Holub, 1995; Thompson & Smolak, 2001).

Anorexia nervosa is typically defined as having a body weight that is less than 85 percent of normal and a refusal to maintain body weight at or above the minimally normal weight for one's age and height. In addition, the DSM-IV-TR (APA, 2000a) criteria for anorexia nervosa include (1) an intense fear of gaining weight, (2) disturbance in perception of body weight and shape or denial of seriousness of low body weight, and (3) absence of three consecutive menstrual cycles in postmenarcheal females. The extreme weight loss and generally drawn appearance typically draws attention to the child with anorexia. This is not the case necessarily with one who is bulimic.

In contrast to anorexia, individuals with bulimia need not have a body weight that is below expected levels. *Bulimia* is typically characterized by recurrent binge eating and the employment of some method of compensating for the binge eating, such as purging by vomiting or the use of laxatives.

The same popular magazines that tout weight loss often have stories of celebrities' struggles with eating disorders. Stories of people such as Karen Carpenter (singer), Cherry Boone O'Neill (Pat Boone's daughter), Cathy Rigby McCoy (former gymnast), and, more recently, Mary-Kate Olsen (actress) have made anorexia and bulimia almost celebrity. But the effects of these eating disorders are not to be celebrated. In addition to major health implications, including possible death, research has demonstrated that students with eating disorders exhibit greater depression, lowered self-esteem, and feelings of personal worthlessness and inadequacy (e.g., Killen et al., 1994).

Although most statistics on eating disorders target late adolescents and young adults, research suggests that concerns about weight are prevalent in children as young as age nine (Cavanaugh & Lemberg, 1999; Mellin, Irwin, & Scully, 1992). Anorexia nervosa affects approximately 2 percent of the North American population; bulimia nervosa affects approximately 4 percent (APA, 2000b). The mortality rate among individuals with eating disorders is high—more than 12 times higher than any other cause of death in females aged 15 to 24 (Cavanaugh & Lemberg, 1999). However, the problem is potentially much bigger than even the statistics suggest.

Although most teens and preteens fail to meet the clinical criteria for bulimia or anorexia, research suggests that many engage in behaviors or possess attitudes and self-percepts that are similar to those with clinical disorders. Researchers (e.g., Davies & Furnham, 1986; Eisele, Hertsgaard, & Light, 1986) report that many adolescent females inaccurately perceive themselves as being overweight and strongly desire to weigh less even though very few are actually overweight. This phenomenon is not restricted to females. Research suggests that about 10 percent of eating-disordered individuals are male (APA, 2000b). Further, eating disorders in males are clinically similar to eating disorders in females (Margo, 1987; Schneider & Agras, 1987).

When looking at the research on treatment, it appears that there is a relatively good prognosis for childhood and adolescent eating disorders if they are treated soon after onset. Given the consensus that early identification and treatment of eating disorders are crucial, school counselors are in a very pivotal position when it comes to prevention, early identification, and intervention.

OVERVIEW

It is essential for school counselors to be sensitive to the early indications that an eating problem may exist, enact effective school-based prevention programs, be aware of empirically supported intervention approaches and strategies for providing support for recovering students, and network with professional programs and personnel who are trained to treat children with eating disorders.

The studies presented within this chapter (Table 19.1) highlight the benefits of cognitive-behavioral interventions, with emphasis on effective prevention programming.

TABLE 19.1 Overview of Studies Presented

TARGET PROBLEM	REFERENCE	K-6	6-9	9-12	OTHER SPECIFICATIONS
Internet-based eating order prevention programs	Zabinski, Celio, Jacobs, Manwaring, & Wilfley (2003)	N	N	Y	Random wait-list control group design
Dietary constraint and preoccupation with body image	Grave, De Luca, & Campello (2001)	Y	Y	N	Randomized control group design
Anorexia	Ball & Mitchell (2004)	N	N	Y	Control group design with manual-based CBT treatment
Etiological eating disorders prevention program	Phelps, Sapia, Nathanson, & Nelson (2000)	N	Y	Y	Random control group design

SAMPLE INTERVENTIONS

Student Bodies—Internet Prevention Program

Author: Marion F. Zabinski, Angela A. Celio, M. Joy Jacobs, Jamie Manwaring, and Denise E. Wilfley

Précis: Presents efficacy findings for two Internet-based eating disorder prevention programs: an asynchronous intervention, "Student Bodies," and a synchronous chatroom.

Introduction

"Student Bodies" is a structured, multimedia, Internet-delivered prevention program developed to reduce identified risk factors for eating disorders, specifically weight and shape concerns, and to reduce unhealthy weight-regulation behaviors (e.g., extreme dietary restriction, excessive exercise).

Intervention

The program uses a self-help cognitive-behavioral approach. The program incorporates cognitive-behavioral concepts and exercises from traditional face-to-face and bibliotherapy programs. Each week, participants are expected to read sections on body image, nutrition, dieting, physical activity, and other topics; complete a cognitive-behavioral-oriented exercise; record thoughts and feelings in their private online body image journal; and post at least two messages on the discussion group per week. The discussion group acts as a "bulletin board" where participants can log in at any time to read messages from the other participants and post responses. The program "Student Bodies" was tested using a series of randomized control trials in which the length of follow-up post-intervention varied up to three months in length. (Celio et al., 2000; Winzelberg et al., 2000; Zabinski et al., 2001). In each of these studies, approximately 30 female students were randomly assigned to the Student Bodies program and a comparable number were randomly assigned to a wait-list control group. Results indicated significant improvements among Student Bodies participants over control participants on measures of eating disorder pathology and concerns related to shape and weight in all trials to date.

Reflection

The use of the Internet as a means of providing therapeutic support and prevention programming has the added value of removing geographic constraints, ensuring anonymity, and even expanding the hours and days of support available. As noted by the authors, the use of such online intervention may be particularly suitable for those working with individuals with eating disorders. In the absence of the need to meet face to face, some of the pressure and self-consciousness about one's appearance that may have served as a deterrent to seeking treatment is removed. The use of the Internet as a medium for distributing information and providing support would allow the school counselor to expand the population serviced to include those students who, although not manifesting clinical symptoms, may be experiencing body image and weight concerns.

Source: Zabinski, M. F., Celio, A. A., Jacobs, M. J., Manwaring, J., & Wilfley, D. E. (2003). Internet-based prevention of eating disorders. *European Eating Disorders Review, 11*, 183–197.

SAMPLE INTERVENTIONS

Primary Prevention Program for Middle School

Authors: Riccardo Dale Grave, Loredana De Luca, and Gabriele Campello

Précis: Evaluated the efficacy of a school-based eating disorder prevention program designed to reduce dietary restraint and level of preoccupation with regard to shape and weight.

Introduction

A school-based prevention program involving six two-hour sessions was implemented and assessed using a control group design; 106 (61 females and 45 males) 11- to 12-year-old students were evaluated, 55 of whom participated in the program (experimental group). An additional 51 students formed the control group. Those in the treatment program demonstrated an increase in knowledge and a decrease in attitudes associated with risk of eating disorders.

Intervention

Six group sessions were administered once a week for six weeks during school hours to the experimental group. Each session lasted 2 hours: the first 30 minutes were dedicated to educational materials; the remaining time was devoted to practical activities, group discussions, and revision of homework. The program was formulated around a cognitive-behavioral perspective on eating disorders. A variety of educational techniques were used, including overheads and handouts. At the end of each session, a summary poster, written by the student, was posted to the wall of the classroom. Whenever possible, ideas and suggestions were elicited from the students, and sharing of information with each other was encouraged. A story about a young girl was used throughout the prevention program to illustrate the points addressed in the course. The sessions took a friendly approach to cognitive restructuring: beliefs about the overriding importance of eating control, shape and weight (thinness), and self-evaluations were usually highly valued. Group discussions were followed by homework assignments on the pros and cons of using eating control and thinness and self-evaluation.

Reflection

Although the program reportedly increased the knowledge of those in the experimental group and decreased certain negative attitudes, the preventive value of such a program is difficult to assess. It is important to note that those involved in the program had not exhibited evidence of having an eating disorder, nor did they show early warning signs that they were at risk. As such, the value of the program may only be able to be assessed as the researchers follow the progression of these students into adolescence.

However, the program does seem to provide a cost-effective mechanism for the school counselor to provide important health information and teach cognitive restructuring strategies that could prove useful in preventing obsessive concerns about weight and body image.

Source: Grave, R. D., De Luca, L., & Campello, G. (2001). Middle school primary prevention program for eating disorders: A controlled study with a 12-month follow-up. *Eating Disorders, 9*(4), 327–337.

SAMPLE INTERVENTIONS

Cognitive-Behavioral Treatment for Anorexia Nervosa

Authors: Jillian Ball and Philip Mitchell

Précis: A randomized control study to evaluate the effectiveness of a 12-month manual-based program of CBT in treating anorexia.

Introduction

The purpose of this study was to investigate the effectiveness of CBT for the treatment of adolescents and young adults with anorexia nervosa in an outpatient setting. The study contrasted the effect of a manual-based program of CBT with behavioral family therapy as the comparison group. Twenty-five adolescents and young adults with anorexia nervosa, currently living with their families, were recruited into the study with both treatment groups (i.e., CBT and behavioral therapy) receiving 21 to 25 sessions of therapy. Outcome measures included nutritional status, eating behaviors, mood, self-esteem, and family communication.

Intervention

The individual CBT program was based on the treatment manual developed by Garner and Bemis (1982) and modified in the present study to address maladaptive core beliefs often associated with feelings of failure and inadequacy. Sixty percent of the total sample and 72 percent of treatment completers had "good" outcome (defined as maintaining weight within 10 percent of average body weight and regular menstrual cycles) at post-treatment and at 6-month follow-up. No significant differences between treatment groups were found. The results suggest that outpatient therapy may be appropriate for the majority of patients with anorexia nervosa.

Reflection

This is one of the few studies to assess the benefits of outpatient CBT for anorexia nervosa. More important (for school counselors) is that the study included a broad range of individuals encompassing the full spectrum of anorexia nervosa—from those in the subclinical range to those in the poor prognostic group.

The manual-based format of the CBT allows for replication; however, the length of the sessions and the presumed specialized training of the therapist most likely preclude the use of this approach by most school counselors. What is valuable about this type of study is that it provides counselors with a knowledge base against which to evaluate potential referral sources in their own communities. Counselors need to identify programs and individuals trained in effective techniques such as CBT.

Source: Ball, J., & Mitchell, P. (2004). Randomized controlled study of cognitive-behavior therapy and behavioral family therapy for anorexia nervosa patients. *Eating Disorders, 12,* 303–314.

DETAILED INTERVENTION

Eating Disorder Prevention Program—A Controlled Study

Introduction

It is generally believed that there is a link between sociocultural pressure and the acceptance among preteens and teens of a thin, unrealistic ideal. As a result of internalizing this unrealistic standard, many students have developed body dissatisfaction and strong motivation to manage their weight, regardless of method. The use of restrictive dieting and stringent control methods increases the risk of developing an eating disorder. Although many "prevention" programs have focused on the negative impact of such restrictive dieting, the current investigation also targeted the development of protective factors (e.g., physical self-esteem and personal competence). Using an etiological model, prevention programming was directed toward female adolescents (ages 11 to 16) and young adults (ages 18 to 25), with an orientation toward increasing factors that attenuate risk status while reducing elements that place these young women in jeopardy.

Method

The researchers used a randomly assigned control group design (control group = 159 students, experimental group = 153 students). A six-session program was then completed with ninth-, tenth-, and eleventh-grade females (ages 13 to 16). Sessions were incorporated into the physical education curriculum. Data suggests that participation in the six-session program had a notable effect on changing participants' (a) attitudes and beliefs about sociocultural mores, (b) unwillingness to engage in dysfunctional disordered eating behaviors, and (c) future intentions regarding weight control. Likewise, the qualitative feedback from the students and the classroom teachers was positive.

The program was intended to promote resiliency factors while mitigating risk factors that had been identified earlier by hierarchical multiple regression analyses and subsequent path analyses from a large epidemiological sample (Phelps, Johnston, & Augustyniak, 1999). Using this etiological model, the program was successful in (a) facilitating an acknowledgement of the ubiquitous pressures for attainment of the model skeletal look; (b) changing attitudes about standards of beauty; (c) altering the participants' current and future intentional use of pharmaceutical aids or disordered eating behaviors (e.g., fasting, strenuous dieting, purging, excessive exercise) as methods of weight control; (d) building physical self-esteem and personal competence; and (e) reducing body dissatisfaction.

Intervention

The eating disorder prevention program was designed and integrated within the existing school curricula. The program utilized active participation by classroom teachers and consisted of six sessions.

Session 1: Reducing the Internalization of Sociocultural Pressures

- Discussion of the impact of sociocultural mores for thinness. The definition of beauty and acceptable weight limitations were examined to see how they have changed over the last 50 years. Photos of Betty Gable, Marilyn Monroe, and Twiggy were used as examples. Students shared their own perceptions of current mores.
- Examples from age-appropriate magazine ads were displayed (e.g., *Seventeen, Vogue, In Style,* and *Cosmopolitan*) to demonstrate the role of media, peers, and family modeling in disseminating weight-control messages.

Session 2: Increasing Physical Self-Esteem

- Group facilitators provided examples of constructive feedback regarding such qualities as hairstyle, eye color, athleticism, etc. Then each attendee had to complete the open-ended statement: "What I like about my physical appearance is . . . " Group members were encouraged to provide positive feedback to one another.
- Encouragement for improvement of personal physical fitness and strength was provided. Alternatives to dieting and fasting were provided with the focus on physical fitness rather than weight. Information on caloric expenditure as a result of various physical activities was presented and information on local fitness centers was disseminated.

Session 3: Building Personal Competence

Group leaders guided a discussion highlighting the importance of self-determination as opposed to responding to external influences as a way of increasing internal locus of control. Discussion also focused on constructive ways to respond to external pressures.

Session 4: Reducing Body Dissatisfaction

- The group was provided information about the biological aspects of puberty and group members shared feelings about their own height and weight gains.
- Pictures of normal-weight teenagers were presented and discussed and compared to photos of extreme thinness. These models were identified as meeting one criteria of anorexia; that is, they were 15 percent below expected body weight.

Session 5: Weight Control

- Information was provided about the negative consequences of restrictive dieting and other weight reduction/maintenance techniques that create the "yo-yo" effect. Information on set-point theory was presented.
- Group worked on identifying healthy techniques for remaining fit, which included frequency and duration of exercise as well as proper eating habits.

Session 6: Q&A

A young adult women who had recovered from an eating disorder shared her story and answered questions.

Reflection

The program provided a successful and relatively easy way to assist students to critically evaluate current sociocultural mores, clarify personal values, and enhance resilience. The use of six time-limited sessions that can be incorporated into an existing curriculum makes this program especially doable for school counselors. Further, the treatment detail provided by the authors makes for ease of replication.

As with all prevention programs, the real value of this intervention can only be assessed at a later date. For counselors implementing this program, it is essential to prepare to do long-term follow-up to test the efficacy of the program. It is important to determine if programs such as this one truly result in significant reduction of eating disorder symptomatology and whether booster sessions may be necessary.

Source: Phelps, L., Sapia, J., Nathanson, D., & Nelson, L. (2000). An empirically supported eating disorder prevention program. *Psychology in the Schools, 37*(5), 443–452.

FROM THE FIELD

The following recommendations come from counselors working in the schools. However, they have not been tested using experimental design. As such, application of these suggestions within the school-counseling setting should be carefully monitored for evidence of effectiveness.

Working with Students

- Listen, listen, listen. Students need to feel that they can discuss their concerns (about self, eating, body image, etc.) without criticism.
- Express your concerns in a forthright and caring manner.
- Do not overreact or indict the student; negative reactions typically stimulate the desire to pursue the problematic behavior.
- Educate. Help students understand the potential impact of their eating patterns.
- Depending on the length and intensity of the "eating disorder," the student may need medical treatment. Get the student to seek professional consultation and treatment by calling the family doctor.
- Have information about treatment programs and counselors and physicians that you can refer students and families to.
- Support students who are in treatment.
- Try and increase the student's awareness of his or her actions. Have the student monitor his or her eating habits—when, where, and the feelings accompanying eating.
- Help the student develop a sensible and realistic meal plan that will ensure regular eating patterns.
- Have the student journal thoughts about eating, weight, and personal value. Use this journal as the focus for teaching cognitive restructuring.
- Get rid of the diets! Gradually help the student to expand the range of food he or she eats.
- Introduce stimulus-control techniques. Narrow the range of cues associated with eating and reduce the possibility of impulse eating. Such techniques include eating only in an appropriate, designated eating place; preplanning meals; storing food in opaque (rather than clear) containers; and avoiding other activities (e.g., watching television) while eating.
- Teach healthy eating. Healthy eating behaviors include consuming regularly scheduled meals, decreasing the pace of eating through increasing number of chews per bite, taking smaller bites, and putting the fork down between bites.
- Teach students how to identify and define problems, develop reasonable goals, brainstorm possible options, assess options with regard to their consequences and barriers, and then implement a chosen option.
- Offer assertiveness training to help the student feel more control, empowerment, and self-esteem.

- Offer stress management and coping-skills training. Eating behaviors are sometimes attempts at coping and managing stress. Teach the student stress reduction and relaxation techniques.

Working with Teachers

- If prevention programs are to be successful, they need to be implemented. Teachers are a valuable resource for implementing prevention programs, but the programs need to fit their schedules, needs, and classroom demands.
- Discussions with teachers and coaches who discuss weight reduction and ideal weight with students will help the school counselor identify possible biases or unfavorable societal views that are promoted in classes. Re-evaluation of personal weight concerns and revelations about the dangers of dieting may assist teachers in promoting a more healthy perspective to students.
- The counselor presents a classroom guidance unit focusing on issues related to nutrition. Lesson topics could include body-esteem and self-esteem, locus of control, approval-seeking behavior, body image and nutrition, excessive exercise, and perfectionism.
- Teachers can also integrate weight concepts with other classroom subjects. A sixth-grade teacher has her students use the Internet to survey and exchange height/weight data with other sixth graders in the state. This larger population group helps to illustrate the great variability of growth and development in this age group. Increased self-esteem results as students learn that their sizes are not that different than others their age.
- Teachers need to be educated as to the extent and seriousness of the problem of eating disorders.
- Teachers need to be trained to identify early signs of eating disorders.
- Collaborate with the teacher to incorporate decision-making aids, health information, and self-esteem-building information into their lesson plans.
- Provide information that teachers can refer to quickly and distribute within their classes.
- Help teachers to feel comfortable talking and listening to their students for whom they have special concern.
- Collaborate with teachers to make the referral process easy.

REFERENCES

American Psychiatric Association. (2000a). *Diagnostic and statistical manual of mental disorders* (4th ed., Text Rev.). Washington, DC: Author.

American Psychiatric Association. (2000b). Practice guideline for the treatment of patients with eating disorders (rev.). *American Journal of Psychiatry, 157*(1), 1–38.

Ball, J., & Mitchell, P. (2004). Randomized controlled study of cognitive-behavior therapy and behavioral family therapy for anorexia nervosa patients. *Eating Disorders, 12,* 303–314.

Cavanaugh, C. J., & Lemberg, R. (1999). What we know about eating disorders: Facts and statistics. In R. Lemberg & L. Cohn (Eds.), *Eating disorders: A reference sourcebook* (pp. 7–12). Phoenix, AZ: The Oryx Press.

Celio, A. A., Winzelberg, A. J., Wilfley, D. E., Springer, E. A., Dev, P., & Taylor, C. B. (2000). Reducing risk factors for eating disorders: Comparison of an Internet and a classroom-delivered psychoeducational program. *Journal of Consulting and Clinical Psychology, 68,* 650–657.

Davies, E., & Furnham, A. (1986). The dieting and body shape concerns of adolescent females. *Journal of Child Psychology and Psychiatry and Allied Disciplines, 27,* 417–428.

Eisele, J., Hertsgaard, D., & Light, H. (1986). Factors related to eating disorders in young adolescent girls. *Adolescence, 21,* 284–290.

Garner, D. H., & Bemis, K. M. (1982). A Cognitive-behavioral approach to anorexia nervosa. *Cognitive Therapy and Research, 6*(2), 123–150.

Grave, R. D., De Luca, L., & Campello, G. (2001). Middle school primary prevention program for eating disorders: A controlled study with a 12-month follow-up. *Eating Disorders, 9*(4), 327–337.

Killen, J. D., Hayward, C., Wilson, D. M., Taylor, C. B., Hammer, L. D., Litt, I., Simmonds, B., & Haydel, F. (1994). Factors associated with eating disorder symptoms in a community sample of sixth and seventh grade girls. *International Journal of Eating Disorders, 15,* 357–367.

Lucas, A. R., & Holub, M. I. (1995). The incidence of anorexia nervosa in adolescent residents in Rochester, Minnesota, during a 50-year period. In H. S. Steinhausen (Ed.), *Eating disorders in adolescence: Anorexia and bulimia nervosa* (pp. 3–19). Berlin: Walter de Gruyter.

Mellin, L. M., Irwin, C. E., & Scully, S. (1992). Prevalence of disordered eating in girls: A survey of middle class children. *Journal of the American Dietetic Association, 92,* 851–853.

Phelps, L., Johnston, L. S., & Augustyniak, K. (1999). Prevention of eating disorders: Identification of predictor variables. *Eating Disorders, 7*(2), 99–108.

Phelps, L., Sapia, J., Nathanson, D., & Nelson, L. (2000). An empirically supported eating disorder prevention program. *Psychology in the Schools, 37*(5), 443–452.

Schneider, J. A., & Agras, W. S. (1987). Bulimia in males: A matched comparison with females. *International Journal of Eating Disorders, 6*(2), 235–242.

Thompson, J. K., & Smolak, L. (2001). Body image, eating disorders and obesity in youth—The future is now. In J. K. Thompson & L. Smolak (Eds.), *Body image, eating disorders and obesity in youth: Assessment, prevention and treatment* (pp. 1–18). Washington, DC: American Psychological Association.

Winzelberg, A. J., Eppstein, D., Eldredge, K. L., Wilfley, D. E., Dasmahapatra, R., Dev, P., & Taylor, C. B. (2000). Effectiveness of an Internet-based program for reducing risk factors for eating disorders. *Journal of Consulting and Clinical Psychology, 68,* 346–350.

Zabinski, M. F., Pung, M. A., Wilfley, D. E., Eppstein, D. L., Winzelberg, A. J., Celio, A., & Taylor, C. B. (2001). Reducing risk factors for eating disorders: Targeting at-risk women with a computerized psychoeducational program. *International Journal of Eating Disorders, 29,* 401–408.

Zabinski, M. F., Celio, A. A., Jacobs, M. J., Manwaring, J., & Wilfley, D. E. (2003). Internet-based prevention of eating disorders. *European Eating Disorders Review, 11,* 183–197.

ADDITIONAL RESOURCES

INTERNET

www.amhb.ab.ca. A resource for promoting healthy body image.

www.something-fishy.org Web site devoted to eating disorders. Contains information on causes, prevention, and treatment. Provides a treatment-finder service and advice for families and friends of people with eating disorders.

www.healthyplace.com/Communities/Eating_Disorders/Site/. Includes advice on approaching someone with an eating disorder, chat and support groups, a resource center, and a "words of experience" column focusing on individuals' struggles with eating disorders.

http://caringonline.com/. A Web site you can use to find the resources to help yourself or someone you love who suffers from negative body image or any of the following eating disorders: anorexia, bulimia, binge eating, or compulsive overeating. Site features treatment centers, support groups, and audio/visual resources.

PRINTED MATERIALS

Barrett, P., & Ollendick, T. (Eds.). (2004). *Handbook of interventions that work with children and adolescents; prevention and treatment*. Chichester: Wiley.

Burby, L. (1998). *Bulimia nervosa: The secret cycle of bingeing and purging*. New York: The Rosen Publishing Group, Inc.

Smith, E. (1999). *Anorexia nervosa: When food is the enemy*. New York: The Rosen Publishing Group.

CHAPTER 20

SUBSTANCE USE AND ABUSE

The Monitoring the Future (MTF) study—the University of Michigan's annual study of eighth-, tenth-, and twelfth-grade students—has reported an overall stabilization or decline in substance use among U.S. youth in recent years (Johnson, O'Malley, & Backman, 1998). However, this information needs to be viewed within the proper context. Levels of substance use, including nicotine use, are higher than they were a decade ago (Piazza & Ivoska, 2002).

Fifty four percent of students report having tried illicit drugs by the time they finish high school (Johnson, O'Malley, & Backman, 2001). Although marijuana is the most widely used illicit drug, 29 percent of those surveyed reported using other illicit drugs (including ecstasy, heroin, and steroids) by the end of twelfth grade. Add these statistics to the 63 percent of students reporting cigarette use by twelfth grade, and the 62 percent of twelfth graders and 25 percent of eighth graders who have reported being drunk at least once in their life (Johnson, O'Malley, & Backman, 2001), and it becomes clear that substance use and abuse among students is a serious issue. Further, the use of these substances, even when the level of use falls short of a clinical definition of abuse or dependence, can have serious consequences, and as such requires a response on the part of school counselors.

OVERVIEW

As in the case with the counselor's response to eating disorders (see Chapter 19), it is essential for school counselors to (1) be sensitive to early indications that a student may be using drugs and alcohol, (2) enact effective school-based prevention programs, (3) be aware of empirically supported intervention approaches and strategies appropriate for school-counselor implementation, and (4) network with professional programs and personnel who are trained to treat children with substance abuse problems. The studies included in this chapter (Table 20.1) provide strategies for intervention and risk reduction. It is this author's opinion that it is in the role of preventionist that the school counselor may be of most value when it comes to student use of drugs and alcohol.

TABLE 20.1 Overview of Studies Presented

TARGET PROBLEM	REFERENCE	K–6	6–9	9–12	OTHER SPECIFICATIONS
Marijuana and alcohol abuse	Liddle, Dakof, Parker, Diamond, Barrett, & Tejeda (2001)	N	N	Y	Random control group design
Binge drinking	Botvin, Griffin, Diaz, & Ifill-Williams (2001)	N	Y	N	Block randomized design, 29 schools
Marijuana use	Battjes, Gordon, O'Grady, Kinlock, Katz, & Sears (2004)	N	Y	Y	Pretest, posttest noncontrol group design, manual-based treatment
Drug and alcohol prevention	Losciuto & Steinman (2004)	Y	Y	N	Pretest, posttest random control group design

SAMPLE INTERVENTIONS

Multidimensional Family Therapy

Authors: Howard A. Liddle, Gayle A. Dakof, Kenneth Parker, Guy S. Diamond, Kimberly Barrett, and Manuel Tejeda

Précis: Study tested the efficacy of MDFT, a relatively short-term, multicomponent, multitarget, family-based intervention, in significantly reducing adolescent drug abuse and facilitating adaptive and protective processes.

Introduction

The clinical picture of adolescent drug abuse is as complex as its etiology. Students will turn to the use of drugs for a variety of reasons, including social pressures, self-medication, experimentation, and other psycho-emotional issues. However, most would argue that family factors are influential in the genesis and exacerbation as well as in the protection against adolescent drug abuse and behavioral problems (Brook, Whiteman, Nomura, Gordon, & Cohen, 1988; Kaufman, 1985). The current study tested the effectiveness of a treatment regimen that included family member involvement.

Intervention

Random assignment was made of 182 clinically referred marijuana- and alcohol-abusing adolescents to one of three treatments: multidimensional family therapy (MDFT), adolescent group therapy (AGT), and multifamily educational intervention (MEI). All treatments were based on a manual and were delivered on a once-a-week outpatient basis.

MDFT is a family-based, developmental-ecological, multiple systems approach (Liddle, 1994). It is a comprehensive, multicomponent, stage-oriented therapy. Treatment addresses the individual characteristics of the adolescent (e.g., cognitive mediators, such as perceptions of the harmfulness of drugs); emotion regulation processes (drug use as coping or as a manifestation of distress); the parent(s) (e.g., parenting practices, parental stress) and other relevant family members (e.g., presence of drug-using adults); as well as patterns of interaction (e.g., emotional disconnection) that link to the development and continuation of drug use and related problem behaviors (Liddle & Diamond, 1991).

In the present study, MDFT consisted of 16 total sessions delivered on a weekly basis in an office-based setting over an average of 5 months. Results indicate that those receiving MDFT showed superior improvement overall. MDFT participants also demonstrated change at one-year follow-up in the important prosocial factors of school/academic performance and family functioning as measured by behavioral ratings. Results support the efficacy of MDFT in significantly reducing adolescent drug abuse and facilitating adaptive and protective developmental processes.

Reflection

The study represents one of the few clinical trials in which randomized assignment to treatment was employed. Not only does this study support the efficacy of MDFT, but it did so by contrasting it with treatments commonly used as interventions. Of special note is the finding that the treatment effect remained at one-year follow-up.

Although the nature of the intervention (involving student and family) and the duration of the sessions (16 sessions over 5 months) most likely place this outside the role and function of the school counselor, it is important for counselors to know of interventions that have demonstrated effectiveness when making referrals.

Source: Liddle, H. A., Dakof, G. A., Parker, K., Diamond, G. S., Barrett, K., & Tejeda, M. (2001). Multidimensional family therapy for adolescent drug abuse: Results of a randomized clinical trial. *American Journal of Drug & Alcohol Abuse, 27*(4), 651–688.

SAMPLE INTERVENTIONS

Preventing Binge Drinking

Authors: Gilbert J. Botvin, Kenneth W. Griffin, Tracy Diaz, and Michelle Ifill-Williams

Précis: Study examined the effectiveness of a school-based prevention program on reducing binge drinking in a sample of minority, inner-city, middle school students.

Introduction

The study investigated the impact of a school-based drug abuse prevention approach using a randomized control group design. The authors reported that rates of binge drinking were compared among youth who received the program beginning in the seventh grade (n = 1,713) and a control group (n = 1,328) that did not. The prevention program had protective effects in terms of binge drinking at the one-year (eighth grade) and two-year (ninth grade) follow-up assessments. The proportion of binge drinkers was over 50 percent lower in the intervention group relative to the control group at follow-up.

Intervention

The study used a block randomized design, in which schools from identified target populations were assigned to receive the intervention (16 schools) or be in the control group (13 schools). Students in the intervention group received 15 sessions in the seventh grade and 10 booster sessions in the eighth grade. Students in the control group received the substance-use curriculum normally in place in New York City schools.

Intervention materials included a teacher's manual with detailed lesson plans, student handouts, and video material demonstrating the skills taught in the prevention program by same-age minority adolescents. The program was implemented by regular classroom teachers who had attended a one-day teacher training workshop.

Using techniques such as group discussion, demonstration, modeling, behavioral rehearsal, feedback and reinforcement, and behavioral "homework" assignments for out-of-class practice, participants were taught a variety of cognitive-behavioral skills for building self-esteem, resisting advertising pressure, managing anxiety, communicating effectively, developing personal relationships, and asserting one's rights.

Reflection

What is of particular value for the school counselor is the fact that regular classroom teachers, after only one day of training, were able to effectively implement this program. Clearly, the ease of using predeveloped materials, handouts, and lessons plans facilitated the teachers' compliance with the program. The possibility of a counselor spending a day of valued time but positively impacting 1,700 students is quite impressive.

Source: Botvin, G. J., Griffin, K. W., Diaz, T., & Ifill-Williams, M. (2001). Preventing binge drinking during early adolescence: One- and two-year follow-up of a school-based preventive intervention. *Psychology of Addictive Behaviors, 15*(4), 360–365.

SAMPLE INTERVENTIONS

Group-based Substance Abuse Treatment Program for Adolescents

Authors: Robert Battjes, Michael Gordon, Kevin O'Grady, Timothy Kinlock, Elizabeth Katz, and Emily Sears

Precis: Study examined the effectiveness of a manual-guided, outpatient, group-based treatment for adolescents.

Introduction

The authors noted that adolescents' compliance with treatment programs is often less than desirable due to a number of factors. Adolescents are often in treatment as a result of an external requirement rather than an internal motivation, and of those who do engage in treatment, many tend to drop out. The model presented within the current study attempts to address the influences of motivation and other personal characteristics of adolescents that may interfere with the treatment process.

Intervention

Using a pretest, posttest noncontrol group design, the effectiveness of a manual-guided, outpatient group-based treatment program was tested on a sample of 194 adolescents. The authors reported that participants significantly reduced marijuana use at 6 months and that these reductions were largely sustained at 12 months.

The treatment, Group-Based Treatment for Adolescent Substance Abuse (GBT), was a 20-week program involving group counseling and limited individual and family counseling. A detailed treatment manual was employed (see Katz, Sears, Adams, & Battjes, 2003).

The treatment began with an individual session designed to prepare members for the group sessions. Group sessions focused on drug education (4 sessions) and skill training and relapse prevention (15 sessions). A minimum of three individual sessions was required, with the focus on developing a treatment and discharge plan, and a minimum of four family sessions focusing on parent education and reduction of family conflict were required.

Reflection

As reported by the authors, GBT was highly successful in retaining the adolescents in the treatment program, and their involvement in the group treatment appears to be associated with their reduction in marijuana use. Although the results are encouraging, they should be viewed with caution given the absence of a control group. The group format and the structure provided by the manual add to the utility of this program for school counselors.

Source: Battjes, R. J., Gordon, M. S., O'Grady, K. E., Kinlock, T. W., Katz, E. C., & Sears, E. A. (2004). Evaluation of a group-based substance abuse treatment program for adolescents. *Journal of Substance Abuse Treatment, 27,* 123–134.

DETAILED INTERVENTION

Project PRIDE: A Counselor-Administered Drug and Alcohol Prevention Program

Introduction

The present study examined the effectiveness of Project PRIDE, a school-based, counselor-administered drug and alcohol prevention program. PRIDE is a primary prevention program intended for use at or before the early stages of drug and alcohol abuse (sixth and seventh grades). It is based on the premise that preventing drug and alcohol use with younger (e.g., middle school) populations will reduce the probability of drug abuse among the same individuals as they move forward into adolescence.

Project PRIDE was first inaugurated in the Philadelphia School System in 1969. The logic model or theoretical basis for the program reflected the idea that certain dysfunctional or negative influences presented by family situations, peers, schools, and the media led to negative behaviors, such as drug abuse. Further, it was thought that these influences could be countered or mitigated by exposing preadolescents and early adolescents to a combination of "affective education" and resistance skills.

Method

The study employed random assignment of schools and classes to treatment and control conditions, using a total of 270 students. Outcome was assessed by specifically designed and pretested instruments based on operational definitions of Project PRIDE's goals and process measures collected throughout the treatment period—especially assessments of "dosage," or degree of student participation. The authors reported that Project PRIDE participants demonstrated greater pretest to posttest gains on five of six outcome measures compared to control students.

Interventions

Project PRIDE was implemented in small groups (8 to 12 participants) and was conducted by school counselors or master's level prevention specialists. The programs consisted of 12 modules, administered during one class period per week over a 12-week period. The modules emphasized the development of specific resistance skills and other social competencies as well as cognitive units on drug education, peer norms, and media pressure.

The modules addressed each of the following:

- Positive communication and social competence
- Self-control and resistance skills (multiple sessions)

- Specific drug education
- Normative education
- Advertising pressure education
- Stress management

Reflection

Even though the program appeared to have a significant impact on participants' knowledge and attitudes regarding drugs, drug use, and methods of resistance, data reflecting the participants' actual use of this knowledge and skill as tools for avoiding drug use were absent from this study. Follow-up research testing the actual impact in terms of behavioral change and change in decision making for those who participated in the curriculum is needed.

One of the interesting characteristics of this program that distinguishes it from other teacher-implemented school-based curricula is that Project PRIDE calls for counselors to use their skills to maximize flexible initiatives and response to student problems and issues relevant to drug use. This use of the counselor as a group facilitator provides the counselor with an opportunity to assess students who may be at higher risk and in need of individual intervention. It also offers counselors the opportunity to be available to students who may have other concerns and problems and to be responsive should urgent issues arise that need immediate and appropriate attention.

Source: Losciuto, L., & Steinman, R. B. (2004). A re-evaluation of Project PRIDE, a redesigned school-based drug abuse prevention program. *Journal of Drug Education, 34*(2), 155–166.

FROM THE FIELD

What follows are recommendations from those working in the schools. As personal suggestions, they need to be employed with caution and their impact monitored.

Working with Students

- Support a positive health-promoting culture. Involve students, teachers, and staff in life style assessment and behavior change activities, model healthy behaviors, and provide reinforcing consequences for behavior change.
- Establish healthy alternatives (e.g., drug-free graduation parties) within the school.
- Establish peer-helper training programs to provide youth who are interested in talking with their peers with a "first stop for help" and information about referral resources and professional help. Training in helping skills benefits the helpers and promotes a positive peer culture.
- Establish support groups for those youth screened as "at risk" as a result of the assessment process and ongoing monitoring of their behaviors.
- Provide groups to focus on "addictive behaviors" for low-incidence addictive behaviors where the numbers warrant.
- Develop reentry programs, including support groups and a tracking system, for those youth returning from treatment programs.

Working with Teachers

- Help teachers integrate prevention programming into the curriculum. Such programming should present information regarding models of addiction, commonalities among addictions, specific addictive behaviors, and consequences of addiction.
- Offer in-class guidance lessons targeting comprehensive life skills training that emphasize personal and social skills and the opportunity to practice these skills. The program should not be based on specific addictive or problem behaviors, but focus rather on choices and decision making and immediate payoffs rather than long-term consequences.
- Help teachers identify children at risk by noting changes in social affiliation, interaction patterns, and engagement in class.
- Help teachers, especially those in secondary classrooms, to monitor their own discussions (with colleagues) in regards to "partying" or "celebrating" so as not to model such behavior.
- Highlight the importance of *not* indirectly reinforcing drug and alcohol use by teasing students in regards to their weekend behaviors, using comments such as "what's the matter Jim, a little too much last night?"

REFERENCES

Battjes, R. J., Gordon, M. S., O'Grady, K. E., Kinlock, T. W., Katz, E. C., & Sears, E. A. (2004). Evaluation of a group-based substance abuse treatment program for adolescents. *Journal of Substance Abuse Treatment, 27,* 123–134.

Botvin, G. J., Griffin, K. W., Diaz, T., & Ifill-Williams, M. (2001). Preventing binge drinking during early adolescence: One- and two-year follow-up of a school-based preventive intervention. *Psychology of Addictive Behaviors, 15*(4), 360–365.

Brook, J. S., Whiteman, M., Nomura, C., Gordon, A. S., Cohen, P. (1988). Personality, family, and ecological influences on adolescent drug use: A developmental analysis. In R. H. Coombs (Ed.), *The family context of adolescent drug use* (pp. 123–163). Haworth Press: New York.

Johnson, L. D., O'Malley, P. M., & Bachman, J. G. (2001). *Monitoring the future national results on adolescent drug use: Overview of key findings 2000.* (NIH Publication NO 01-4923). Bethesda, MD: National Institute on Drug Abuse.

Katz, E. C., Sears, E. A., Adams, C. A., & Battjes, R. J. (2003). *Group-based treatment for adolescent substance abuse.* Bloomington, IL: Chestnut Health Systems (Online). Available at www.Chestnut.org/li/bookstore.

Kaufman, E. (1985). Family systems and family therapy of substance abuse: An overview of two decades of research and clinical experience. *International Journal of Addiction, 20,* 897–916.

Liddle, H. A. (1994). The anatomy of emotions in family therapy with adolescents. *Journal of Adolescent Research, 9,* 120–157.

Liddle, H. A., & Diamond, G. (1991). Adolescent substance abusers in family therapy: The critical initial phase of treatment. *Family Dynamics of Addiction Quarterly, 1,* 63–75.

Liddle, H. A., Dakof, G. A., Parker, K., Diamond, G. S., Barrett, K., & Tejeda, M. (2001). Multidimensional family therapy for adolescent drug abuse: Results of a randomized clinical trial. *American Journal of Drug & Alcohol Abuse, 27*(4), 651–688.

Losciuto, L., & Steinman, R. B. (2004). A re-evaluation of Project PRIDE, a redesigned school-based drug abuse prevention program. *Journal of Drug Education, 34*(2), 155–166.

Piazza, N. J., & Ivoska, W. (2000). *ADAS student survey for Toledo, Lucas County, and Northwest Ohio.* Toledo, OH: Alcohol and Drug Addiction Services Board.

ADDITIONAL RESOURCES

INTERNET

www.nationalyouth.com/substanceabuse.html. National Youth Network. Includes a definition of substance abuse, symptoms, diagnosis, treatment, and tips for what to do if you suspect your child is abusing substances.

http://open-mind.org/Drugs.htm. Includes information on substance abuse and addiction research, therapies, news, and events. Also offers treatment resources for drug and alcohol addiction, including 12 step and other programs, residential centers, and holistic approaches. Includes links for drug-related slang, drug abuse signs and symptoms, and personal recovery stories.

www.netwellness.org/healthtopics/substanceabuse/. Net Wellness: Consumer Health Information provides links for alcoholism and drug abuse, treatment, and screening. Also provides information on helping teens make good choices.

PRINTED MATERIALS

Connors, G. J. (2001). *Substance abuse treatment and the stages of change: Selecting and planning interventions*. New York: Guilford Press.

DiClemente, C. C. (2003). *Addiction and change: How addictions develop and addicted people recover*. New York: Guilford Press.

Miller, W. R. (2002). *Motivational interviewing: preparing people for change*. New York: Guilford Press.

Monti, P. M., Colby, S. M., & O'Leary, T. A. (Eds.). (2001). *Adolescents, alcohol, and substance abuse: Reaching teens through brief intervention*. New York: Guilford.

INDEX